LEARN THE SECRETS OF SUCCESS IN THE **NEW ECONOMY**
FROM TODAY'S LEADING ENTREPRENEURS & PROFESSIONALS

SUCCESSONOMICS

Published by CelebrityPress®, Orlando, FL

CelebrityPress® is a registered trademark.

Printed in the United States of America.

ISBN: 978-0-9912143-8-9
LCCN: 2014941001

This publication is designed to provide accurate and authoritative information with regard to the subject matter covered. It is sold with the understanding that the publisher is not engaged in rendering legal, accounting, or other professional advice. If legal advice or other expert assistance is required, the services of a competent professional should be sought. The opinions expressed by the authors in this book are not endorsed by Celebrity Press®, Steve Forbes, or Forbes Magazine, and are the sole responsibility of the author rendering the opinion.

Most CelebrityPress® titles are available at special quantity discounts for bulk purchases for sales promotions, premiums, fundraising, and educational use. Special versions or book excerpts can also be created to fit specific needs.

For more information, please write:
CelebrityPress®
520 N. Orlando Ave, #2
Winter Park, FL 32789
or call 1.877.261.4930

Visit us online at: www.CelebrityPressPublishing.com

SUCCESSONOMICS

CELEBRITY PRESS®
Winter Park, Florida

CONTENTS

CHAPTER 1

THE U.S. ECONOMY: HOW TO RAMP UP OUR RECOVERY AND STABILIZE OUR FUTURE

BY STEVE FORBES

In 2008 we were hit by the possibility of a complete meltdown of our financial system. Since then things have, of course, calmed down tremendously, but the U.S. economy is still a source of much speculation. Is its current growth enough? Will that growth continue? The answers, of course, are important to all of us, whether you're a CEO, an entrepreneur or someone concerned about keeping their job – or getting one.

As of this writing, the U.S. economy has grown more in 2013 than it grew in the past three years and should end the fiscal year with an overall annual growth rate of 3%, barring any kind of international crisis. That's a better rate than we experienced during the previous three years, which was roughly 1.5% to 2%.

However, that growth is still not what it should be. I liken it to a talented baseball player, who has been routinely striking out for the last month or so. Now he's hitting .250 – but, with his natural abilities, he should be hitting .350. In other words, he remains competitive, but he's certainly not going to lead his team to the World Series. Our current economic progress is far from championship caliber.

We should, of course, acknowledge the positive signs. Private credit is beginning to flow again; the housing marketing has shown some improvement; and retail sales aren't too bad. The automatic budget cuts that triggered the Sequester did cause the government to take fewer resources from the economy than it had been, but those cuts were made in the worst way possible.

As far as job creation goes, when you look at what's called the Household Survey – which, I believe, measures small-business creation better than the so-called Corporate Survey or Establishment Survey – there are some heartening signs as well.

But, again, we're the guy who's only hitting .250. Because we're not achieving at a higher level, we're still very vulnerable to outside threats – and we must learn how to connect with the ball on a more consistent and powerful level.

INTERNATIONAL THREATS

Of course, to continue the baseball analogy, if we want to get our average up, there has to be a ball for us to swing at. Unfortunately, there are still some ominous clouds on the horizon that could rain out this game and put us right back in the dugout.

For example, the Middle East almost exploded in the spring of 2012. Everyone is now focused on Syria, but, as we all know, Egypt remains an ongoing question, and Iran and Israel continue to butt heads.

Then there's the lunatic who runs North Korea. The scary thing about Kim Jong-un is that he was brought up in a bubble. We have no idea how he sees the world; we only know that it's not our world. No one knows what he will do next - especially if he doesn't succeed in shaking down the U.S., Japan, and South Korea for another round of money. In that case, he may do something that has unforeseen consequences for the world.

On the financial side, Cyprus, a little country with a population of 800,000, established a truly frightening precedent. With the connivance of the European Central Bank, the IMF and others, Cyprus' government seized private citizens' deposits from the banks. The consequences of this? Anytime there's the threat of a financial crisis in any of the southern

European countries, the first thing people will do is pull their money out of the bank for fear that the government might seize it before rightful owners can withdraw it – and that, of course, makes any financial crisis worse.

Yes, we live in an uncertain world. Even China is having financial hiccups at the moment. But, having looked outward, let's do some inward soul-searching and analyze the reasons for our own weak economic growth.

THE REASONS BEHIND OUR WEAK RECOVERY

Here's the question we really need to answer: Why is this the feeblest recovery from a sharp economic downturn in American history?

Many of you don't remember the 1970s, but, during that decade we had three recessions in a row, each more severe than its predecessor. Each was followed by a sharp upturn. This kind of up-and-down shockwave made many wonder if our economy was sustainable.

It wasn't until the early 1980s when, with the Reagan reforms of the Federal Reserve, we finally got a sustainable boom of historic proportions. Remember the Great Depression, the worst economic disaster in history – at least in American history – did not finally bottom out until the early 1930s. After the initial crash, there was actually a sharp uptick in the economy. It didn't last, but, as had always happened previously, when there was a sharp downturn, we always got a subsequent sharp upturn.

But this time, it didn't happen. Why?

Here's the big thing that stands in the economy's way – monetary policy. Now, this is not the most exciting subject in the world, so I hope you had some caffeine to get through this. Better yet, let me put this in terms you might find a little more interesting. Think of it as you would a magnificent automobile you own and love to drive. Now, if you don't have enough fuel for that vehicle, it stalls. Of course, if you pump the gas pedal and give it too much fuel, you also stall, because you flood the engine. The ideal situation is, of course, to have the right amount of gas so you can move forward smoothly without any complications.

Well, the same is true of our economy. It may be a magnificent one, or at least, a very sturdy and usable one, but if the Federal Reserve doesn't supply enough money to meet the economy's natural needs, well, the economy is going to stall out.

However, just as too much fuel stalls your car, too much money from the Fed stalls the economy. And that's just what's been happening since the early part of the last decade. The Fed has been creating so much money that it has undermined the integrity of the U.S. dollar. People start distrusting our currency, and we don't get a sustainable recovery. This is a historical fact that's been proven time and time again, but memories, at least at the federal level, are very short.

WHEN YOU MESS WITH MONEY

Now, money is simply a means to simplify the ways in which we carry out transactions with each other. Wealth-creation happens through people conducting these transactions in the marketplace. Before there was a currency, we could only deal with each other through a barter system. Three thousand years ago, if I were to sell an ad in FORBES, the advertiser might have paid me with a herd of goats.

But let's say that things worked that way still, and I want to buy iPads for each of our writers. I go to the Apple store with a very large herd of goats. Naturally, this would take a lot of very obliging cab drivers, but let's not get too bogged down in the details. Anyway, the Apple store manager sees my goats and says, "I've got enough goats. What I need is sheep."

Now, I have to figure out how to exchange my goats for sheep to get the products I want. After I get the sheep, I have to hire a shepherd to make sure the wolves of Wall Street don't eat the sheep. But the available shepherds want to be paid in wine. I only have red wine, they want white. As you can see, this could go on forever – and that's without even considering the logistics of depositing a cow into an ATM.

So, 2600 years ago in Athens, Greece, which was a great commercial center, money was created in the form of coins. It made it easier to buy, sell and invest. But, let's remember, that for money to work, *it has to have a stable value,* just as all of our other weights and measures in the marketplace do.

For example, when you go to a store and buy a pound of apples, you expect those apples to weigh 16 ounces, not 15 or 10 (18 would be nice, of course, but unfair to the seller). Solid measurements ensure both sides are treated equally well. When you want a 2,500 square foot house, you don't expect the builder to suddenly assume there are only 11 inches in a foot.

So why in the world would we allow money – arguably, the most important system of measurement used – to be tinkered with?

What if the Federal Reserve did to clocks what it does to the dollar? Let's say they "floated" time. One day, there were 60 minutes in an hour and the next day, only 42. Now, say you hired someone to work for you at $15 an hour, you'd have to figure out whether that was a New York hour, a Texas hour, a Thailand hour or a Congo hour? You wouldn't know. It would be hard to even bake a cake – the recipe says, "Bake the batter 45 minutes." Do you have to adjust those minutes for inflation?

The goats, in comparison, are starting to look simple, right?

Whenever you engineer an environment in which people can't trust the fixed nature of money, the first problem is that capital gets misdirected. Investors suddenly lock it into hard assets. Why? To preserve what they have, instead of investing in a very uncertain future. When you invest in something, it may be three or more years before you get a payout. An investment is risky enough without having to worry about the uncertainty of what the dollar is worth when you actually get your payout. Will you be collecting it in dollars that are worth 100 cents? 80 cents? 20 cents?

This is the kind of thing that fueled the housing bubble in the early 2000s. Everyone thought, because the Fed had undermined the dollar, that prices would keep going up forever. It became the norm for the value of homes to always rise. Of course, that's not reality, but everyone's mindset was corrupted, which caused the bubble to grow until it finally blew up in everyone's faces.

CHEAP CREDIT = LESS JOBS

Today, you routinely hear about 0% interest rates, which distorts the credit markets. It brings to mind an old joke about the Soviet Union: "Healthcare is free, but you can't get any." And 0% interest rates absolutely direct capital to certain parties at the expense of others.

Who benefits by what Ben Bernanke's done at the Federal Reserve? First of all, the government itself, by creating cheap deficits. Who else gets helped? Fannie Mae and Freddie Mac, which are government-sponsored enterprises. They're, in effect, coining money, because the Fed's buying all these mortgage securities. Big companies also have access to cheap credit. Their balance sheets are spectacular today, probably the strongest in American history because of this.

Now, who gets hurt in this era of cheap credit? Small companies do, because they simply don't have reliable access to it. It is instead being directed to big players and to hard assets, as already noted, which is why we've had a weak job-creation environment. As you know, most jobs are created in *small* businesses. In an uncertain credit environment, job-creation is hurt. That's why only now, four years into the recovery, are we starting to see some real signs of life in terms of employment numbers.

That's beginning to change thankfully, because it looks like the 0% interest rate policy is finally coming to an end. It's hurt the recovery, not helped it. The Federal Reserve underestimated – or, to recall a Bushism, "misunderestimated" – the consequences of its policies. They thought of it as a stimulus, but all it did was create our current $2 trillion overhang. By printing money that went to preferred borrowers, such as Fannie and Freddie and the Federal Government, our national balance sheet has gone from $800 billion to more than $3 trillion.

THE PRICE OF UNCERTAINTY

Where is this ultimately going to lead, here and around the world? Well, this may sound very strange, but I believe, in the next few years we're going to see something that hasn't been since since the 1970s: The dollar is going to be relinked to gold. In the U.S., that link was in place for 180 years of our existence.

Why gold? Yes, it fluctuates in terms of dollars, but the value of the gold itself doesn't change - it's the *perception* of the value of the dollar that does. Gold retains its intrinsic value better than anything else – better than silver, better than copper, platinum, or you name it. It's the best thing we have, and its worked for 4,000 years.

Frankly, we need a hard and fast ruler with which we measure our money's worth. In a vibrant economy gold doesn't restrict money creation; it makes sure the currency's value remains consistent. It's like when building a highway, you know when construction begins that there are 5,280 feet in a mile. It doesn't restrict the number of miles or highways that you can build. It just means the mile is a fixed measure - the same as gold.

If a proper gold standard were in place, what would it mean? Well, let's assign it a random value of, say, $1200 an ounce. That means that if the price of gold rose above that $1200 an ounce, the Federal Reserve would stop creating money. If it fell below $1200, the Fed would create *more* money. The amount of money would be practically and accurately measured.

You might ask, "Can it actually be that simple?" The answer is "Yes." This is the essence of how a gold standard works. Does it hurt money creation in a vibrant economy? Absolutely not.

Here's a statistic that will make you sound profound the next time you attend a cocktail party. Start by pointing out that from the time we declared America's independence in the 1770s, when the U.S. was a small agricultural and relatively poor nation of 3.8 million people, to about 1900, when we had grown to 76 million people and had become the mightiest industrial nation in the world, the amount of gold mined in that period had increased the world's gold supply by a little more than three times. And even though the dollar was fixed to gold in terms of measurement, the money in the U.S. actually increased by *160 times*. This makes it clear that a gold standard would not be an anchor around our economic neck; it would bring a much needed stability to the value of our money, while still providing the flexibility to meet the needs of our economy.

And isn't that better than putting all our trust in the bureaucrats and politicians in Washington?

CHAPTER 2

THE WALL STREET SHUFFLE

BY BLAIR AARONSON

When I was informed I would be writing a chapter in Steve Forbes' upcoming book, I experienced two instantaneous emotions. The first was great pride, knowing I'd attained a kind of hallmark moment in my business career. The second was trepidation, as I could hear that inner voice whisper, *"How can you impact the everyday investor in a few short pages?"* I had to get that feeling in a headlock to give me the inspiration to move forward.

"Yes," I said to myself, *"it is possible to shift the belief of the everyday investor—provided I show solid facts and give them an interesting learning experience!"*

So, without further ado, let's take a little trip in the newly-upgraded time machine.

NOW BOARDING!

Watch your step as you climb in, now. Grab a window seat if you like. We're setting our course for New York City, New Year's Eve, 1972. Everybody in? Buckle up...Here we go!

There now. That wasn't so bad, was it? I know things look a little different in 1972. Lord knows the music is different! Oh, look. There's the stock exchange. Let's take a stroll over there. One thing that hasn't changed in four decades is the non-stop hype surrounding the market.

We're going to visit today with William Broadmore, a successful builder.

This New Year's Eve is quite different for the Broadmore family. You see, William is retiring this year. Yep, he's calling it quits after 35 years of breaking his back. He's got the world by the...well, you know what I mean.

(Now remember, we have to follow a few simple rules on this journey. We can't disclose we're from the future. For some, it may be hard to keep quiet and not reveal what we know to be the truth. This is a case where self-control is the word of the day.)

We're meeting with William and a few of his buddies at the club for lunch. The talk at the table centers on what it's like to be wealthy in the 1970s. Sitting to my right is William's stock advisor, Anthony Brown, who also advises all of William's buddies. I took a deep breath and demurely asked, "What do you think of this market, Anthony?"

Without even waiting till he finished chewing his dinner roll, he blurted out, "Lovin' it. Lovin' it!" How I wanted to say, "You're a fool who's about to learn a hard lesson!" But I held my tongue.

The conversation at the table continued in a back-and-forth rhythm. "You know, William," Anthony said, "we've been averaging about 9-10% a year for quite a while now. It'll be smooth sailing if we only have a 5% withdrawal rate to cover you and Dorothy through retirement."

I almost used one of those dinner rolls as a gag to stop myself from using Anthony's tie as a noose! You see, William had been taught by his co-workers, his golf buddies, his tax advisor and his brokers the "qualified plan." You know, the tax-deferral route was the only way to go. After all, tax-deferred is almost like tax-free, isn't it? (I know, I know—that's a different conversation.)

So, after 35 years of work, William has about $2 million in the latest and greatest mutual funds, all hand-picked by Anthony the Great! Anthony reasoned that $100,000—which is 5% of the plan he recommended plus Social Security and Dorothy's little pension—should be plenty to take care of the couple for their remaining years.

Unfortunately, the conversation William hadn't had with any of his trusted advisors was the one about sequence of returns. Since my first days as an advisor in 1985, I have yet to see Wall Street recognize the major importance of this issue. The focus has always been on average rate of return and the "buy and hold" mantra.

Before we leave New York, you'll see firsthand the foolishness of ignoring sequence of returns!

AIR-SICK BAGS ARE IN THE SEAT BACKS.

As the New Year's Eve celebration comes to an end, the business of life proceeds apace. With no more income from the business, William begins to take his needed distributions from his IRA. Just as he prepares to deposit his first distribution check, the U.S. economy hits a snag. By the end of 1973, the S&P 500 suffers a dramatic loss of 16.58%.

Now pay attention as the lesson unfolds before us. In prior years, that 16.58% downturn would have had absolutely no impact, as William would have had ample time to recover. But those days are gone, as he's now in distribution mode. William is forced to take his distribution in the midst of this pullback; thus he's now selling and locking in a loss.

As a matter of fact, after year one, our account value of $2 million is sitting at $1,565,980, and we only took out $100,000. Of course, Anthony is singing his favorite tune: "Hang in there, William. Market's coming back. Remember: We're in it for the long haul!"

The Broadmore family has no idea of the financial Titanic that awaits them. In a sad comparison, once the iceberg was spotted, no one thought it capable of bringing down such an engineering marvel—just like one bad year was never thought to be enough of a force to destroy 35 years of saving and planning!

A quick trip just one year ahead, folks. Enjoy the snacks we've provided in the seat pockets (that's also where you'll find the air-sick bags).

New Year's Eve 1974 brought more chill to the coast, and along with it, devastating continuation of the perfect storm. The S&P 500 ended the year down an additional 27.57%, and the Broadmore account now sits at $1,051,191. That's a million-dollar loss after taking only $200,000 in distributions.

It's probably painful for you, even as mere observers, to see the stress lines in William's face and his attempt to remain positive in front of his family and friends. Anthony is holding fast to his "buy and hold" mantra, and William is just too overwhelmed to do anything but maintain his unwavering faith in Anthony – and of course, in the market. Sadly, $100,000 is no longer a 5% withdrawal rate; it's now 9.51%—an almost impossible rate to keep pace with.

(I see some of the group is looking a bit bewildered. Is this new information for you? I apologize for forgetting that most advisors don't have this conversation with their clients during the planning phase of retirement.)

I suppose we should get on with the outcome here. It's time to set a new destination: New Year's Eve, exactly 20 years from whence we started. That's it—1993! Thank g-d there won't be any more bell bottoms and disco. At least we can have some sushi on this pit stop!

Sorry for the bumpy landing. With 1993 just hours away, let's look over William's shoulder, as he is currently in a closed-door meeting with Anthony and his attorney. You see, William's account now sits at a mere $171,423.00. He will be broke in one year! And YES, it was 100% avoidable if he had been working with someone who understands what I understand!

Pardon me for being direct, but this is what separates me from Anthony and every other advisor who is ignorant about how money works in distribution mode during retirement!

HISTORY OF THE S&P 500 INDEX

December 29, 1972	15.6%
December 31, 1973	-17.4%
December 31, 1974	-29.7%
December 31, 1975	31.5%
December 31, 1976	19.1%
December 30, 1977	-11.5%
December 29, 1978	1.1%
December 31, 1979	12.3%
December 31, 1980	25.8%
December 31, 1981	-9.7%
December 31, 1982	14.8%

December 30, 1983	17.3%
December 31, 1984	1.4%
December 31, 1985	26.3%
December 31, 1986	14.6%
December 31, 1987	2.0%
December 30, 1988	12.4%
December 29, 1989	27.3%
December 31, 1990	-6.6%
December 31, 1991	26.3%
December 31, 1992	4.5%
December 31, 1993	7.1%

I see some of you hanging your head watching William's wife Dorothy in tears as their accountant and attorneys bring her out of the dark and reveal the unthinkable. The reality is that they are broke—just a stone's throw from destitution.

But wait! When we get back home, will some of you still insist on wearing the same shoes as William Broadmore and drinking Anthony's blend of Wall Street Kool-Aid?

When I left the Wall Street mindset after 16 years, I vowed I would never utter the phrase "Hang in there, Mr. or Mrs. Jones! The Market's coming back; you're in it for the long haul!" As I write these words, I can honestly say I've never broken that promise (after fourteen years and two stock market meltdowns).

So, I ask you: What if you found out that what you thought to be true about retirement planning turned out not to be true? When would you want to know? I wish I could have been there for William and Dorothy, but to be honest, I see their carbon copies several days a week! Unfortunately, it's a very hard lesson that too many people have yet to learn.

HOME SWEET HOME

Oh, I see the shuttle has arrived to take us back to the time machine. All of you will be given a voucher good for a complimentary evaluation of your retirement plan. (This will be an hour well spent, if I do say so myself!) I'd like to take this opportunity to thank all of you for accompanying me on Retirement Thru Design's Reality Check Tour, where you get to see how your belief system really panned out for other like-minded folks!

While we're loading the bags, I'd like to take a moment to tell you a bit about some of our other tours:

1. **Is Paying Off Your Mortgage In Your Best Interest?** This is a three-hour tour where you'll be able to see and validate that the rate of return on home equity is 0%. This tour is not for the squeamish, as you will witness two couples who used very different mortgage strategies. Sadly, one couple subscribed to the American Dream of the 1940s and learned they had given up 100% of the control of the equity in their home after retirement. The other couple built a side bucket of money that was 100% accessible, and it was tax-free. (A light meal is served on this tour.)

2. **Was a 401K/IRA My Best Retirement Option?** This is by far our most popular tour, as it's only two hours long. We'll visit three individuals and watch two of them experience the devastating reality of a higher tax bracket in retirement combined with market risk and inflation risk. The third individual is the one who paid taxes and built a large bucket of tax-free funds in a maximized life insurance policy. It's a powerful tour that gets right to the heart of the greatest lie ever foisted on the American worker: tax deferral (or as I like to call it, tax postponement). Who would ever sign a blank check that will only be cashed 30-40 years down the road? No one knows what bracket they will be in or the tax write-off they will have. (Beverage service only; 24-hour reservation required due to demand.)

3. **Will You Unknowingly and Unnecessarily Transfer Away $500,000 Through Poor College Funding, Mortgage Structure, and Retirement Planning?** When I read that Facebook founder Mark Zuckerberg had just refinanced his house, I began to wonder if his advisor had taken one of our tours recently. Fortunately, the everyday mom-and-pop investor can use the very same planning strategies that super-wealthy investors have used for the last 100 years. In the words of one of our favorite tour guests, "It's quite elementary, dear Watson: You are either a customer of the bank, or you ARE the bank."

4. **It is estimated 90% of Americans still believe compounding money in a taxable account is both prudent and sure fire way to build wealth!**

Join us on our flagship tour as we reveal the lie that truly is the "Dark Side of Compounding." We will follow two families. One who had chosen to follow the "let it re-invest" long term and we will just pay the tax out of our pockets. The other family was well aware of the nightmare this creates and chose to roll the money over a period of years into a tax-advantaged account. This simple strategy not only minimized the taxes due every year but also substantially scaled back the lost opportunity cost on those dollars! The final outcome will raise your blood pressure for sure! If you are prone to outbursts of anger due to lack of proper advice from your C.P.A. or advisor we do NOT recommend this tour!

On that note, I'd like to share a quote from my favorite Doctor!

Sometimes the questions are complicated and the answers are simple.
~ Dr. Seuss

Be well.

Blair Aaronson
Retirement Thru Design
Woodland Hills, CA

About Blair

Blair Aaronson, Founder of Retirement Thru Design has been helping So.Cal. investors reach their retirement and estate planning goals since 1985. Over his 29-year career he has worked for the largest brokerage firms in Beverly Hills, Los Angeles and Century City. Blair has also worked with several of Southern California's largest law firms that regularly refer their clients to Blair.

His concepts are straightforward and have proven to be 100% effective during the most trying markets in the last Quarter Century. Blair is a Certified Estate & Trust Specialist. Blair currently has his own radio show *The Financial Bottom Line* every Saturday morning at 8:00 am on local radio KEIB 1150 AM The Patriot. The radio show is educational where listeners are taught about Wealth Transfers that are occurring and how to re-direct this funds back in to their lifestyle to enjoy!

Blair receives cards and letters on a regular basis giving thanks for protecting his clients during 2008/09 when not one of his clients lost a PENNY! Blair believes the brokerage community has failed terribly at protecting the senior's life savings. Sometimes a second set of eyes can shed new light on the existing plan and bring new valuable information to the table.

And remember...It's NOT what you DON'T know that can hurt you, but rather what you thought you did know! Blair is also an award winning pianist and composer.

CHAPTER 3

THE ULTIMATE RETIREMENT BLUEPRINT
"THE 7 SECRETS TO A STRESS-FREE RETIREMENT"

BY DAVID REYES II

I have been a Financial Architect for nearly two decades and am honored to share with you my experience helping hundreds of families and business owners create retirement plans that have stood the test of time. Early in my career, a life-changing event altered forever the way I look at money, investing, retirement and most importantly, families. Being raised by a single parent, I was blessed to have my grandmother, Edna, to help raise me.

After she passed away, my grandfather Kermit, who had worked for Sears most of his life and saved quite well, eventually entered a nursing home.

In less than 3 years my grandfather was broke and soon passed on to be with my grandmother. After this experience I promised myself that I would do everything in my power for the families I had the privilege to advise, to prevent their life's dreams and life's work from ending in this way.

SECRET #1
PLAN TO LIVE NOT TO DIE

Having a plan for retirement is of great importance. One of the greatest risks you will face by not having a plan is the risk of longevity. The average life expectancy is 78.7 years. Couples now have a 50% chance that one or both will live to age 88, a 20% chance one or both will live to age 94. Do you have a plan to ensure that you will not outlive your retirement savings? Can you afford NOT to have a plan?

According to a study by the Certified Financial Planning (CFP) Board in 2011, less that 1/3 of all retirees had a written retirement plan.

Why is this? The dirty little secret is that most advisors are not really planners; they are product sales people or investment managers who are either not qualified or licensed, to do planning. But most importantly, they are not getting paid to create a plan for you, they are getting paid to invest your money.

An investment plan is not a retirement distribution plan. It does not take into consideration taxes, inflation, health care costs, life expectancy, your family budget and many other considerations.

When choosing an advisor to implement a comprehensive family retirement distribution plan, only work with someone who is a fiduciary. I will tell you who is not a fiduciary: a stockbroker, insurance agent, or banker. The only true fiduciaries are CFPs (Certified Financial Planners) and RIAs (Registered Investment Advisors), who are required by law to put their clients' interest first and must disclose any conflicts of interest. If your advisor is not a fiduciary, find one ASAP!

SECRET #2
WINNING BY NOT LOSING

Rule # 1, don't lose money. Rule #2, don't forget rule number #1.
~Warren Buffett

Many Americans lost close to 50% in the early 2000's Tech Wreck and the "2008 Financial Crisis." To recover would have required a 100% return just to get back to even. If you had received only 30% of the upside of the stock market and no downside, you would have BEATEN the stock market! You cannot afford to have a "passive" portfolio and watch it lose value again.

Most of our clients are near or in retirement and have already "won the game" or are close to it – with enough assets to retire comfortably because of proper planning and a proactive Risk Management Plan. A Risk Management Plan is NOT a passive 60/40% stock and bond portfolio; you do not need a professional or any expertise to implement this plan. According to Morningstar, "If you have a 60/40 portfolio at a 4% withdraw rate you have a 50% chance of running out of money during your retirement." Do not accept those odds with your life savings.

Is there a better way to increase the odds of not running out of money? Yes! In addition to asset allocation, there are three additional ways of protecting and maximizing your income during retirement:

1. Guaranteed Investments: Social Security is really an annuity and a great one if used properly. If you have less than $2M-$3M dollars you are likely a candidate for a guaranteed income stream investment for a portion of your portfolio. Some of these products pay 5% to 6% over the lifetime of both you and your spouse. Annuities are a complex topic and not all annuities are created equal.

2. Using Options to Protect Downside Risk: Most investors do not have much experience using options in a portfolio and consider options to be risky. Used properly, options can be very safe. Option strategies are used as insurance to protect against severe market downturns. As the market goes down the value of the option goes up, reducing the amount of loss and in some cases actually creating net gains in the portfolio. For example in 2000-2002 when the market was down over 40% one of our institutional managers who manages investments for major pension funds was actually up over 20% during that severe bear market.

3. Tactical Unconstrained Investing: This strategy gives the ability to be in the market when the manager feels it is favorable based upon the rules of the investment or to be in cash when markets are less favorable. Most investors do not realize that most brokerage houses do not get paid to be in cash and do not consider this a legitimate alternative asset class. One of our portfolio managers using this method in 2008 when the market was down -37%, was

actually up over 5%, because he had the ability to move to cash when the market was not in a favorable position.

Can you financially and emotionally handle another financial crisis? If not what are you doing about it? If you knew there were strategies to protect and grow your portfolio and have not included them in your retirement plan how would you feel in the next market downturn having done nothing to protect yourself?

SECRET #3
INCOME FOR LIFE

Auto Insurance is designed to protect our cars...Health Insurance for keeping medical costs down...Life Insurance to protect and provide for our families...How about Investment Insurance? Why?

When planning to retire, you need to have "Inflation-Protected, Predictable and Guaranteed Income Streams" through Social Security maximization and guaranteed income stream-type investments which help minimize the risk of outliving your money.

Did you know that Social Security is basically an annuity? A great annuity. With proper planning, your Social Security can grow at 6% to 8% including increases for inflation. What other assets do you have that grow at that rate, guaranteed?

There are investment strategies that offer some of the features of Social Security and provide you with growth and lifetime income streams for you and your spouse. Anyone with assets below $2M to $3M, should have some of their investments in an annuity. There I said it, the "A" word. Although you won't admit it, you love the idea of what an annuity can do, but don't understand it. It is not your fault, annuities are complex and confusing, as there are fixed, indexed, variable, deferred and immediate annuities. There are three main reasons why most of you do not like annuities:

1. You believe they have high fees (The fees in an average variable annuity range from 4% to 6%).

2. You believe that you won't make any money.

3. You believe that your heirs will not get what is left of your money after you have passed.

Many annuities do have these negative features and I do not recommend them. I recommend products that have very low fees, often less than 1%, earn a good return, and allow the balance to pass to your heirs. Also, you have access to your money with lifetime payouts that survive both you and your spouse. A major benefit of choosing the right kind of annuity is the payout rate; the lifetime income you collect. Someone in their 60's could receive payouts of 5% to 6% for life. According to Morningstar, "This is extremely important since the average retiree can only take out about 2.8% of their portfolio without running out of money."

If you are considering an annuity for your retirement portfolio, I urge you to work only with a fiduciary, who must put your interest first, and who does not work for an insurance company. This will assure an honest assessment of the annuity appropriate for your situation.

SECRET #4
GET WHAT YOU PAID FOR

Can you afford to make a $250,000 mistake?

Maximizing your Social Security is crucial to getting the most out of your benefits. Making an incorrect choice can be costly!

Did you know there are more than 527 ways to claim Social Security? There are more than 2000 rules and over 100,000 rules for those rules. Social Security is more complex than the Federal Tax Code and on top of that, the Social Security Administration is not allowed to advise you on which option may be best for you.

If you were born between 1943 and 1954 with a full benefit of $2,466 and choose to retire at age 62 you would only receive 75% of your Social Security benefits for a total of $1,850.

Would you like to increase your monthly Social Security benefit of $1,850 to a monthly benefit that could equal $3,255 - $4,060?

If you wait until age 66 to receive benefits, you receive 100% of your benefit. Instead of $1,850, your monthly benefit will equal $2,466. If you can afford to wait to age 70, the maximum age to wait to receive Social Security, you will receive 132% of your benefit. This means your monthly benefit will equal $3,255 to $4,060, which also includes Cost-of-Living Adjustments! Because of lack of understanding and planning, most Americans do not receive this much money.

To maximize Social Security, you need a comprehensive retirement distribution plan, an integrated plan that includes Social Security, 401k's, IRA's, pensions, your expenses, everything. The best choice for taking Social Security may be waiting to start taking benefits. Between the ages of 66 and 70 your Social Security income grows between 6% and 8%, with cost-of-living adjustments. What assets do you have that grow like that and are guaranteed! You must determine the proper time to begin taking Social Security benefits.

SECRET #5
KEEP YOUR UNCLE OUT OF YOUR POCKET!

Your least favorite uncle, Uncle Sam, is a vested partner with you in your retirement. Protect your retirement assets from being eaten up by taxes.

Did you know that up to 85% of your Social Security Income may be taxable?

Minimize taxes now and during retirement to protect your nest egg and increase and protect your income, using strategies such as proper asset location, tax-loss harvesting, and Roth conversions.

1. *Asset Location:* Most investors are aware of asset allocation but not familiar with *asset location*. Placing investments in tax-deferred accounts vs. taxable accounts makes a huge difference. As an example, most bond interest is taxed at ordinary income tax rates, which could be as high as 50% depending upon your tax bracket. Proper asset location planning allows deferring interest and tax thus increasing the overall performance of your portfolio with no additional risk.

2. *Tax-Loss Harvesting:* This strategy may increase the rate of return of your portfolio between 1% to 4% per year with no additional market risk. Tax–Loss Harvesting is a strategy to actively manage a portfolio to gain tax benefits using losses written off while still remaining invested in the market. An example would be owning Coca-Cola stock which incurred losses. Coca-Cola would then be sold and Pepsi stock purchased. Thus, you are still invested in the market and sector desired, but would achieve an increased rate of return on the portfolio by taking the loss.

3. *Tax-free Income:* One of the best ways to maximize income in retirement is to take advantage of Roth Conversions. This is a strategy used to pay taxes once and never again. This strategy is used only when your current tax situation is favorable. One example, losses that are carried forward such as NOL's (net operating losses). For example, with $100,000 in losses you could convert $100,000 into a Roth IRA and pay no taxes on the conversion, saving you on average $25,000 in taxes. As a general rule, do not make conversions while working when your income and therefore your tax bracket is highest. Most Roth conversion strategies should be used when you are retired and paying less taxes, thus paying less tax on the conversion.

SECRET #6
THE SILENT KILLER

Inflation is as violent as a mugger, as frightening as an armed robber, and as deadly as a hit man.
~ Ronald Reagan (1980)

Inflation erodes your purchasing power. A cost-of-living adjustment must be included in your retirement budgeting in order to continue buying the same goods and services, including medical and food costs. As discussed in #4 above, there are "Inflation-Protected, Predictable and Guaranteed Income Stream type investments" that will minimize the risk of outliving your money.

Assuming an inflation rate of 3.5% you will need to double your income in 20 years in order to maintain the same lifestyle you have today.

What should you not invest in today? Due to our national debt of around $17 Trillion and the Federal Reserve "tapering" there is extreme risk of higher interest rates in the future. Thus, bonds are potentially the worst investment. Every 1% increase in interest rates can reduce the amount of your principal between 5% and 15% depending on the type and duration of your bonds. For example, if you held 20-year bonds in 2013, you lost nearly 10% on your bond portfolio.

Bonds promoted as offering risk-free returns are now priced to deliver return-free risk.
~ Warren Buffett

SECRET #7
PROTECT YOUR NEST EGG

Did you know that you will spend on average of over $250k during your retirement on healthcare? And on average, you will spend another $250k on long term care? Unfortunately, if you are married, there is more than a 60% chance that you or your spouse will be in a long term care facility for an average of 2.5 years.

Not having long term care insurance exposes you to the risk of depleting all your life savings. Long term care insurance provides a means to protect your nest egg and pay necessary long term care expenses. Protect yourself and your family!

I believe that my experience helping people like you with their financial planning will make a positive difference in the quality of your life, especially in your retirement years. My goal is that you achieve the highest quality of life possible in retirement, with a true sense of security after a lifetime of hard work. Thinking back to my grandfather, if he were alive today, he would likely lean over and tell you "Plan to LIVE and do it NOW."

*(Any guarantees are based upon the claims-paying ability of the insurance company.)

About David

David Reyes II is the Founder and Chief Financial Architect of Reyes Financial Architecture, Inc., a Registered Investment Advisory Firm. He specializes in working with successful families and business owners by helping them achieve their personal and financial goals. As a fiduciary, David takes his role as an advisor personally and passionately. He is an expert in tax reduction strategies, asset protection, retirement and generational wealth planning. David works in collaboration with leading CPA's, attorneys and financial advisors to ensure that all planning is not only implemented but also integrated. This collaborative team approach ensures the highest probability of success.

David has been an advisor for over twenty years and holds multiple licenses and registrations in the fields of investment, real estate and insurance. He has been featured in many magazines and publications including Kiplinger's Personal Finance and has co-authored two books on estate and retirement planning. Currently David is working on a new book, *The Ultimate Retirement Blueprint, the 7 Secrets to a Stress-free Retirement*. He also is the host of *The Retirement Architect* radio show heard every Sunday morning at 9:00 on KFMB AM 760 in San Diego and is the financial expert on the weekly television show, *The American Dream*.

David graduated from UCLA's Personal Financial Planning program (Distinguished) and from the Wharton Business School's Retirement Income Planning certification program.

David and his family live in San Diego, CA, where he is an active member of his church and an avid tennis player.

CHAPTER 4

THE THREE-QUESTION SUCCESS FORMULA

BY BRAD MARTINEAU

I'm the 6th of 10 kids. There are roughly 19 years and 42 days between my oldest and youngest sisters. That's a new kid about every two years on average. That fascinates most people. More than anything, they wonder how we functioned and how we maintained any level of sanity or normalcy. I like to joke that I'm not sure we did.

So picture yourself in a house with 10 kids who are the following ages: 19, 17, 16, 14, 13, 11, 8, 4, 2, and a newborn. That was my house growing up. A common response I get is, "your poor mother." Nothing could be further from the truth, but more on that in a minute.

So skipping ahead past diapers, elementary school, and high school, we get to 2004, when I was working as an Admissions Counselor at an online university. I got a call from two of my brothers and my brother-in-law saying they were looking for some help at this little five-person software company they had started called Infusionsoft (if you're not familiar with Infusionsoft, it's an extremely powerful software tool that helps small businesses improve their marketing, sales, and client management).

At the time I hardly understood anything that they did, and the offer was for less money then I was currently making with no benefits. So, I did the only natural thing to do in that situation…I took the job. I'm not convinced that given that scenario again, I would make the same decision, but I'm extremely grateful I did.

That decision kick-started the journey I've been on for the last 10 years of really coming to understand and love entrepreneurship, as well as getting a taste of what it takes to be truly successful.

That journey has been somewhat of a roller coaster ride. I spent six years as part of the core leadership team of a growing software company that now employs over 500 people. I left to start my own business and woke up two years later with literally no money in my bank accounts. Then I started a new company and we did seven figures in a little over nine months. Like I said, a roller coaster ride.

I've learned a TON over the last ten years, but I believe the core underlying principles of my success can be traced to three questions that I've found to be absolutely critical to what I've been able to accomplish.

And it all starts back in the house with 10 kids:

"WHAT DO WE WANT TO HAVE HAPPEN HERE?"

My parents are literally two of the most amazing human beings that have ever walked the earth. Now, I can't say that I always held that viewpoint; in fact at one point I thought they were outright crazy.

You see, when I was growing up, my dad had this question he would ask over, and over, and over. I kid you not, before every family activity, family planning meeting, family anything, he would say the same thing. I even remember him saying it as we were heading to a movie as a family.

"What do we want to have happen here?"

Growing up, he might as well have said it in Spanish, German or French. I had NO idea what he was trying to say. No joke, Pavlov would have been impressed by how my dad could get me to roll my eyes on command.

I'm a firm believer that most of life's important lessons cannot be taught, but rather must be learned. This was no exception for me. It wasn't until I was married, had a few kids, spent six years at Infusionsoft, and failed at my first business that I realized the power of that phrase:

"What do we want to have happen here?"

In fact, it reminds me of a scene from Alice and Wonderland where Alice is talking to the Cheshire Cat:

Alice went on. "Would you tell me, please, which way I ought to go from here?"

> "That depends a good deal on where you want to go," said the Cat.

> "I don't much care where," said Alice.

> "Then it doesn't matter which way you go," said the Cat.

> "So long as I get somewhere," Alice added as an explanation.

> "Oh, you're sure to do that," said the cat, "if you only walk long enough."

About half our waking hours are spent working. The question is, towards what? What are we trying to make happen?

Not what are we trying to do, but what are we trying to make happen?

I fear that most of us don't actually know. We've convinced ourselves that our goals to "make more money" or "work less" or "lose more weight" or "buy a nicer car" or "get a bigger house" actually count as goals.

I think any goal that includes the words "more" or "less" is a copout. It's a lazy goal. Instead of actually deciding on a goal, we've decided to just point ourselves in a direction.

How *much* money do you want? How *many* vacation days do you want to take? *Which* vacations do you want to take? How *much* weight do you want to lose? *Which* car do you want to drive? How *big* of a house do you want? In *which* neighborhood?

The answers to those questions are goals. The problem is that most people can't answer them. Most people have directions, not goals. But then again, most people aren't successful.

The first step to hitting a target is to know which target you're trying to hit.

So pull out your list of goals (if you don't have a list of goals already written, that's a pretty good sign you have some work to do). How many of your goals have the words "more" or "less" in them? Which of your goals do you need to make more specific and more concrete?

Once you have clearly defined what success means for you personally, you can get to work.

And that leads us to our second question.

"WHAT IF I JUST DIDN'T DO THIS?"

So 2012 was our first full year in business at SixthDivision, and we were blessed to crack the seven-figure mark right out of the gate. That didn't happen without a lot of craziness, travelling, and being away from family. It was so bad, that our stated objective for 2013 was literally to grow the business by at least a penny, but to cut the pace in half.

At the end of 2013 we were doing our annual planning, and part of that planning involved a step where we made a list of all of our accomplishments for the year. We did a LOT in 2013. But as my business partner and I were reviewing our list of accomplishments, I had a very scary thought pop into my head.

What if we just hadn't done half of this stuff? Would it have changed where we finished the year? Or could we have just not done certain things, and gone home at noon every day? Or, could we have reinvested all that time into other activities that would have actually impacted our ability to meet our goal?

We were patting ourselves on the back for our list of accomplishments, but we weren't asking ourselves whether those accomplishments actually mattered in the first place. It wasn't that any of the accomplishments were inherently bad or wasteful, but when put in the context of our goals, they became completely unnecessary. I made a commitment right then that I would never get to the end of the year and look back and say, "I could have just not done half of what I did last year and I'd still be in the same place."

That was when I realized that simply asking, *"What do we want to have happen here?"* isn't enough. Every day when you show up to work, there is a second question you must be diligent in asking: *"What if I just didn't do this?"*

If the answer to that question is NOT a massive reduction in the likelihood that you're going to accomplish your goal, then you probably shouldn't do whatever you were about to do.

A good exercise is to pretend that you can't actually do any of the work yourself. All you can do is spend money to get work done to accomplish your goals. Would you spend the money as easily as you spend your time?

What I've found is that as soon as I have to part with my money, I become very serious about whether or not that money is going to produce a return. For some reason though, that part of our brain doesn't engage when it comes to our time.

So the next time you're about to start working on something, consider whether you'd be willing to write a check to get the work done as quickly as you're willing to spend your time.

Then ask yourself, "What if I just didn't do this?" And if the answer doesn't make you panic, go find something more important to do.

Now, on to the last question…

WHAT CAN I DO RIGHT NOW?

So let's jump back to 2010 when I had just left Infusionsoft. At that time, there wasn't a human being on the planet that knew more about Infusionsoft and how to leverage it to grow a business than I did. I had literally spent over six years actually building the product and implementing it for small businesses.

In a market where my skillset was at a premium, I should have been massively successful. Literally all I had to do was package my services, and then go sell them. Yet despite all that, within about 19 months, I was writing this in my journal:

> "I have enough money to make it through the end of the month.
> If we don't start driving some serious revenue, I'm screwed,
> with no real backup since I already burned that being stupid.
> I'm about $20k in debt."

Then, within a couple of months after that journal entry, I had started a new business and we were on our way to making seven figures. As I pondered what was different from my first business and my current business, I came to a very interesting realization.

Most people are more comfortable trying to solve any problem other than the first problem.

Let me explain what I mean. For any goal you have there are first problems, and then there are the rest of the problems. The first problem is the most important, and is easily recognizable because it's the one you can take immediate action to solve. The rest are problems (or potential problems) that we can only think about solving.

Most of us don't like addressing the first because it takes work. So instead we jump on the other problems because it's comfortable to just think about them. That's what happened when I started my own company. The first problem was deciding how I wanted to package and sell my own services. Everything else was secondary to that problem.

What did I do though? I went about 47 problems down the line and I started to worry about what my logo would look like, what shade of blue I should use, and how I was going to scale. Scale? Really? I didn't even know what I was going to sell, or whether I even needed to scale.

When we get sucked into trying to address the "other" issues, we do a lot of thinking, doubting, guessing, and getting frustrated. You know when you're trying to solve a problem and you start to feel helpless? That's a telltale sign that you're addressing the "other" problems and are skipping the first problem.

The first problem is always solved with action. So if you feel yourself getting stuck, ask yourself the third question: *"What can I do right now?"* The answer to that question is the solution to the first problem. In my case, the answer was, "create a service offering and sell it." Period. There was nothing else more important than that, and the only way to solve it was to take action.

It reminds me of one of my favorite quotes, "Action breeds confidence and courage. Inaction breeds doubt and fear. If you want to conquer fear, do not sit at home and think about it. Go out and get busy."

The solution is always to take action.

So the next time you find yourself going in circles and getting frustrated with the same problem, ask yourself, *"What can I do right now?"* Then, go do it.

This three-question formula has proven to be massively helpful for me in my business as well as my personal life. And while the questions themselves are not earth-shattering, actually going through the process of asking and answering them can produce dramatic changes and results.

I would recommend asking yourself those three questions when you feel overwhelmed, overworked, or just need a clearer vision of where you're going. It took me 25 years to understand the value of this formula, so take the shortcut and start practicing it now.

About Brad

Brad Martineau is the CEO and Chief Baller at SixthDivision, a small business consulting organization that specializes in helping entrepreneurs build better businesses. More specifically, he and his team are experts at helping entrepreneurs get clear on what success looks like for them, articulating a plan to accomplish that success, and then most importantly, actually implementing the plan.

Brad's introduction to the world of small business and entrepreneurship came back in 2004 when he was hired as the sixth employee at Infusionsoft to run their entire support team. He got a firsthand view of what it takes to be successful as an entrepreneur as Infusionsoft grew from 6 to 150 employees, and then ultimately to over 500 employees.

After six years at Infusionsoft, Brad teamed up with another former Infusionsoft veteran, Dave Lee, to launch SixthDivision and PlusThis (a software company that helps entrepreneurs). Within nine months they had built a seven-figure company that has continued to grow every year since. Each year they help hundreds of entrepreneurs build more successful businesses so they can enjoy life as they see fit.

In 2014, Brad was featured on NBC, ABC, CBS, and Fox television affiliates speaking on marketing automation and small business success, and was quoted in Forbes Magazine as one of America's PremierExperts™. He has also been featured in CNBC, Reuters, MarketWatch, and Yahoo Finance, among other notable news outlets throughout the country.

Brad is married with five (yes, five, you read that right) kids. When he's not helping entrepreneurs tap into the power of marketing automation, you'll find Brad building his fitted hat collection (you'll very rarely see him without a hat on), playing basketball, snowboarding, and spending time with his family.

You can connect with Brad at:
Brad@SixthDivision.com
Linkedin.com/in/BradMartineau
Twitter.com/BradMartineau
www.SixthDivision.com
Facebook.com/SixthDivision
Twitter.com/SixthDivision

CHAPTER 5

7 KEYS TO CHOOSING THE RIGHT FINANCIAL ADVISOR... FOR LIFE

BY C. GRANT CONNESS AND ANDREW COSTA

One day after we conducted an educational financial speaking engagement, a man flagged us down to talk for a bit. He was a retired teacher, who we will call Mr. Thompson, who had lived and worked in NY. He had recently moved to South Florida. Mr. Thompson had his life savings from teaching sitting in a bank account, and he was interviewing financial planners to determine who would manage this important piece of the rest of his life.

Many clients approach us to ask how we will manage their money and how they can get in contact with us. Mr. Thompson, however, explained the process through which he was going and wanted our advice. "What should I ask potential managers of my nest egg so I know that I am choosing the right person?" said Mr. Thompson.

Mr. Thompson's question struck a chord with us. Our personal motivation to start our firm was a close family member who hadn't known what to ask her financial planner. The result was unsatisfactory investments that ate up her retirement savings too quickly. Her personal experience drove us to create a firm that is plan driven. We devise a formal, tangible financial income plan for every client.

People should know what they can expect from their financial advisor.

The number one question that every investor should ask is, "Are you going to put together a tangible plan for me to guide me through the rest of my life?" If there is no plan, there will be no accountability. No accountability can equal retirement disaster. It can mean that you get a retirement of nightmares, not the retirement of your dreams.

Mr. Thompson helped us to realize that establishing a firm that meets the individual retirement needs of each of our clients is not enough. We need to go further to educate investors and retirees how to find a reputable financial advisor with whom they can plan their retirement and beyond.

With Mr. Thompson, our own relatives and countless future clients in mind, we developed seven keys to selecting the right financial advisor. When interviewing an advisor to whom you will trust your life savings, make sure you address these seven items.

KEY#1
WHAT KIND OF PLAN WILL YOU CREATE FOR ME?

What an advisor will do with your money to help you make it to and through your retirement should not be a secret. Having an income or financial plan in place makes all the difference. All day, everyday, we meet with people who invested in various financial vehicles over their lifetime. They have pots of money here and there but no physical plan for how everything works together and how to spend it to make it last.

If you have amassed $1 million, you need to have a plan to spend or generate income from those million dollars in a logical way. A plan holds your advisor accountable to something. Your financial plan is a roadmap. It creates the ability to stay on track with the goals you have set and to see clearly when you have taken an unexpected detour. You can say to yourself and to your advisor, "Here is where I am supposed to be according to the plan" and see how to get back on course.

Surprisingly, people will hire an attorney to handle their estate planning needs such as trusts and wills, but they won't hire a financial planner to develop a formal retirement income or financial plan that clearly documents how their investments will be managed, painting a clear picture of the rest of their life. Seek an advisor who is paid the same way your estate attorney is compensated, a fee-based advisor with fees for service. A fee-based advisor will be accountable to you and not the company for which they sell. Salesmen work for free in hopes they can sell you something as an end result. That is generally not the type of relationship you are looking for and it may not be in your best interest. Look for a specialist that will put a plan together to solve your retirement needs—not someone that will push a product on you that may not solve your needs. We bet you would not hire an attorney who telephoned you unexpectedly to offer you a new living will or estate plan because that's the special of the month at his firm.

Make sure the advisor will put a diversified plan in place and that your income producing accounts really do produce the income you need. Moreover, plan for a long life, not a short life. You might defy the genetics in your family and live to 99. Plan accordingly.

KEY #2
DOES YOUR ADVISOR HAVE AN INTEREST IN YOU OR ONLY YOUR MONEY?

An advisor you are interviewing should ask about your goals and expected returns. He or she should also ask you:

Do you have a will or trust? Do you own a home? Do you have a pension? Are there major life changes on the horizon for you? Do you have any debt? How is your health? What are your retirement goals? Essentially, you want them to ask anything and everything that will help them get to know you.

Do not be afraid of an advisor that pokes and prods into the depths of your financial life. This usually indicates that they are doing their job and attempting to create solutions that are in your best interest as opposed to theirs. This is similar to going to a doctor; you want the doctor to be thorough and ask you a lot of questions—not just prescribe you a drug without understanding your ailment.

The Advisor should also ask, "What is a reasonable rate of return for you?" Does your income currently meet your monthly expenses? Do you help support your children or grandchildren? How much can you stand to lose in a year? If you are likely to suffer a heart attack at a 5% loss, then we will build a different plan than we would for someone who is unafraid to lose 10-20%.

All of these factors must be considered in the creation of your plan. Additionally, questions such as, what happens to your pension when you die? Is there a provision for continued payments to your spouse, or will those payments cease? How will you cover loss of social security income from the spouse if that spouse dies? It's all about the bigger picture. We solve for the need based on the problems that could arise, not just the situation as it stands now.

We have a client who has $800,000 in investments. She lives frugally and can comfortably retire without having to utilize that $800,000. She may not require any income from that money, so we could invest it differently than we might for someone who has only that money to live on in retirement. However, our client conveyed that she has a strong desire to always be able to help her kids if they have money needs. Therefore, we kept most of her money liquid so she can help her children financially as needed. If we had not asked about her intentions regarding her children, her money might not have been accessible when she wanted it.

Some people want to "bounce their last check" and some want to leave money for their kids or charity. Asking the right questions and getting to know a prospective investor creates better outcomes.

KEY #3
MAKE SURE A REPUTABLE CUSTODIAN HOLDS YOUR ASSETS.

Ask the advisor, "Where is my money being held?"

Make sure your advisor is aligned with a reputable custodian and that your funds are held by a reputable investment firm, not in their personal or corporate bank account. This can really save you from fraudulent activity. (Anyone remember Bernie Madoff?) Fidelity, TD Ameritrade or Schwab accounts are a few examples of reputable custodians and they generally carry enough insurance to cover your accounts even in the event of advisor fraud or misrepresentation. Checks should not be made payable to the advisor or the firm. Always write your checks directly to the investment fund or custodian. Our custodian is Fidelity.

KEY #4
COMMUNICATION: QUARTERLY OR SEMI-ANNUAL ACCOUNT REVIEWS.

You will hear from some advisors all the time when the market is up, but then never hear from them when the market is down. Your advisor should contact you and review your plan with you quarterly or semi-annually to make sure that you are sticking to your plan. It is prudent to make adjustments along the way. Salesmen and brokers might be less incentivized to check in with you because they were paid up front. They don't have a need to check up and, in fact, they receive no additional compensation for checking in. In actuality, they might be hiding from you.

It is fair for you to contact your advisor and ask, "How have my accounts done?" How do they compare with the general market? If you are conservative, you might be doing really well at a 7% increase even if the market is averaging a 20% return. Just make sure you stick to your plan. Ask the advisor, "How do you feel about the next quarter?" Is there anything I can or should be doing differently going forward, to help me stick to my financial plan? Excellent communication is good for the client and the advisor because it forces the advisor to stay on point. It fosters a system of checks and balances for the advisors.

KEY #5
WHOLESALE OR RETAIL? AND WHO IS MINDING THE HEN HOUSE?

Your goal with any product or service should be to pay wholesale prices, not retail. This concept should be no different with your investments. A fee-based advisor with the appropriate platform can cut out all of the middlemen on investments and save you money in the end.

Wholesale or retail depends on who is managing your money for you.

Ask, "Who is managing my money?" The advisor might say that he or she is managing the money. You would think that would be good, right, to have the trusted advisor also manage your funds. In our experience, it is inefficient. You want to find out if they have an institutional management team who manages the money so a busy day for the advisor doesn't mean your money took a day off. You don't want them stuck in an easier-to-manage mutual fund with hidden fees and less than stellar performance.

Know who is minding the hen house. We believe a dedicated chief investment officer and their team can better manage client investments while also being able to secure wholesale pricing that saves investors money. A mutual fund is one example of the many expensive financial retail products packaged and sold by somebody else. They are the convenience food of the investment world. An advisor who has been in the field meeting with clients all day might sustain himself and his clients on mutual funds. A broker might choose to sell you that product, and you will have no idea who is actually managing your money within that mutual fund. In contrast, separately managed accounts in which the firm manages all the transactions are generally wholesale, transparent accounts. Wholesale, transparent accounts do not have the hidden fees often associated with mutual funds, variable annuities, brokered bonds, whole life insurance and many other packaged expensive retail products.

KEY #6
MAKE SURE THE ADVISOR CLEARLY DEFINES HOW THEY ARE BEING PAID FOR THEIR SERVICES.

We refer to this as transparency. You shouldn't have to ask them. Advisors are either getting paid commissions, charging fees for their time, or doing both. Get that information up front because no one works for free.

Beware of undisclosed fees. Mutual funds, variable annuities, bond funds, variable life insurance policies, and whole life insurance are permitted to hide their fees. What are the real costs? Instead of a variable annuity, you can choose an indexed annuity. Instead of a mutual fund, you can choose an Exchange-Traded Fund (ETF). Find the lower cost alternatives. If someone is working with you and planning through all these things, the right advisor will not want to waste your money because their fees are tied to the value of your account. If they place you in a high cost investment, they are not only hurting you, but also themselves. If you see any of the above high cost products—run.

KEY #7
VISIT THE ADVISOR'S OFFICE.

Think back to when your children were small and you wanted to scope out a new friend's home and meet their parents before you would allow your child to play there. The appearance of their office will tell you a great deal about the scope and viability of their practice. This is not an exact science, but a firm with large amount of assets under management generally will mean an advisor will have full-time staff of some sort. Beware of house calls and cold calls. How many times has your CPA, attorney or doctor visited your house? Accommodating you occasionally does not make them a bad advisor; however, some things can tip you off. You want to see the office and verify that they actually have staff and that their office is not their car. Proper due diligence will help safeguard your nest egg.

If an advisor with whom you have no previous contact randomly called you at 7pm tonight, beware. Cold calls are not the norm. If you do randomly hear from an advisor and are interested in pursuing a business relationship, you can investigate them via the SEC website (sec.gov), FINRA broker check (www.finra.org), Better Business Bureau (bbb. org) or the National Ethics Association (ethics.net). Cold calling from an advisor or broker might mean they have too much time on their hands or offers that might be too good to be true. If the product were truly amazing, every financial advisor would be promoting it.

Choosing the right advisor to manage your assets for life can be a daunting task. Your financial advisor should be a trusted friend who understands not only your retirement goals but also your life goals. No one should work their entire life scrimping and saving for retirement, only to lose a substantial portion of their investments due to improper planning and advisor selection. We hope that our 7 Keys will help you find and interview the right financial advisor for life.

About Grant

Radio Talk Show host, financial co-author, and South Florida native, C. Grant Conness services affluent South Florida individuals and families whom he advises and consults with on their retirement and estate planning aspirations. Mr. Conness brings trust, integrity and service when working with his clients.

Grant's dedication has earned him the respect of the South Florida community, of which he has been a part for over 30 years. He values the opportunity he had to ring the NASDAQ closing bell in 2013 and has been invited to ring the NYSE opening bell with his team at Global Financial Private Capital in 2014 as personal and professional achievements over his career.

Grant Conness is the Co-Founder of Global Wealth Management and an Investment Advisor Representative of Global Financial Private Capital an SEC registered investment advisor ranked nationally in the Top 50 by Forbes in 2013 in the Wealth Management Category: Fastest Growing RIAS. He is the Co-Host of the financial radio show *The Global Wealth Show*, airing on WiOD—South Florida's Number 1 Talk Radio Station. He was previously an accredited course instructor with the Florida Bar on 1031 Exchanges. Grant Conness has been featured and quoted in major publications such as *The Wall Street Journal*, *USA Today*, and *Newsweek* and has appeared on major television network affiliates such as NBC, ABC, CBS and FOX as a recognized investment advisor in his field.

Grant resides in Ft. Lauderdale with his wife Jessica and four children. He is a passionate sports fan and enjoys boating, surfing, paddleboarding, coaching his kids' youth sports teams and spending quality time with his family.

About Andrew

Andrew Costa is a financial co-author and co-Founder of Global Wealth Management, who has worked extensively in the field of Financial Management.

Andrew Costa is the co-host of the financial radio show *The Global Wealth Show* on 610 WiOD and iheartradio.com. He has been featured and quoted in major publications such as *The Wall Street Journal*, *USA Today*, and *Newsweek* and has appeared on major television network affiliates such as CBS, NBC, ABC, and FOX as a recognized professional in the investment management business. Moreover, he has been invited to ring both the NASDAQ and NYSE bells on Wall Street.

Andrew and his wife Liz have been married since March 2008 and have been residents of Ft. Lauderdale for more than 25 years. They are proud parents of two sons, Dylan and Austin. Andrew's hobbies include spending time with the family, golf, boating, scuba diving, traveling, and his passion for sports.

CHAPTER 6

LIFE LESSONS —THE PROPER NURTURING AND GROOMING OF FUTURE LEADERS

BY ROSIE RODRIGUEZ

I begin my title of this chapter by indicating there is a "proper" upbringing of a child and a sort of "how to." The truth is that there is no "proper" way to grow leaders. The growth is in the hurdles or life lessons that will be taken away from life experiences. That being said, can we as parents instill some key ingredients at an early age by not just what we say, but what we do? In this brief chapter, I will demonstrate the direct relationship between early life lessons, and how if we internalized them at the time, they become the foundation in your career and business!

By age 13, my father, who had been disabled due to kidney failure, and suffered from diabetes, died while on dialysis. If you ever want to learn a lesson on work till you drop, here is one. This story would inspire you, parents. The way you live your life, the choices you make will determine the views on life and values that your children will carry throughout life. This value system shows up in business every day. In the case of my father, I remember they had to force him into disability. He literally passed out at work while operating heavy machinery and they had to call an ambulance to take him to the hospital. Talk about dogmatic conviction. For a Hispanic male to not be able to take care of his family was like death. His physical and emotional health began to deteriorate at this point until his passing.

Lesson: Let the man work.

What I mean by that, is I do not know what brought my father personal or creative joy; however, I do know that being able to provide and care for his family brought him deep, deep satisfaction. Once he felt that was taken away – once you take a man's (or woman's) purpose – in a sense, he/she will be left with very little to keep him/her motivated in life.

IT'S MY DREAM STAY OUT OF IT!

I loved and respected my father for the man he was. I remember having a dream about my father, and him telling me in the dream that he was ok, that it would all be ok. That dream gave me comfort and peace. I remember a neighbor talking to me and telling me he was gone and that I had to accept it. I shared my dream with her and remember that she attempted to discount the validity of the dream or the message, and what it meant for me. I refused to listen to her. I remember being upset. Who was she to tell me what I was to believe?

Lessson: Guard your Dreams.

Do not let anyone tell you what is real and what is not. Don't let anyone else's beliefs become you own. At the time, that dream kept me going through a very confusing and emotional time. To this day I believe my father did come to me in a dream to bring me comfort. Whatever you believe to be true for you is yours. It's that easy. Learning that at an early age helped me completely ignore the nay sayers and dream poopers. What you believe is 100% true for you. No questions asked. So if you believe you can sell squid ink to monks, go for it!

STRENGTH – A WHOLE NEW MEANING

Difficult as it was, our family kept going. Just six months after my father's passing, my mother's cancer had returned (previously diagnosed and she had a masectomy) this time, the tumor was in her brain. Unbeknownst to me, she had been given six months to live. All I knew at the time was that mom was sick and that she was losing her hair because of the treatment. Can you imagine being a recently widowed woman, left to care for three children, not speaking the language and never having worked a day in this country? On top of all of that, now having to fight for your life, literally. She went through several chemo sessions, eventually became bedridden, and passed away 18 months later. Never once did this woman complain. Never once did she let on the gravity of what was happening. Her positive outlook and determination were unlike anything I have or will ever experience.

I remember having to make a phone call to the doctor to find out whether I could mix her morphine with the other medication she was on. The doctor proceeded to tell me that at this point in her illness, she had outlived her six months and could take whatever made her comfortable. I was silent. I left the room for a moment to process what I had just heard while holding back the tears. It was at that moment I knew my mother was not just sick, she was dying. My mother knew me well, she asked what the doctor had said, and I said simply that it was fine to mix the medication. The only thing she said to me was that doctors did not know anything, not to believe what they said, and that everything was going to be ok. I left the room because I did not want her to see the pain on my face or the tears that were stuck in my throat.

I think it was in that moment that I learned how to be strong for someone else. My mother's faith in God was the source of her strength. Even then, I cannot imagine how she held back from crying, from stressing, from being angry at the world. I wonder how many silent tears she must have shed in her moments alone. So if you are wondering where my inner strength came from, it is from her. All from this woman. She kept it together till the very end. I was the last one to see her alive. She was at the time on an airbed in the hospital, and we would take shifts being with her. She waited till I left, then went peacefully.

Lesson: Take nothing or no one for granted.

My father's passing was my first real experience with death. I was not prepared for it. I had to grieve like everyone does. In those moments, you think that things cannot get any worse. Seeing my mother bedridden and suffer was worse. Although it hurt beyond words, her passing brought me a sense of peace because I knew she was no longer in pain. Life took on a whole new meaning from that point forward. My purpose in life was crystal clear – SUCCEED! In order for me to honor their life and struggle, I had to be everything I could be, and take my brother, age 11, along with me. That was it.

In middle school and high school, kids worry about video games, their hair, the cute boy or girl, the dance…yes, all of those things were a part of my world. But none of it had nearly as much significance as where I was going. Education was the center point of our upbringing. I was lucky to have had a father who constantly reminded me of how I had to go to college so I did not end up a laborer like him. All I had at the time was the memory of what they wanted for us, and an internal focus I was not aware I had, until now that I look back.

That strength and focus was embedded into my DNA and has become the staple of my success—along with adopting gratitude as my source of consolation. I could not hurt any more than I already had. The story I created was about how grateful I was that I had amazing parents, even if it was only for a short while. Some people have parents that abuse them, or are not present. My parents never did. They loved me, and for that I was grateful. They taught me how to work, how to fight, how to love, and how to be grateful. I learned how to appreciate what really matters and ignore the trivial things. All of this prepared me for my journey in business.

LET'S GET TO WORK

I became an entrepreneur at a very young age. Through this time, I knew money was an issue and never wanted to burden my parents with my personal necessities, so I went to work at age 12 on the weekends at a local swap meet. I would wake at 5 am in the morning and put in a 12 hour day for 30 dollars a day – helping vendors set up their tarps and selling their items. Little did I know that would give me my first experience with sales.

Lesson: Hands-on experience.

Literally, I firmly believe that academic education is the core, but that life experience is equally valuable. If you want to raise a hard-working leader to be, let him work. The lesson that a day's work will teach a young person cannot be experienced out of a chapter in a book. The feeling of accomplishment, the budgeting, and the separation anxiety when you spend your hard-earned dollars, all of that, the emotional part, can only be experienced firsthand. Let the child learn firsthand.

RESPONSIBILITIES EARLY ON

How can a child learn to be responsible when growing up, if everything is spoon-fed, or done for him. At 15, I had become responsible for my little brother. Seeing him through adolescence into adulthood became my focus, second only to how I was going to get myself through the next few years to be able to financially care for him. We lived in a terrible gang and drug-infested neighborhood. Once at about age 19, they had the audacity to come to my door and threaten our family with violence if we did not force some kids out of our house and into their hands to beat them. Why? Because my brother and his friends did not want to join the gang. So the gang took measures to ensure they had no choice. Essentially their life was in daily danger, until they got "jumped in" to the gang. I remember the incredible rage I felt that day. I also remember feeling powerless. I could not protect the boys, or I would be risking my brother's safety. I could not call the cops, or I would be risking my entire family's safety, as they would continue to terrorize us. I had to find a way out. I had to find a way to leave and take my brother with me.

Lesson: When push comes to shove, find your way out.

Owning a business will throw so many challenges your way. Your reasons for pushing forward have to be so big and so important to you that you will find the way to get there. I could not tolerate my environment or the thought of losing my brother. The feeling of being responsible for him and the desire to have him succeed was my driving force. What is so important to you, that it will drive you? Take on the challenge and responsibilities that come along with your determination. Sure its scary, but anything worth having, should be.

HERE COME THE BELLS

Not long after, I met this amazing man, now my husband. I had been in a dysfunctional relationship (imagine that) during high school. I had a guy tell me he loved me, during a time I needed it. In whatever shape it came in, I was lucky to have left the relationship and to have found Mr. Right very early on. I was 20 years old and met this fun-loving, caring, enthusiastic, hardworking, kid-loving, 6ft. 1" "hottie." We were married within a year. We were 21 years old and I remember thinking, why marry him now? I had just been accepted to transfer in to USC, was ready to live the college experience. But I could not find a reason not to marry him. I had a choice to make. Short term fun versus long term happiness. I suppose this is when I adopted a true long term approach towards things in life. With my early losses, I knew love was more significant that college parties. I was going to succeed in life; however, meeting the love of my life who had become my support through everything, was the best thing that ever happened to me. We got married and moved out of the "hood". I was able to finish college, start my career, and eventually we started our Mortgage business together.

Lesson: Support Beyond the Bra.

Who do you have in your life that serves that role. Everything that I have accomplished has not been an individual effort. I cannot tell you how many times my poor husband has been woken up at 4 am to hear my great ideas, or the value that my auntie who helped raise us and has continued to support me like a mother. It may be a co-worker, a best friend, a pastor or a teacher – look around. We all have support out there and I so appreciate my support system. If it wasn't for all the people that I have found in my life and the people that have been behind the scenes, I cannot imagine being in this blessed place I am today.

WHAT'S YOUR MOTIVATION?

Soon after I Graduated from USC (go Trojans), I began my career in Mortgage lending, When my husband and I purchased our home which closed the first week of our marriage, I was terribly confused by the process. I did not understand the terms, fees, charges, etc. I had decided that once I graduated college, I would learn this business. At college, we had lost our family home to foreclosure. I was not in control of the process and so was extremely disappointed and hurt. In retrospect, I am kind of glad. That home was full of painful memories and I hated the neighborhood, the gangs and the drugs. The home represented my father's hard work. But after some time, it took on a different meaning to me. Losing the home increased my interest on how loans worked, on top of the fact that years prior when we bought ours, I did not understand that either.

Once graduated, I chased the loan officer who helped us during the home loan process and agreed to work for $500 a file on a commission-only basis. I was thrilled! Yes, USC college grad, able to secure a normal high paying salary, but no, I wanted to be in this field. It was not about the money. You see I never had any, so can't tell you I needed it. I wanted to learn. Unfortunately the lender hired me, and then never called me back. So I found an ad in the paper, applied and was hired, on a gut feeling. (Apparently I did not score really high on an assessment.) In my first month I beat the top producer. Three months later I was training new hires, another three months and I was promoted to manage a new branch in the West LA area. I am grateful because I learned so much about my field: managing, hiring, firing, auditing, phone systems, client care, etc. It was a fabulous experience.

Lesson: Learning is more valuable than the money it will bring.

When you are starting in a new career, the single most important thing you should look for is a place you can learn. Look for a mentor – someone who is wildly successful and will give you the opportunity to learn from them. Whether they pay you or not. Understand they are doing you a huge favor. One you can never repay. If they are willing to take their time and teach you, you will have everything you need to succeed.

SHORT LIVED HIGH

I hit company records and had enormous success. However, after a year of being with the company, learned that their practices where not entirely ethical. I became highly demotivated. My job was to teach others how to sell like I did, and close deals knowing that the product was not in the best interest of the client. I could not. I remember the moment one of my loan officers asked me to help him close a deal. I walked in to the room, looked the man in the eyes, and decided to resign. I did not "close the deal" I actually told him to keep shopping. I then proceeded to give notice and moved on to my next chapter.

Lesson: You must be completely aligned with your core.

Ethics are a huge part of your internal drive. You must be congruent with who you are to experience joy with success. How many times have you heard of highly successful business men and women who are divorced, ill, or worse, commit suicide. Those who truly succeed find that alignment and excel ten-fold over those who don't – because it becomes easy. It requires zero effort to feel good about the service or product you are delivering. As a matter of fact, you free yourself up to actually enjoy what you do on your way to the top, what a novel concept, aye?

THE NEXT STEPPING STONE

Soon after I left the company, I went to work for a small broker. The opportunity was enormous. Working under a broker I was able to offer my clients a variety of products that served their needs while making a living for myself. It was awesome! It was awesome until I hit my personal peak and wanted to build a team. My broker at the time was focused on his passion, investing. I was ready to build a team. I went to him to ask for advice on how to become my own broker, how to set up the company, what CPA's to consult, etc. He was very resourceful and supportive.

Lesson: Be Transparent.

Thinking back and having had experience as the "boss," I can appreciate the relationship my broker and I had. It was a very open and mature business relationship. I never realized that people on both sides of the table, the boss and employee, don't always conduct themselves in that manner. I really do not understand why both employers and employees feel the need to hide company information or plans to seek other careers. I believe that comes from within you. It's a great big world inside and outside of us. If you work under someone, be upfront and honest about your career goals. If your employer can help support that growth, awesome, if they become intimidated by it, awesome. It only reinforces your decision to move on. And vice-versa. If as a leader in your organization, your people are onboard with your vision, awesome! If they are not, awesome! If the people in your professional environment do not share your vision, or cannot support it for whatever reason, then you have permission to dismiss them, no matter what side of the table you are sitting on. It is not good or bad, it's just reality. When you are building your career or sharing it with the world, be transparent and enroll support for that dream. When you are completely transparent, you may not make the world happy with your decisions, but you will have peace of mind and a confidence that you are aligned.

READY, SET, JUMP!

Opening up Powerhouse Mortgage was one of the most exciting times of my life. Being self-employed under a broker for two years had given me the discipline I needed to go to work without pay, and the budgeting skills to run my life on a fluctuating income. This was essential. I jumped, but not before going through two years of boot camp, and making sure I had a safety parachute, my financial cushion. I had done very well with my broker, and very quickly. This enabled me to have a financial reserve in place that would carry my personal and business expenses for a good six months comfortably. This was crucial because you never know what unexpected turn may come. Like having a baby! Yes, we were pregnant. After three years and several painful failed attempts, we were finally having a baby. Because of our failed attempts, I put myself on bed rest because I was going to make sure this baby had every chance of meeting her mom. It was a difficult pregnancy, but despite the challenges, we officially incorporated our business two months after my baby girl was born.

Lesson : Be prepared.

Being successful means preparing for all of the life changes that may come your way. My childhood was full of unexpected turns—which helped me mentally prepare for whatever was to come in my adult life and career. If you have a dream, a passion to pursue a business or venture, do it! Do it fast but be smart! Have a plan laid out, your personal finances in order, your business cushion in place, and a Plan "B" in place to carry you through the hurdles.

THE RISE AND FALL

Ten years had passed. I had built an incredibly successful mortgage operation, built a comfortable investment portfolio, grew a successful Real Estate office with over 150 agents, opened an escrow company, and, just for kicks, a chocolate fountain company. What now? Well the market took care of our next life lesson. 2007 had been a horrible year for my companies, the employee morale was floored, our reserves were being depleted month after month, and to top that, we were pregnant, again! As a leader in an organization, you are the visionary...the big picture...you can do it! Let me show you the way people! What cannot be taught is how to be that person. We were losing money like there was no tomorrow, and some of our real estate investments as well. So here is the picture, 3 businesses, 9 months pregnant, bank accounts hemorrhaging, husband had been hospitalized a few times because of a blood count issue, and 2 little girls at home. For most people, that is enough to want to throw yourself over a cliff, right?

Lesson: Have a sense of Humor.

I remember our office administrator at the time, telling us what the cash call was going to be to cover payroll, and my husband and I kind of laughed it off. She asked, "I don't know how you two can laugh about it, when you are losing so much money." Believe me, it was not that we did not stress or worry, or that the financial blow was not substantial. You get to a point in your business during challenging times when you just have to laugh. Really, it is either that or you "die," so to speak. Having come from six people living in a studio apartment and later losing what was truly valuable in my life, this did not compare. It was just money. It was not our life, it was not our health. It was just money. Life is too short.

Having a business...being successful, means that you have to learn to carry things lightly. Don't let any one deal, one month, one client, one challenge – weigh you down. If you do, you will never make it. Successful people learn to laugh at themselves and they keep going. A sense of humor is an essential quality. Be willing to laugh.

WHEN YOU'RE GOING THROUGH HELL, KEEP GOING!

Despite the challenges and the losses, we made it through the storm intact. Sure we were inches away from losing our businesses and a hairline away from a divorce, but we are a stubborn pair. In any trying time, people take for granted those that are closest to us. We just do. Husband has a bad day, wife gets to enjoy his tension, wife has a long day at work, someone is sick at home, the big child is fighting with the little one and someone screams "it's not fair, how come you..." You know the story. It is usually with the people that we care for the most that we let our hair down to, and unfortunately, vent freely. In our case, working together and bearing the same challenge, that was multiplied. To be successful, you have to, have to, have to, be successful in the home. You cannot separate the two for very long. And although my partner (husband) and I were able to laugh, the weight of our employees, the self-blame, the "what-am-I-doing-wrong?" conversation kicked in hard.

Lesson: Leaders take responsibility for the results they experience.

If your business is failing, it may feel like something is wrong with you. Learn to separate your work from your own identity. You cannot control external factors. Do not get so drawn in and take so much responsibility for things over which you may not have any control of, so that you fail to recognize the power of decisions. In retrospect, I should have been a bit more objective and made a few more decisions a little quicker. Had I done that, I would have saved myself and family some grief at that time. Remember that you can only do your best with what you are equipped with at the time. So don't be too hard on yourself when things don't work out the way they were planned.

FULL CIRCLE – THE SINGLE MOST IMPORTANT LESSON IN BUSINESS.

I have to date, in my 30-something-plus-one more years of life (that would be 40) and business, I have learned so many valuable lessons along the way. I could teach a person how to incorporate a business, how to establish your internal processes and secure your public identity, how to market and sell anything, how to protect your assets, and about legal outlets, family support, marriage tools, parenting , building a team, letting people or opportunities go, how to speak in public, how to… how to…how to…But the ONE lesson that has been the most valuable is that of being GRATEFFUL. All the way back to losing my parents, to disease and cancer, to setting up my businesses and almost losing them, to getting married and almost divorced, to rebuilding it all. The single most important tip or lesson that I can share with you is to BE GRATEFUL. Be grateful for what you did have, what you did learn, who you do have in your life. If you stay focused on gifts of growth, your cup will always be half-full. Most importantly, you will enjoy the journey.

About Rosie

Rosie Rodriguez is an entrepreneur and self-made millionaire owning multiple real estate related businesses and investment properties. She enjoys building businesses, teaching, coaching, exercising, and is constantly in the pursuit of higher learning. She is married and ready to celebrate 20 years of marriage, and the mother of three beautiful children. She will begin by telling you in some detail about her childhood, only so that you can understand how crucial the lessons learned early in her life can translate into success or failure of your business.

Rosie was born of immigrant parents many moons ago. As a young child, they lived in a studio apartment (3 adults and 3 children). Their living room was their bedroom and their dining room. She never knew the definition of poor or rich, and never saw herself as any different than other kids. What she remembers most about her childhood was how hard her father worked, and how much she was loved. She never "thought" about how she was going to succeed, what her career was going to be—it was all about living in the moment, celebrating, and being part of her family.

Little did she know what life lessons were ahead of her.

CHAPTER 7

BEING UNREALISTIC AND BEING UNREASONABLE

BY MIKKEL PITZNER

I'm currently house-hunting, and as it happens, I've found a house that appeals to me. Unfortunately I'm not in a position to acquire a mortgage since I do not have the required US history as yet in terms of W2s, nor do I have the visa status that would even allow me to apply (that application is still awaiting approval with the Immigration Services and the State Department).

But like I said, I found the house that I like, and as one can only expect with my taste and my desire for a certain upscale lifestyle, the house is somewhat costly—making a cash buy a little bit out of reach for my current liquidity, having just sunk a lot of my money into several new start up businesses.

The region in which the house is located is experiencing a pretty great demand, and it has, unlike so many other locations in the U.S., enjoyed a fairly warm housing market the last couple of years. In other words, sellers here are sticking to their prices and guns in negotiations – because they know that they'll probably make their sale if not to one buyer then to another.

So when I spoke to my real estate agent about the possibilities of temporary owner financing, she immediately told me that I could completely forget about that and that no one would do that. I reminded her that no one can be sure of the other person's situation or temperament and that everybody's mentality, attitude and situation changes, depending on what else might have happened or is currently happening in their lives. She responded she was just being realistic and that she lived in the real world.

Well, as it happens, she kind of shot me down, but that lasted only for a little while. I'm usually not one to give up.

I kept thinking about the house, and as I looked at other houses, none of them appealed to me like this one. Now, I honestly am not the person with too much patience, especially when it comes to a person who exudes limited mindsets. I've also learned from the experience of so many business negotiations over the years that unless you direct yourself with authority and from a place of certainty, well, then you really don't stand a very good chance of obtaining what you want.

So it wasn't long before I drove by the house I wanted and had another look. The realtor sign outside had changed and there was now a new realtor representing the buyer. I thought to myself, "To hell with it, why not?"

I picked up my phone, dialed the seller's realtor and introduced myself. I told the agent that while I did have an agent representing me, I didn't want what I was going to propose to be muddled up along the way (quite frankly, if I had been able to reach the seller directly then that's what I would have done. Not to cheat out the agents, but to ensure that they wouldn't mess up what could end up in a mutually-beneficial deal).

I clearly explained my situation and my sincere interest in the house and then I laid out my suggestion for a deal. That suggestion entailed a very large cash down payment (almost 60%) and then the balance to be financed by the seller. However, I would then pay a monthly payment that I calculated to be equivalent to at least double a monthly mortgage payment for a mortgage based on a sum corresponding to the remaining balance. My monthly payment would draw down the remaining balance that I owed the Seller and when the two years were up a balloon payment of what was left would be fully payable. Before the two years would be up, my visa situation would be in place and so would my W2 history, and I would qualify for a mortgage. With so much equity in the house already by that time, obtaining a very favorable mortgage would not pose a problem.

The Sellers realtor was a little astounded judging by the sound of it, and her response, as she stated that this sounded highly unusual and out of the ordinary. However, I had said everything in no uncertain terms, showed complete conviction and used appropriate tonality and I relayed everything as if this was the most natural and sure deal in the world, so she had no other choice than to actually present it to the Seller.

She called me back the following day and informed me that the Seller actually had agreed to the offer with some minor adjustments. She was completely taken aback by this experience. Now, we haven't actually closed on the house as of yet, but the story illustrates a number of points, including the point of being unrealistic.

Here's the truth as I see things: I have not achieved my best results that I have experienced throughout my lifetime and my entrepreneurial life spanning many businesses, industries and even continents, by being realistic. In fact, my best results have been achieved when I've been completely unrealistic and stretched much farther than one would normally even dream could be possible.

I have completed a marathon (42.2 km/26.2 miles) with just a single training run prior in the six months leading up to the race. Now granted, it wasn't my personal best result by far (about 50 minutes slower), but I accomplished it.

I have likewise completed an Ironman (3.86 km/2.4 miles swim, 180.25 km/112 miles bikeride and 42.2 km/26.2 miles run) with just a few 10 kilometer (approx. 6 miles) runs, about 8 or 9 bikerides leading up to it, and a total of three 1.5 kilometers (just less than 1 mile) swims, and completed it in a respectable time (everything considered) of 13 hours 10 minutes, which I could probably have done a full hour faster had I not turned a bit lazy along the way.

I have completed a bike race that stretched over several mountain passes including over the highest paved mountain pass of Europe (Stelvio), and which spanned three countries in about nine hours with less than two months training and less than 750 km/468 miles bike training rides prior—beating several much more trained friends by more than 30 minutes.

In business, my biggest results have come from times when I dared to take on bigger assignments than I have ever done before; such as the time when I had in excess of 200 limousines on the road for the Climate Summit a few years back. This was at a time when, after we had gathered about 85 chauffeurs and cars, it seemed as if absolutely no more cars nor qualified drivers could be found. I was unrealistic and we made it happen (we had to source cars from outside the country to fulfill).

Currently, I'm unrealistically engaged in about twelve new business ventures—all start ups and all in completely unrelated industries or business areas. I say 'about' cause I'm actually considering about two or three more businesses. All have been started in the past 6 months or less and my part of them is either 100% ownership or 50% ownership.

All this is in process while I also help a few other companies, sit on about nine boards, already am partner of six other companies, am engaged in at least three book collaborations, and in the process of writing two of my own books—and reading between three books a week to one book a day. And also, while studying at least twelve programs, and building several online information programs of my own—including one on how to achieve the lifestyle of The Automated Millionaire (www. theautomatedmillionaire.com)—and while fully engaged and spending lots of time with my two small children and my wonderful wife (not to mention traveling, vacationing, procrastinating, being lazy and more).

Now, can I be certain that all my new ventures will be successful? No, and judging from statistics and even my own track record, probably not. But do I believe they all stand a pretty decent chance of success? Absolutely. I wouldn't otherwise have engaged in them or started them. Could I reach better results quicker in a single one of these if I devoted myself just to that one? More than likely, yes. But it wouldn't be as much fun for me as I think it is to do several. Would I recommend engaging in physical challenges of the kinds described above without decent training having led the way prior? Absolutely not—and my results would of course also have been better and the experience probably a lot more fun too.

But the bottom line is, you should be highly unrealistic if you want to achieve much greater results. Setting unrealistic goals make you stretch farther. Much farther than you otherwise thought possible. Unrealistic goals make you seek out unusual avenues and solutions. Unrealistic aims make you come up with more imagination and resolution that you probably have seen in yourself before. Unrealistic reaches make you grow, expand and evolve.

Now, I do not wish for me to make this chapter a write up on Goal Setting (www.thegoalsettingacademy.com), but it's probably fair to mention that there is basis for a discussion of whether unrealistic goals could make you depressed or demoralized along the way, since they would seem so unrealizable and that smaller partial goals along the way would be more recommended to keep up your spirits along your struggle towards the "finish line."…And I would agree with that a great deal.

You've probably heard of the SMART goal setting, in which you set goals that are Specific, Measurable, Attainable, Realistic and Time-Bound. But honestly, sometimes I would say "to hell with SMART goals." Specifically, "to hell with the Realistic part of it." I find that human beings, when setting Realistic goals, tend to underestimate their true potential and abilities, and I should like to see them stretch way farther. Simply stated, they flat out set their goals way too low.

No, what the world needs is Big Hairy Audacious Goals (often called BHAGs). Those who set BHAGs often come up with the most unique solutions, and in the process find huge advantages, advances, huge innovations and often leapfrog typical development and progress.

Great examples of this can be seen with Elon Musk's fully electronic vehicles of Tesla—that not only made electronic cars sleek, stylish and sexy, but also supplied great performance, not just in respect to how the cars drive, but also in terms of the performance of the Tesla business, while most other car companies struggled. Not convinced by the Tesla story, well, then just look a bit further and see how his Space X efforts are completely outperforming other 'conventional' space programs in cost, in speed of getting results, and well, in results.

Peter Diamandis also stretched himself when he preposterously put up a $10 million prize (the largest prize in history when it was put up) with his first X-Prize project in his X Prize Foundation, and that at a time when Peter Diamandis himself hardly had a dime himself, and had yet to find any real sponsor to the purse.

The result: To win the prize, famed aerospace designer Burt Rutan and financier Paul Allen led the first private team to build and launch a spacecraft capable of carrying three people to 100 kilometers above the earth's surface, and twice within two weeks.

The late Steve Jobs of Apple also set unrealistic goals. He wanted to make a dent in the Universe. The results? He completely transformed and revolutionized not just one industry, but six: The personal computer industry, the animated movie industry, the music industry, the mobile phone industry, the tablet industry and the digital publishing industry. In fact you might add a seventh—that being the retail industry.

Elon Musk and Steve Jobs have been rewarded by their unrealistic goals. They both became billionaires and they probably share some of the same traits as several other billionaires. I've had the pleasure of meeting a few billionaires myself and if I were to draw a few parallels without knowing them very closely, I would venture to say that not only do they all seem to make some rather unrealistic if not completely unrealistic goals, but what's more, they often seem from the outside to be completely unreasonable.

Now, I'm not saying this as a negative, and necessarily as in treating other people in unreasonable fashion (although we have probably all heard about certain character flaws of the late Steve Jobs and possibly several other eccentric billionaires now and then), but unreasonable compared to the typical mindset and opinions that people carry, and unreasonable in their thinking of what's possible and what's possible how soon and at what cost. Yet, aren't they often the ones who bring us the greatest advances? Aren't they usually the ones who accomplished the most? If nothings else, they built big businesses and reaped the biggest financial rewards. Study some of the most successful and wealthy and you will find a lot of them came from nothing. ...Foster home kids even, and upbringings in poverty. I venture to say they wouldn't have gotten this far had they not been unrealistic and unreasonable.

Perhaps there's something in that for the rest of us to learn from, if we wish to gain greater results and reach a higher level.

About Mikkel

Originally from Denmark, Mikkel Pitzner turned the car rental company, Pitzner Auto, into the fourth largest, quadrupling the number of locations. Its leasing department doubled under his leadership and he led it to becoming the Budget Rent A Car licensee for Denmark. He was instrumental in the challenging sale of the company, which comprised a split of the company to three different buyers.

From late 1996 up until the end of 2010, he owned and operated the largest limousine service company in Denmark, for which profits grew 3200% during the first year of ownership alone. The company served the most discerning clientele, including three recent US presidents—George Bush, President Clinton and President O'Bama—and numerous embassies, countries, royalties, celebrities, multi-conglomerates, etc.

He successfully ran an import and distribution company of scuba diving equipment and sold it to a German distributor just a few years following the foundation. He is a partner of Freetrailer (comprising Freetrailer Denmark, Freetrailer Sweden and soon Freetrailer Germany and other nations) and of a very unique advertising and marketing bureau, Aksel & Ko, while helping several US and international businesses in a challenging economy.

Recently Mikkel Pitzner has founded several new businesses including Pivot Point Enterprises, which has created an online business platform on which to build, collaborate on and manage all of your business processes. New is also RetailWise USA which builds on special and unique expertise that at roughly the same price you would typically pay for mystery shopping, you'll get ExitShopping® that combines the very best from mystery shopping, customer satisfaction and competitor analyses, loyalty rates, efficiency measurements, etc., all in one smooth operation.

A sought after professional board member, Mikkel Pitzner currently sits on boards of companies spanning the US, Denmark, Sweden and Poland - privately held as well as publicly traded companies.

Mikkel is a multiple best selling author (six best selling books published so far) and speaker. He teaches entrepreneurs how to create a business that provides for the lifestyle of your choice while taking you off the treadmill of your job, so you can spend your time on things of your choosing. Here's list of Mikkel Pitzners books:

• *The Art And Science Of Success, Vol 2*

• *The Only Business Book You'll Ever Need*

- *The Success Secret*

- *Marketing Miracles*

- *New Rules Of The Game*

- *Mikkel Pitzner's Trade Secrets For Marketing Your Business Online*

- *Masterminds's Insights To Business Success*

Mikkel has several new books in the works due out during 2014, including *Breaking Through* and *The Automated Millionaire.*

Mikkel Pitzner has been featured on CNBC, ABC, CNNMONEY.com, Entrepreneur, Fox News, CBS News, *The Wall Street Journal, Fortune, Fast Company, SmartMoney, USA Today* and NBC, America's PremierExperts, Børsen, Berlingske Tidende, Erhvervsbladet and Näringsliv. Mikkel Pitzner was also a guest at the Brian Tracy TV Show, Amino TV, *The Secret Entourage* and radio program *Money for Lunch.*

Residing in beautiful Colorado with wife Olga, son Gabriel and daughter Angelica.

To learn more about Mikkel Pitzner, please visit www.mikkelpitzner.com

Contact:
Mikkel Pitzner
888-988-2489
info@mikkelpitzner.com

CHAPTER 8

A NO-NONSENSE GUIDE TO HIGHER SALES

BY PAUL EDGEWATER

K.I.S.S.

The acronym "Keep It Simple Stupid," has been attributed to Kelly Johnson, who back in the 1950s and '60s was the lead engineer at Lockheed in their top secret division, "Skunk Works." This was the enterprise that developed the U2 and SR71 reconnaissance aircraft for the U.S. military; the most successful and effective aircraft of their kind. The K.I.S.S. principle is based on the concept that systems are most efficient and effective when kept as simple as possible. All business functions should adhere to this same principle.

Sales processes should not be complicated. Selling is simple. That is not to say that it's easy and it's easy to miss that notion. Winning a marathon is a simple process; just be the fastest person in a group of about 45,000 runners on that day. Simple equation? Yes. Easy? Of course not, but anything worthwhile is challenging. Most people and organizations that fail in their endeavors do so because they make them too complicated. The basics are the essence of success in any pursuit. Keep things simple. This isn't rocket science.

SALES IS NOT A DIRTY WORD

In Brian Tracy's, *The Psychology Of Selling,* he reminded those of us in sales to be proud of being sales people. Being a salesperson is to hold one of the most important and crucial positions in any organization. Without sales, there is no manufacturing, no HR, no R&D, no marketing, no distribution; there is nothing without sales. If there are no sales, there is no enterprise; it's that important. If you are in sales, hold your head really high; you're employing everyone around you.

Some people get a job in sales until they get a 'real job.' They do sales because there isn't a position currently available in their field and when that position becomes available, often the sales job is wantonly dropped and they dive headfirst into the job they prepared for. That's fine, but many of these people walked away from a career that may have proved to be far more lucrative and rewarding than the other course of action. I'm not suggesting the reader shouldn't follow his or her dreams. By all means, do. But know that whatever your field of study or expertise is in, please realize that there is a sales component present. Even if you aren't on commission, having basic sales skills will assist you in any endeavor. You may not have to get someone to sign on the dotted line to collect a check, but we all have to sell our ideas to others and convince them to see things our way. Sales skills are needed in all walks of life.

GET TO THE POINT

Brevity is the soul of wit. A great book for learning this skill is, *How To Get Your Point Across In 30 Seconds Or Less* by Milo Frank. It's vital to understand and appreciate how busy prospects are these days. An example I like using to illustrate the importance of brevity today is with advertisements. In television's infancy, commercials could be as long as two minutes. Viewers were so enamored of their TV sets in those days, that even watching commercials was entertaining. That evolved into 30 to 60-second spots. Fast forward to the present day. I recently gave a talk to an entrepreneur class at Columbia College and asked the students for a show of hands: "Who has watched a network television commercial in the last 12 months?" Not one student raised their hand. The advertisements young people are noticing (or ignoring) these days are online and when the ads give the viewer the option of skipping the spot in five seconds, almost all the students exercise this option. Does that open your eyes? It did mine. We have to respect our prospect's time, and we need to get to the point and get to it fast.

THE MORE THE MERRIER

Nike reminds us: "Just Do It." Don't overthink sales, or how you're going to approach prospects. The worst thing that'll happen if you don't close the deal is that you will learn how to not close the deal and you'll get it right the next time. A perfect example of this was back in the late 1980s, I was the Chicago sales manager for Metagram America, a long defunct, alphanumeric paging/answering service, which at the time was the cutting edge in communications technology. It was a 24/7 live answering service that would answer your calls with a customized greeting and then send the user, what would today be called a text message, on a device that looked like a beeper. Remember those? All of our sales reps were issued one of these pagers and were tasked to hit the pavement. Many of the reps would sit in the office and spend hours figuring out their strategy for the day before getting in their cars and going on sales calls. At best, they would see about three to four prospects before coming back to the office to complain that they hadn't closed any sales.

My number one salesman had a different strategy. I hardly ever saw him. The only time he would ever come in the office would be to get more literature and business cards. The rest of his time was spent talking to people about Metagram America. He would talk to hundreds of people every week and he sold more than anyone in the country. He 'just did it.' He didn't over think it. He would strike up casual conversations with people he met at the bus stop, train station, at the grocery store— whenever and wherever he was. He didn't take the process too seriously and his commissions were seriously large. I'm not suggesting that every company has a product or service that lends itself to this type of approach. I'm aware that some things can't be closed without a lengthy and involved consultative process. But in all industries, a salesperson can still vacillate too long before getting the ball rolling.

The bottom line with regard to the numbers game is to do the math. There is a very good chance that you will double your sales if you pitch twice as many people. You will triple your sales if you pitch three times as many people and so on. Ask yourself how big of a raise you'd like, set your goals, do the math and hit the pavement.

ASSUME THE SALE

One of the greatest salespeople ever, Elmer Wheeler, used to instruct his students, "Don't ask if, ask which." In other words, don't give your prospect a choice between something and nothing. Rather, give them a choice between something and something else. Instead of asking, "Would you like one of these knick knacks?" – ask instead, "Which one of these knick knacks would you like?" or "How many knick knacks would you like?" or "What color/size knick knack would you like?" Often when someone says "no thank you" to your offer, it isn't because they're not interested; it's because you gave them the opportunity to say "no," which often times is just a conditioned response. When you ask an "if" question, you are giving the prospect a choice between "yes" and "no." This is what we call a 'closed-ended question.' These are to be avoided whenever possible. At worst, they end the sales process immediately with a "no" response and at best, you won't have much to go on with a "yes" response. As salespeople, we are always trying to engage our prospects in conversations that reveal their needs and wants. If someone just gives you a "yes," you now have to ask another question to dig deeper. Assuming the sale begins with asking open-ended questions that start with "Which," "When," "Where," "What" and "How." These will get your prospect reflecting, responding and revealing their real needs and wants to you.

Another part of 'assuming the sale' is to have the right attitude about your product or service. If what you are selling isn't something that you're completely sold on, you'll have a hard time selling it. You should start your day with the assumption that since you're sold, everyone else will be too. If you have reservations about what you're selling, your prospects will be able to tell. If you are not sure about how you feel about this, do a little research into your product(s) and service(s) and do a little soul searching too; you may have to work somewhere else, or sell a different product or service to succeed. Anthony Robbins discusses this in his best-selling book, *Unlimited Power.* We have to be congruent to have the influence we desire. As salespeople, we have to be fully aligned in this area.

HOW TO GET MORE YESES

Let's examine the "Yes, yes, yes" method of closing the sale. At first blush, this tip may seem like a contradiction of what we just discussed where I suggested that you never ask a closed-ended question (one that could be answered with a 'yes' or 'no'). So is this a contradiction to our last training? No.

In sales and business, you have to try everything until you find what works for you and depending on your personality and your ability to persuade, this "yes, yes, yes" tactic can work wonders. Legendary sales trainer Brian Tracy, says that when people answer "yes" to a series of questions, they are more likely to say, "yes" to your ultimate proposition. The trick is to make certain that the questions you ask will indeed illicit a "yes" response; nothing that requires a commitment by the prospect. Come up with some 'safe' questions. For instance, if it's nice out, ask the consumer, "Isn't this a beautiful day?" They answer, "yes." If your home team just won a big game, ask, "Isn't it great that xxxxx won??" Again, they answer, "yes." Then when it comes to asking someone to make a purchase, they are on a 'yes-roll' and the likelihood of getting them to make a purchase goes up exponentially (factoring that you still ask "which," not "if," during your close). I'm suggesting that you have very upbeat, positive and light-hearted conversations with your prospect.

It's important not to overdo this as you only have a small window of time to properly educate the consumer and too much fluff will annoy them. Formulate your questions in advance so that you're not getting "no's" about anything. It's a highly effective tactic that will go a long way to increasing cooperation and compliance in all areas of our lives, not just when we're selling.

BODY LANGUAGE

We've all heard, "It's not what you say, it's how you say it." We wield far more influence with our words when they are accompanied with positive body language. I'm not going to delve too deeply into this, as this is a study in and of itself. If you'd like to learn more about this subject, I would suggest that you study NLP (Neuro-Linguistic Programming).

For this chapter, I'll highlight what I have found to be the salient points of body language that have helped me in my sales career:

- Smile! Pretty simple: Just wear your best smile as often as you can. Make sure it's genuine and warm.

- Listen intently by maintaining eye contact.

- Subtly nod your head to communicate an affirmative message to your prospect—whether or not you agree with them (more on that below). A little nod is letting them know you're present and paying attention.

- Pace your prospect's style of speaking. Speak slowly if they do. Speak quickly if they do. Speak loudly if they do. Speak softly if they do. People like people who are like them and one of the quickest ways to establish rapport is to have a similar speaking pattern. Be careful not to mock them; do this with stealth.

This is the tip of the iceberg. I strongly encourage you to do your research on NLP and body language.

EMPATHETIC SELLING

Everyone likes to get an education, but no one likes to be schooled. When we are selling, we are educating our prospects. If and when they have a concern or an objection to our proposal (erroneous or otherwise), it behooves us to educate them gently. Dale Carnegie taught us that "A person convinced against their will, is of the same opinion still." Tom Hopkins teaches a great method to address this; it's called the 'Feel-Felt-Found' system.

If someone raises a concern, immediately agree with them and tell them, "I know how you feel." Incidentally, you can say this with conviction because they indeed shared their concern with you, ergo you know how they feel. This works because it takes the 'fight' out of the prospect. The last thing they expect a salesperson to do is not throw a clever rebuttal back at them. It also shows them that you are listening to them and acknowledging their concern as valid. We then follow up with something akin to, "Most folks I speak with have felt the same way." This lets the prospect know that they are not the only ones with this concern. The last part of this equation is to preface your response with, "But what we have found is…" and here you can list all the reasons why your prospect need not be concerned.

If you skip the 'Feel-Felt-Found' method and go right into your rebuttal, it's going to feel like a game of ping-pong to your prospect. They will think you have a 'canned response' for everything they say and you'll lose them. The 'Feel-Felt-Found method gives you an opportunity to really hear them and give them the best solution for their needs and wants, which is what selling really is all about.

DON'T GIVE UP

Jim Rohn would ask audiences during his talks, "How long would you give your baby to learn how to walk, before you just told him or her to stop trying?" The reaction was unanimous: "As long as it takes! My baby will keep trying until they walk!" Tony Robbins used this same analogy and made the observation that this is why every able-bodied person on Earth learns how to walk; our parents didn't give up on us. Later in life, whenever we set our goals in any endeavor - be it sales or even losing weight - we need to get it done with the same resolve we used to learn to walk as children; keep working on it until we succeed. Earl Nightingale reminded us to keep working at our goals—no matter how long it takes to get them accomplished. The time will pass anyway. Do your best for as long as it takes and success will be yours.

About Paul

Paul Edgewater is America's Brand Builder™ and Promotions Powerhouse™. He's an in-demand keynote speaker and a best-selling and award-winning author. He is cofounder and CMO of Busy Bee Promotions, Inc., which opened its doors in 1998. Busy Bee Promotions executes an average of 1,200 events every month in all 50 states.

Paul has been featured on and in *The Wall Street Journal*, *USA Today*, *Promo Magazine*, FOX News, CNN, CNBC, MSNBC, FOX, ABC, NBC and CBS news affiliates. His clients range from start ups to Fortune 100 firms such as Coca-Cola, Whole Foods Market, Ikea, Macy's, Starbucks Coffee, Verizon Wireless, Groupon and many, many more. He is the creator of the Sampling Sales Success System™, the leading method to convert samples into sales in the retail food industry.

Paul is the author of several books including: *I Challenge You To Find A Better Book*, a sardonic scrutiny of awful advertising; *Counter Attack,* co-authored with world-renowned business leader, Brian Tracy; *The Only Business Book You'll Ever Need*, co-authored with Robert G. Allen and Ron LeGrand; *In It To Win It*, co-authored with legendary sales trainer, Tom Hopkins and *The Success Secret*, co-authored with personal development legend, Jack Canfield (all available at: www.EdgewaterConsortium.com).

Paul has more than 40 years of sales, marketing and promotions experience and is motivated by his intense love of the private sector and the free market system. He takes great pleasure in creatively connecting his clients with new customers. Along with his business pursuits, he is a weekend athlete with three marathons under his belt as well as an acclaimed singer and musician.

Paul is available for speaking engagements and consultations worldwide.

For booking information, please visit: www.BusyBeePromotions.com or call Toll-Free (888) 438-9995 X 21.

CHAPTER 9

YOUR RETIREMENT EDGE

BY PHIL CALANDRA, RFC®

I remember back in the mid-1980s waking up early to the smell of fresh-brewed coffee and the rustling of a crisp newspaper. At the time, I lived with my grandfather, a retired Army Colonel and lifelong early riser. He would drink his morning cup(s) of Joe and pour over the stock pages of that newsprint. I asked him once, "What in the world are you looking for in those columns of numbers?" This of course was before the era of unlimited, real-time financial and business news. Granddad said, "Son, I am looking for an edge." "An edge?" I asked. He explained, "I have retired in an envious position, at an envious period in financial history. Your Nana and I have two Social Security checks per month, I have an Army officer's pension (after 32 years of service), and I saved and invested well." He said "I am always looking for an edge, an investment strategy that will protect us. That is why I work with my advisor to stay on top of these stock pages."

In my youth, I didn't quite understand why a "strategy" was so important. From the outside looking in, it just seemed so ideal and natural to live ones retired years the way my grandparents did. It wasn't until years later, as I was working hard for my clients, that I really understand what he meant. Times are certainly different and many things have changed over just a few decades.

Planning your financial future is your responsibility. In today's changing economic environment, it's never been more important to know whether you are on the path to financial security throughout retirement or not.

It's becoming more and more difficult to solve retirement through the conventional method of just investing in a tax-qualified plan, buying a few financial products or following the advice that seemed to work over the past 30 years. Hope and timing is not a strategy.

The most difficult thing to plan for is the unknown. American retirees will always be looking for a solution to the retirement income-planning puzzle. Whether approaching retirement or already retired, everyone faces the increasingly complex challenge of building a retirement income plan to last throughout their lifetime. You have worked hard to nurture and cultivate your savings nest egg. Now the biggest question is, "How do I spend my money and not run out in retirement?" As a retirement planning expert, I want a plan that gives our clients the best chance for success.

FIVE KEY IDEAS THAT MAY GIVE YOU AN EDGE

#1 – Converting Wealth Into Income

Retirement shouldn't mean cutting back on your favorite things. Whether your hobby is playing golf or working in your garden, retirement should be about enjoying your favorite pastimes. However many find themselves worried about money and not having enough money in retirement. With proper planning and execution, retirement should be your time to enjoy the hobbies and activities that have been pushed to the backburner during your working years. Throughout your working life, you've received a paycheck on a set, regular basis. And, you probably knew exactly how much each check was going to be. Now you've retired, and rolled over your 401(k) and other retirement plans into your IRA. You've saved diligently and have accumulated wealth within your plans, but now what? How do you transition your wealth into income to cover your living expenses?

Every retiree must customize their solution to provide a steady stream of income using a defined strategic process and realistic assumptions. Your key objectives must be to maximize income, increase investment options, maintain liquidity, and protect your principal. The retirement funding problem should be viewed as a two-phased problem: accumulation and spending.

Most people understand that there are differences between these two phases of the retirement process. However, the prevailing methodology for the spending phase uses static models that simply extend the investment portfolio of the accumulation phase. These models either continue with fixed proportions portfolio, or a decreasing equity portfolio. The whole idea of retirement is to draw income from savings that have accumulated over time, without having to continue working for wages. Success in this endeavor depends upon several factors: The starting amount, the required spending, the investment results, one's life expectancy and, most important, overcoming the erosion in purchasing power that inflation creates. All retirees must consider certain realities when working with their financial advisor. The real challenges that must be addressed include: inflation, interest rates, liquidity and longevity of spending.

#2 – Generating Your New Paycheck

Once you retire, you'll want to re-evaluate your overall asset allocation, to make sure your portfolio is structured to generate the income that you'll need. Some of the investments that you may want to consider at this point are:

- Bonds
- Dividend-Paying Stocks
- Preferred Stocks
- Mutual Funds
- Annuities

All of these investments have different and unique advantages and disadvantages. As we all know, there is no perfect investment. Therefore, it is important to understand how any and all selected financial products fit into what you are planning to accomplish. Unfortunately, most people succumb to the siren of Wall Street and end up purchasing some financial product because it was a "hot tip" or favorite of some research department. Don't just buy an investment product, completely understand and be comfortable with how it fits into your plan.

I remember when our sons were much younger. We would sit down to work on a jigsaw puzzle, and in many cases they thought two or three pieces of the puzzle fit, when in fact, they did not quite match up. Being young boys, they would try to "make" those pieces fit. Of course, pushing and forcing the puzzle pieces together didn't help render the desired result. Don't make this juvenile mistake with your financial future.

#3 – A Warning About Bonds

Here is a big red flag regarding bond strategies as of this writing. For the last 60 years it has been commonly agreed upon that a bond position adds safety to the investor's portfolio - and that has been generally true. However, investors who own bonds today may be sitting on a ticking time bomb. Consider this. The value of any given bond is driven by the bond coupon (interest rate) and duration (time to maturity). In a falling interest rate environment, bond values will tend to rise. Since the Federal Reserve has been keeping interest rates abnormally low, investors who have held bonds for the last 10 years have done very well. On the other hand, a rising interest rate environment will depress the value of bonds. Do you have any doubt that we will see interest rates rise over the next five to ten years?

For example, if we see just a 2% increase in interest rates, a bond with a 20-year maturity will fall in price by 23%. In other words, a $100,000 bond portfolio just lost $23,000. I don't mean to be a Chicken Little, but let's take this hypothetical one step further. Interest rates rise by 2%. You see your bond holding devalued by 23%. What will you likely want to do in reaction. Sell! What happens to any item where there is a high supply and a low demand? The price is depressed even more. So, why would you be eager to buy and hold an asset that you know will lose money. Understand what I am teaching you, having the proper vision and plan in place may help you avoid making common mistakes that we believe to be conventional wisdom.

#4 – "The 4% Myth"

Once your needs are determined, your financial advisor can help you develop the right distribution strategy for you. If you blindly subscribe to the conventional knowledge that has long favored the "4% withdrawal rule" (which states with a withdrawal rate of 4% of the value of your portfolio at retirement, adjusted for 3% inflation, your money should last for 30 years) then it's time to know the facts.

How much money can I withdraw on an annual basis from my portfolio without running the risk of going broke? This is the kind of question that should keep you up at night. And, it is the exact analysis exercise you should be completing with your financial advisor. We call this type of planning: Results In Advance Planning. Utilizing one of the many software based tools now available, you can "test drive" your retirement plan. Of course, no one has a crystal ball, however, you can simulate how any given investment strategy may perform using the thousands of data points collected over history. This type of retirement income plan allows you to "stress test" what you are currently doing, and it illuminates the changes you must make and why you should make them.

Volatility in the markets, historically low yields, and the fact that people are living longer has many experts questioning the 4% safe money withdrawal rule. Morningstar recently concluded that a retiree who wants a 90% probability of achieving their income goal and having their assets last 30 years should only withdraw 2.8% per year. To look at it in different light, if you retired today, at age 62, and had a portfolio of $1,000,000, you could safely withdraw $28,000 the first year, with 3% inflation the second year it jumps to $28,840 and so on. After that, pray you and your spouse don't live past 92 years old. By the way, a married couple age 65 has a 40% chance that one of them will celebrate their 92nd birthday.

#5 – Cover All Your Bases
When you approach retirement, there are obviously things that will change in your life, one of them is how you think and manage your money. Many people make this major transition without making the necessary change to coincide with their new phase in life. Big mistake! Retirement planning will become increasingly difficult and complex as our economy, markets and political landscapes shift.

Income planning has now become crucial for people in or nearing retirement and you may want to work backwards to figure out what your primary income needs are. When you add your Social Security payments, pension (if you are one of the lucky few) and investment income, there may be a gap in your primary income need. One solution that has been getting a great deal of support lately is to use a portion of your assets to purchase an annuity with a lifetime income rider that will cover the gap and protect against longevity. The income stream may also be adjusted for inflation if desired. By implementing a product allocation strategy combining annuities with a lifetime income rider and traditional portfolio strategies, you may vastly increase the chances of having sustainable income in retirement no matter if you live to be 85 or 105 years old.

However, buyer beware when it comes to annuities. It is imperative that you completely understand the type of annuity you are buying and how it specifically fits into your retirement income plan. In fact, there are more annuity contracts I dislike than contracts I like. You may not need the benefits of an annuity to accomplish your income planning goals. That is precisely why we recommend using a process like Results in Advance Planning to stress check and verify which allocation is going to create the greatest outcome for you.

These days, people are looking at retirement as a whole new chapter in their lives. It is the end of one season and the beginning of something new and exciting. In working with clients, my sincere hope is that they are not robbed of that new and exciting chapter because of worry and anxiety over money. Your retired years are to be filled with the opportunity to travel to places you've never seen or trying hobbies you've never had time for previously. Resolve to be done putting your dreams off any longer.

Along with ensuring that the essentials and needs of life are paid for, strive to enhance your financial well-being, giving you the confidence to live the life you've been dreaming about for the last 20 years. Find your "edge" and "strategy". The hours and the days are yours to live out your retirement dreams, and we want to be there to help make those dreams come true. It is the joy of our profession to make the lives of our clients happier and to help them enjoy the retirement they worked so hard for and deserve.

About Phil

Phil Calandra: Financial Commentator, Author & Advisor

Phil Calandra is the Co-founder and CEO of Calandra Financial Group, LLC and Calandra Wealth Management. Before creating his independent wealth management firm, Phil spent more than 20 years consulting such Fortune 500 companies as Coca-Cola, Walt Disney World, UPS and Georgia-Pacific. Along with his wife and business partner, Jennifer, he now advises clients on issues of crucial importance so they can make the financial decisions needed to retire with peace of mind.

Phil is a Registered Financial Consultant® (RFC), a member of the International Association of Registered Financial Consultants, and is an Investment Advisor Representative. He is also the Chief Investment Strategist at Calandra Financial Group, LLC. and a nationally-recognized expert in Retirement Income Planning and Investment Management. In 2011, American Registry added Phil to the Registry of Business Excellence™ following his selection as one of the 2011 Atlanta Wealth Managers by Atlanta Magazine, who honored him again in 2012. Phil is also honored to have received the highest award the State of Kentucky can bestow, The Kentucky Colonel, and is an American Legion Civic Leadership Award recipient.

Phil has written extensively for the financial press and recently released his second book: *Retirement Unchained: Break Free from Wall Street and a Government Gone Wild!* In this book, Phil shares the financial strategies he has developed over his 20 years of working with Fortune 500 companies and how these strategies can be used to secure your financial freedom.

A native of the Atlanta area, Phil currently resides in Kennesaw, Georgia, with Jennifer, and their four sons. Phil is an active member of Burnt Hickory Baptist Church and enjoys reading, playing trumpet, skiing and riding his Harley-Davidson motorcycle.

Phil, his wife Jennifer, and the Calandra Financial Group, LLC, have appeared on ABC, NBC, CBS and FOX affiliates around the country, and have been featured in articles in a variety of print media and websites including *USA TODAY, Newsweek* and T*he Wall Street Journal, The Huffington Post*, DepositAccount.com, *Little PINK Book* and the *Calgary Herald.*

CHAPTER 10

HOW TO SUCCEED IN MOBILE REVOLUTION – ADAPT OR PERISH

BY PRAVEEN NARRA

It is not the strongest of the species that survives, nor the most intelligent. It is the one that is most adaptable to change.
~ Charles Darwin

ADAPT OR PERISH

Blockbuster was a highly successful brick-and-mortar company in the 1990's that provided home movie and video game rental services. At the peak of their success, they employed 60,000 people throughout 9,000 stores serving over 15 million households. However, because they did not evolve with the new technologies and business models of the time, they were forced to file bankruptcy, and were sold at auction for a mere 320 million dollars.

The mistakes Blockbuster made were multi-factorial, but what really hurt them was they didn't see emerging technologies that were taking over their industry. Nor did they address frustrations their customers were experiencing by having to pay late fees.

In 1997, Reed Hastings rented a movie from Blockbuster. However, he inadvertently misplaced it and was charged a hefty late fee. While on his way to the gym, Hastings realized he paid a flat monthly fee to workout as much or as little as he wanted and that led to an idea that revolutionized the video rental industry.

Hastings launched Netflix, an online movie rental service where people could choose any video they wanted, receive it by mail and then return it in the self-addressed/stamped envelope provided. The best part was there were no late fees.

With this business model, Netflix's sales grew from $1 million to $5 million within a year. Hastings then went to Blockbuster offering to sell Netflix for 50 million dollars. However, to their detriment, Blockbuster remained stuck in their brick-and-mortar way of thinking and underestimated the power of new technologies that was reshaping our world. As a result, their revenue rapidly dropped. They were forced to close many of their company-operated stores and sadly, in September 2010, the 25-year-old company had to file for bankruptcy.

TECHNOLOGY COMPLETELY REVOLUTIONIZES BUSINESSES

Companies who do not adapt are sure to perish. For instance, AOL was another household name back in the nineties. They had 13 million members worldwide using their dial-up Internet services. At peak, they were the leader in instant messaging and email platforms. However, AOL did not see the dark horse of high-speed Internet taking over.

The mistake AOL made was building their infrastructure completely for dial-up and not upgrading to new technology. Then, they merged with Time Warner, a non-technology company. The unfortunate result was their market cap plummeting to less than 1% of its peak.

Here's another story. Sony was founded in 1946 and evolved serving the electronics, game and entertainment sectors. Even though they employed over 146,000 people throughout the world with sales of 78.2 billion dollars in 2013, their market cap was only 17.6 billion dollars. In contrast, a new company called WhatsApp, started up in 2009. They are a cross-platform instant messaging subscription service company – with only with 55 employees and estimated revenue of just 20 million dollars. However, because WhatsApp developed cutting-edge technology that continues to reach millions of people, Facebook recently bought them for 19 Billion dollars! That is 10% more than the market cap of Sony.

That, my friends, is the power of technology.

MOBILE REVOLUTION

Mobile technology is taking over consumers and businesses like wild fire. It took nearly 64 years for telephones to mature in the market, almost 22 years for computers and only 4 years for smartphones. The message is this – unless you adapt to mobile, you will not be able to reach your customers in their preferred way of communicating and doing business, and will eventually perish.

Think about it. There are more people on the planet who have access to mobile phones than toothbrushes or toilets. This is unbelievable, right? 6 billion people have access to mobile phones, where as only 4.2 billion people have access to a toothbrush and only 4.5 billion have access to a clean toilet.

And what about your love life? Imagine your typical day. In comparison, how much time are you spending on your smartphone as opposed to actual time with the your spouse or loved ones? If you are among the average statistics, then the answer is 2.7 hours on your smartphone and less than 30 minutes a day with the most important person in your life. Most people say they can be away from their lover for more than a day, but in a survey, 84% admitted they couldn't go a single day without their mobile phone.

The entire behavior of humanity is changing because of the integration of mobile phones into our society.

Now that you have a taste of the statistics, let me give you the top seven tips that you can implement right now to help your business thrive in this mobile revolution.

TIP #1: HAVE A MOBILE OPTIMIZED WEBSITE

By the end of 2014, more people will be accessing the Internet using mobile devices than they will be from desktop computers.

According to Google, 75% of the website visitors prefer a mobile friendly website. If your website is not mobile friendly, 61% of your mobile visitors not only leave your website, but also go to your competitor's website.

While most businesses have a website, when it is accessed from a smartphone, the website is too heavy with images and videos and not effective because it is designed for large screens.

Think about how your website is going to look on a mobile device. One of the things you can do quickly and easily is to adapt a mobile first strategy and make your website a responsive design, which means that it will automatically adjust its format to fit the size of a screen.

Because more people are using mobile devices than desktops, it is important to design your website to be easily accessible on the smartphone.

TIP #2: USE MOBILE INTELLIGENCE

Smartphones have more functionality than computers. They have features such as GPS, camera, videos, QR code and barcode scanners, gyroscope, accelerometer, receiving push notifications and texting to name a few.

Smartphones can provide a lot more intelligence about your customers and user behavior. It is wise to think about how you can serve your customers better by using this intelligence and providing information that is more relevant and time sensitive. For example, if you are in Los Angeles, it does not make sense to receive information about an event happening tonight in New York. Similarly, based on where the user is located, you can send coupons for services that can be used in their particular location.

TIP #3: BUILD A MOBILE APP FOR YOUR BUSINESS

70 billion apps were downloaded in 2013. That is nearly 10 apps for every person living on this planet and this trend is growing exponentially.

At the time of writing this chapter, there are 2.4 million total apps among four major app stores: Apple, Google, Microsoft and Blackberry. About a million of those are Apple (iOS) apps and 1.1 million are Google Play (Android) apps. There are only 142,000 Windows apps and only 130,000 Blackberry apps.

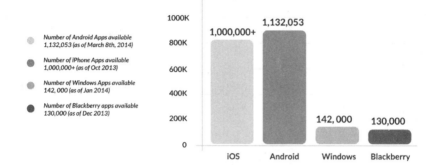

2.4 MILLION TOTAL APPS
on the 4 major app stores

The first place to make an investment is either Apple or Google (or both if your budget supports it). If you have a limited budget, then first evaluate if more of your target customers are using iPhones or if more are using Android phones. People with iPhones typically tend to spend more money than those with Android phones. If you serve both iPhone and Android users, you will cover more than 90% of the market share of smartphones.

TIP #4: LIST YOUR BUSINESS ON ONLINE MAPS
AND LOCAL DIRECTORIES

95% of smartphone users have looked for local information via their smartphone. Therefore, it is vital to have your information available in mobile format and have a presence in places such as Google Maps, Bing Maps, Yellow Pages, etc., since listings from these sources are shown in local business search results.

Another important thing to know is that 90% of smartphone users took action after performing a local search. Compared with other kinds of marketing such as television advertising, although they may reach the customer, the customer rarely takes action. With mobile search, 90% of users take some sort of action, and 70% of those will take an action within one hour. However, if they use a desktop, it will take a whopping one month for maybe 70% of those people to take an action, if you get that much conversion at all.

TIP #5: PROVIDE MOBILE INFORMATION FOR LOCAL SHOPPERS

Traditionally when shoppers were in a brick-and-mortar store, the store was more than likely to do business with them if the right products were offered for the right price. That is not the case anymore. Now, 84% of the smartphone shoppers are using their smartphones while they are physically in the store shopping. Many customers use apps that scan product's barcode and look for the lowest price by searching on the Internet and comparing them to where the best place is to buy. The trend now is for people to view products locally, but then actually buying them online, where the price is typically cheaper.

Not only are your customers able to shop for a better price, but they also are able to get more information online than they are able to get from what is printed on the products.

Another thing to know is that mobile coupons receive a mind-blowing 1,000% redemption rates over printed coupons. Therefore, it is better for you to spend money on providing mobile coupons than it is spending money on printed coupons, right?

TIP #6: USE QR CODES

QR codes are 2-dimensional images that you can scan with your smartphone's camera using QR Code scanner apps. Within it, information such as a website URL address, email address or phone number is embedded so the customer can continue their action there.

Therefore, if you are advertising in print, instead of providing information on a four-page newspaper ad, you can print a smaller ad with a QR code. Then, when people scan the QR code, they can be taken to your website directly from their smartphones where you can show them unlimited information along with images, videos and interactive media.

You can also collect personalized information by asking basic questions. For example, if you are in the insurance business, when people come to your website via QR code, you can ask for their location, age, etc. and then provide them with a customized quote.

Realtors can print only so much information on a flyer and it is not interactive. Add a QR code that takes people to your website, and then you can show as many images of the property as you want along with videos and 360 degree views.

TIP #7: UTILIZE PUSH NOTIFICATIONS

Push notifications are notifications that can be sent to mobile phones. The advantage of push notifications is that they can be customized and automatically sent to your customer depending on various criteria.

For example, imagine you have a store located in the mall. You can use push notifications to provide coupons for your customers when they come to the mall to shop. The app will detect when your customer is nearby and automatically send them your coupon. They then immediately receive it, which gives your store instant recognition. Even if they had no intentions of visiting, when you send your customer a coupon at precisely the point in which they are in proximity of your store, they are more likely to buy from you.

CONCLUSION

We are just seeing the beginning of the extraordinary impact that mobile is having on the way we do business. There will be an estimated growth of ten times the mobile data traffic between now and 2019. Ten times! Unless you adapt your business along with this new age of technology, then your business is sure to perish.

Within change comes the opportunity to take your business to a completely new level. By implementing the latest mobile technologies, you gain the leading edge over competitors who do not have this mobile knowledge. We can help you do that.

About Praveen

Praveen Narra is a serial entrepreneur, author, and international speaker. Praveen Narra is Founder & Chief Executive Officer of Byji, Inc. The vision of Byji is to empower millions of people in this world by providing them software, apps, and tools though a wide range of channels. Byji brings the power of knowledge-sharing, training and coaching to the fingertips of every person with computers, smartphones, and tablet PCs.

Prior to founding Byji, Inc, Praveen Narra founded AppDevelopment.com, Inc. and is a CEO of the company. In his 13 year tenure as CEO of the company, Mr. Narra has lead his team of engineers to successfully complete more than 1200 projects in Software, Web and Mobile platforms. Some of the companies that trusted their software development needs to Mr. Narra's companies include Small and Medium-sized Businesses, Startups as well as Fortune 500 companies, as well as world-renowned business leaders such as Tony Robbins. Mr. Narra is passionate about delivering exceptionally great value for his customers' software development Investment.

Praveen Narra is also Technology Director at Nexus Global's India chapter. Nexus Global is a movement of 2000+ young investors, social entrepreneurs and allies who work to increase and improve philanthropy and social impact investing. Nexus's members are under the age of 40, spanning from 60 countries with a combined wealth of over $200 billion in investible assets. Members include royalty from the EU to Asia, and families such as the Rockefeller's, Kluge's, Bronfman's, Pew's, etc., … as well as young movement leaders and entrepreneurs.

Prior to founding Indyzen Inc. dba AppDevelopment.com, Inc., Mr. Narra has consulted for Microsoft Corporation, TechLead, ICL Fujitsu, as well as Dillard's. Mr. Narra holds a masters degree from Birla Institute of Technology & Science, Pilani.

Visit: PraveenNarra.com to learn more about him.

For more information, scan the QR Code below
or visit www.AppDevelopment.com/Successonomics.

CHAPTER 11

LEAVING A LEGACY OF FINANCIAL EDUCATION

BY JAMIE NOWAKOWSKI

As a young mother of three boys, I owned and operated beauty salons for a number of years. It was during this time that I developed a lot of interpersonal relationships with women and became an excellent listener. I learned very quickly how to align with people and understand how they were feeling and what they were thinking. Little did I know at the time how important those listening and interpersonal skills would be when I transitioned into a new career.

As my children became older, I entered the world of banking and excelled at a rapid pace. I found myself gravitating toward the investment side of the industry and eventually became licensed to assist our banking customers with their investment portfolios.

As a result of developing my interpersonal skills in prior years, very early in my financial services career I was able to narrow down who I am and with whom I was able to work well. I find it very important that when a client is looking to work with an advisor they must feel the advisor is a fit for them and the advisor must feel the same toward the client. I came to learn that there are many moving parts to the market and not all aspects of the market relate directly to every individual in the same way. As I continued to acquire the right clients, I was able to deepen those relationships to better understand the specific financial goals and objectives of my clients.

I find that people are often emotional and unclear about their description about money. Sometimes what they say is not always what they mean. So it's extremely important for an advisor to be able to ask the right questions to determine the exact intent of the client. People may say they don't want one thing or another. But, when you begin to probe deeper into their thought process, they often don't have a good explanation as to why they think the way they do. Sometimes they don't fully understand what they do or do not want. They may have heard something from a friend or on television that caused their mind to be set in a certain direction.

Often people are afraid when they talk to an advisor about their money. They may be afraid that they will be taken advantage of, so they don't want to come across as unknowledgeable. I pride myself in being able to get to know my clients, earn their trust, and work with them to pursue their long-term financial goals. I will always be honest with my clients about our working relationship because there has to be an understanding and trust between us. If I don't understand them and they don't understand me, then it's just not going to work.

Since I began in this business I have positioned myself as an advisor to qualified investors and their families. In general, my clients are baby boomers and are very similar as to their goals and financial status. I feel that I'm able to be more efficient as an advisor if I'm not spreading myself too thin by trying to capture clients in all stages of wealth advancement. By concentrating on keeping current with all the financial products and services that are designed for that carefully chosen group of investors, I find that I'm able to better serve each one individually and address how their unique situations and goals best interact with the complexities of the market.

As a parent now of three adult boys and a grandparent to my three-year old grandson, I know how important my children's and grandchildren's futures are to me. I also know that I'm not alone with this parental emotion and that many of my clients are very concerned about their children's futures as well. These are "millennials"— the X and Y generations. I believe they are a neglected generation for many reasons. Financial advisors typically tend to concentrate their efforts on the more established investors. However, I feel a great sense of responsibility to help my clients **and** their X and Y generation children.

Financial advising with baby boomers is a lot easier than it will be for the next generation. Unfortunately, I believe the millennial generation is destined to experience much more disparity and greater challenges than their baby boomer parents ever realized. Yet, all is not lost. If these children are educated properly in financial matters and embrace a savings nature, then they will be in a position to support themselves through retirement. On the other hand, there will be a large segment of that generation that will not be educated financially and they will struggle when it comes to retirement.

As I mentioned before, I see the younger generation as a neglected segment of the population and they are going to be facing untold challenges throughout their lifetime. Many of today's companies are not offering the pension plans that the baby boomer generation experienced. In fact, pension plans will probably soon be non-existent. 2014 will likely be a big year for companies to de-risk their pension plans then offload the plan to an insurer. In a few short years the young person starting in the workforce will probably have no idea what the word "pension" even means. It's quickly going the way of the dial telephone or the "dial" on the television.

Companies evolved from offering pensions to offering 401K matching funds. Now the current trend is away from offering matching funds for a company's retirement plan. The baby boomers also had high hopes for social security. But today there is great uncertainty about the future of social security for the next generation. At minimum, it will undoubtedly look much different for the millennial generation.

The housing market is also very different today. The baby boomers were able to buy a home and watch it appreciate over their lifetime. We now have millennial generation first-time homebuyers with mortgages higher than the value of their home. They also are facing things such as lack of jobs in many areas, high unemployment rates, astronomical student loan debt, the uncertainty of the market, and the list goes on. They seem to have so much against them. Many of them are literally starting out in a position of deficit.

In order for the millennial generation to navigate through the financial roadblocks and detours they are going to have to be educated. They need to understand the power of saving early and prioritizing for the long term.

I have asked many millennial generation young people what concerns them and what keeps them from saving. Their answers are usually related to the complexities of the market and the uncertainty of what to do. The investment products available to them are all over the board. You turn on the television and one person is telling you not to do what another person on television is telling you to do. Then the experienced advisors, who they really need, don't want to deal with someone that doesn't have a substantial amount of money to invest now. My business practices are unique in that that I am willing to help educate these younger people even if they don't have large sums of money to invest right now. I take a "whole family" approach. I want to help educate the adult children of my baby boomer clients.

When I talk to them I encourage them to begin to harness the power of compounding interest. Albert Einstein once noted that the most powerful force in the universe was the principle of compounding interest income. I have compounding interest calculators on my website that I refer them to so they can see the substantial power of this factor. I also introduce them to the basics of interest, interest rates, the time value of money, taxable vs. tax-free vs. tax-deferred, how to evaluate an investment and its performance, risk measured by standard deviation, etc. We need to equip them with the right tools.

The most important thing in our lives is not our money; it's our children and their future. People often want to leave a legacy and making sure your children are educated about their financial future should be part of your legacy. You might think of it as legacy planning from a different angle. We can't all guarantee that we will leave our children enough money to take care of them through their retirement. However, the legacy every parent can leave for their children is to make sure they are equipped with the financial knowledge they need to make informed decisions about the security of their future.

I have worked with many of the children of my clients, helping to educate them regarding the investment choices they can make in their life right now given their current circumstances and level of income. I may not even hold their investments, but I can direct them to where they can obtain the investment I'm recommending for them. Sometimes it involves helping the adult child of my client understand their 401(k) options because he or she just obtained a new job. I do my best to debunk the myth of just investing enough to maximize the company's match. I encourage them to put a bigger emphasis on their future and begin as early as possible to save as much as possible in the most tax efficient manner.

I am of the persuasion that families with young children need to bring the piggy bank back into their children's lives. I spent much time explaining to my children while they were growing up why we don't spend all our money on things that are frivolous and unnecessary. It didn't matter how their friends' families were spending their money, our strategy was to follow a disciplined financial plan and if that meant making certain sacrifices, then that's what we did. That was sometimes a difficult lesson for them to understand, but it has definitely paid off for our family. We have been through some tragedies that would have left us financially devastated if we had not been disciplined in our savings and investing practices. If we weren't prepared, we could have lost everything for which we have worked.

My husband, who owns his own business, was riding his motorcycle one day in 2003 when another driver crossed the centerline and hit him. As a result he lost one of his legs. He was in the hospital for a month and was unable to work. As you can imagine, there were horrific medical expenses and a tremendous amount of emotional stress placed on the family during that time. I wasn't able to work as much because I needed to be home with him after he was released from the hospital. However, we were able to survive this situation because we had a plan in place. We had the appropriate insurances in place to mitigate our financial exposure and we had enough savings to help us through that very difficult and trying time of our lives. The 25-year old who was at fault in the accident only had minimal insurance coverage that wouldn't even cover the emergency helicopter flight from the accident scene – let alone any of the other major medical and rehabilitation expenses. There were no large settlements because the individual had no assets from which to collect and we chose not to sue the young driver for future wages. The accident was tragic enough and we didn't want to ruin the rest of the young man's life.

The good news is that my husband is fully recovered and gets along well with a prosthetic leg. Because we had the right financial plan in place my husband was able to be off work for an extended period of time and I was able to take time off to help him as needed until he was fully recovered. And, we were able to pay all of our medical expenses.

You can see how this situation could have dealt a devastating blow to a family if the proper planning wasn't in place.

To sum up the principles of this chapter, I offer the following recommendations:

1. Find a qualified financial advisor to help you build a financial strategy – don't try to do it on your own.

2. Work with the right financial advisor – make sure you understand each other.

3. Trust is vitally important in a client/advisor relationship – work with someone with whom you have complete trust.

4. Leave a legacy of financial education for your children – the millennial generation needs your help.

5. Begin saving early and prioritize for the long term – this is key to financial success.

6. Understand and harness the power of compounding interest – it will serve you well.

7. Put risk mitigating strategies in place for your protection – you will need it someday. No one is invincible.

8. Be highly disciplined in your financial plan – discipline today may pay you well in the future.

The baby boomer generation as well as the millennial generation can benefit from these principles. You can be influential in leaving a legacy of quality financial education for your heirs that may prove more valuable than a monetary legacy. The financial success of future generations may depend on it.

This chapter was written by Jamie Nowakowski, Senior Financial Advisor

Wells Fargo Advisors Financial Network, LLC in Uncasville, Connecticut.

Wells Fargo Advisors Financial Network did not assist in the preparation of this chapter, and its accuracy and completeness are not guaranteed. The opinions expressed in this chapter are those of the author(s) and are not necessarily those of Wells Fargo Advisors Financial Network or its affiliates. The material has been prepared for informational purposes only and is not a solicitation or an offer to buy any security or instrument or to participate in any trading strategy.

Investments in securities and insurance products are: NOT FDIC-INSURED/NOT BANK-GUARANTEED/MAY LOSE VALUE

Wells Fargo Advisors Financial Network, LLC, Member SIPC, is a registered broker-dealer and a separate non-bank affiliate of Wells Fargo & Company.

About Jamie

Jamie Nowakowski, CRC®, Senior Financial Advisor

With 12 years of experience in financial services, Jamie is dedicated to helping individuals meet their financial needs by developing investment plans around their long-term goals and risk tolerance. Her extensive experience - throughout major shifts in the markets - enables her to help her clients structure balanced portfolios to address their specific financial goals.

Jamie began her financial services career as a Financial Advisor with Bank of America Investments in 2002. She joined Citizens Investment Services in 2007 where she worked for 5 years. She then moved her financial practice to Wells Fargo Advisors Financial Network. Backed by a full-service investment firm, she has access to an array of resources to help her remain fully invested in her clients' success.

In addition to applicable securities registrations, Jamie is a certified Retirement Counselor. She is committed to helping her community prosper. Away from the office, she also enjoys riding her horse, Golfing, Gardening, Cooking and traveling. Her husband Steve and herself live in East Hampton, CT with their grandson, Oliver.

Making sure your wealth continues to work in support of the goals you have established takes careful planning. Such planning is not a single event – it is a process. As your life circumstances change, so must the investment strategies she uses to stay on course toward meeting your objective. That is why she works with you, one-on-one, to design investment strategies targeted to your specific needs and goals. Although she does not provide tax advice, she will help you stay current with tax law changes and estate planning issues to help preserve and protect your wealth - now and for generations to come.

Wells Fargo Advisors, LLC, which traces its roots to 1879, grew over the years through mergers with some of the industry's most respected regional and national firms. Throughout their histories, Wells Fargo Advisors' predecessors were known for exceptional service based on trust and knowledge and for corporate cultures that put client needs above all else.

Contact info:
Jamie Nowakowski, CRC®, Senior Financial Advisor
620 Norwich New London Turnpike, Uncasville, CT 06382
860-682-4879
Jamie.Nowakowski@wfafinet.com

Investment and Insurance Products: >NOT FDIC Insured> NO Bank Guarantee > MAYLose Value

Photo by Paulette Mertes Studios, Hartford

CHAPTER 12

EMPOWERING SMALL BUSINESSES, THE LIFE-BLOOD OF THE MARKET, THROUGH ALTERNATIVE LENDING — TURNED DOWN FOR A LOAN BY THE MAJOR FINANCIAL INSTITUTIONS? DON'T FRET. THERE IS A SOLUTION!

BY HERSCHEL AND NICK BENTLEY

IF SMALL BUSINESSES ARE THE BACKBONE, WHY WON'T OUR BANKS FUND THEM?

In August 2010, President Obama travelled to Seattle and met with three local small business owners – who operate a bakery, a hotel and a pizzeria – in a roundtable discussion about strengthening the economy and creating jobs. Acknowledging that small businesses create two out of every three new jobs in America, Obama was quoted that day as calling small businesses "the backbone of our economy and the cornerstones of our communities."

In November 2013, in a post on the official blog of the Department of Housing and Urban Development called the HUDdle, Secretary Shaun Donovan echoed the President, writing that "Small businesses are the backbone of the American economy and the cornerstones of our Nation's promise. In fact, today over half of America's workers either own or work for a small business, and small businesses have generated 64 percent of net new jobs over the past 15 years. Small businesses create two out of every three new jobs in America."

If this is the case, and our top officials in our government are so enthused by the power of small businesses to drive our economy - why, as The Restaurant Finance Company recently reported, do major institutional banks turn down well over half of the small business loans applied for?

The RFC says that since the beginning of 2011, banks have turned down 60 percent of applicants in the U.S. With the down economy, many small business owners face poor sales and are in dire need of capital. According to an article they cite in The Wall Street Journal, many businesses that would have traditionally turned to banks – or have already been turned down by them – have instead sought funding from cash advance providers. In exchange for a certain amount of future sales (and hefty borrowing fees), cash advance providers are giving money to those who are willing to risk entrance into this highly unregulated market for quick access to capital regardless of personal credit.

In 2012, Forbes cited a study of 1,000 rejected small business loan applications (conducted by credit marketplace Biz2Credit) and found that the biggest culprits as far as rejection percentage were Bank of America (13.5%), JP Morgan Chase (11.6%) and Wells Fargo (11.2%). The article concludes that the lending environment "still looks dicey with the most recent National Federation of Independent Business optimism survey showing more entrepreneurs with a negative outlook in obtaining credit."

THE RISE OF ALTERNATIVE LENDING

So in light of all this, we have to ask ourselves: What is the value that small businesses bring to the economy and how important is it for growing companies to have access to financing to grow in that space? What happens in the lending realm impacts small businesses around the country, and what the owners do with that money in growing their business has a rippling effect on their communities.

Agreeing that small businesses are the lifeblood of the small middle market and sharing the frustration that accessing cash is proving to be more difficult than ever, we created Bentley Capital Ventures, an alternative lending space that allows us to provide capital solutions through strategic relationships. Our portfolio of capital partners includes corporations, institutional investors, mid-level firms and private investment. Many of our clients who were at the end of their rope going through traditional lending channels are surprised to know that companies like ours exist – but it's a necessity if small businesses are going to have a chance to thrive in the 21st Century. We're pleased to offer some of the industry's best rates, service and loan options available.

Consider the benefits and efficiency of alternative lending. With traditional lending, you're in a position where everything has to be perfect in your business life, starting with your credit rating. And we all know that such perfection is rare if not impossible. So what companies like ours do is help business owners leverage strength in their business cash flow, which is one of the things we can lend off of.

DIFFERENT TYPES OF LENDING AND FINANCING FOR DIFFERENT LEVELS OF SMALL BUSINESS

Companies like ours are positioned to help small business owners acquire finances when they have no other options – without everything having to be perfect. That can range from the salon and restaurant owner to a guy who owns 300 properties and needs $7.5 million to fund more.

1. Account Receivable Financing

A business owner came to us with terrible credit but with a very important task. He was in charge of changing the Sprint Towers in his area from 3G to 4G but couldn't get financing despite contracts he had secured from Sprint. He had already attempted to go the traditional lending method through Wells Fargo but was turned away due to credit. At the time he was unable to pay the upfront cost and service fees to continue working on the cell towers. He was stuck with a project that would pay dividends in the long run, but he just needed a way to make it through the first few phases of the project. Through our Account Receivable Financing service, we were able to front him $300,000 in accounts receivable to cover expenses and help him complete his project. Clients can access up to 80% of invoices within 48 hours and instantly correct the "Cash Flow Drain" problem with being paid on net terms.

Without that loan, our client would not have been able to offer a bid on the project and would have missed out on potentially millions of dollars. The irony in the communications industry, huge as it is, is that many of the guys bidding for large projects have poor credit and only have enough capital on hand to make small deposits on their bids. Major banks obviously want them to have more deposits on hand.

Account Receivable Financing is the cheapest type of financing available, with a rate of 2.25%. This is why our client was able to get the loan because they don't take into account the credit score of the contractor, but are relying on the obviously stronger score of the corporation (in this case, Sprint). This type of financing provides your business with flexible and immediate cash that will give your business the opportunity to grow, restructure, take advantage of supplier discounts, hire additional employees or even fund payroll.

It's all about having the ability to access cash without having to give up equity in your company, and of course it is less restrictive and expensive than equity financing. This process helps you free up valuable time and allows you to service your customers and generate new business. It's proven to shorten payment turnaround time, which in turn, ensures better cash flow for your company and reduces interest expense. And because this form of financing allows you to access more cash as your business grows, or less if you need less, you can always ramp up or scale back as you see fit.

2. Business Revenue Lending

We work a lot with restaurant owners because this is one of the best industries out there. So let's say we're dealing with Mr. Smith, an owner who has bad credit and needs cash yesterday, but doesn't have time for funds to come in. Then his stove blows, and it's an unexpected $20,000 expense, but he doesn't have the money. But he believes if he gets a new one, he can generate an additional $12,000 a month once the equipment is up and running. He can call us and get approval on a $20,000 loan, with very reasonable terms: a nine-month loan with a daily payment of $135.75. All we need is a one-page application and six months of bank statements and we can issue the loan the same day. Within a few days of the approval, Mr. Smith is able to purchase the stove.

The math of the deal is pretty straightforward. Mr. Smith believes with his $20,000 stove he'll be able to increase revenues from $32,000-40,000 to $44,000-52,000 every month. His loan has been approved with a $135.75 daily payback. There are 22 business days in a month. This equals $2986.50 as a monthly payback to us and/or our affiliates. During the first month, Mr. Smith virtually covers 50% of the loan in new revenue because he can use the new stove to generate revenue at a rapid pace.

Companies like ours care more about deposits than credit scores. The client's score only affects how much he or she will be approved for and the fee. People with a 500 credit score will never get a traditional bank loan, but we've worked with clients who have scores in the 400's. Our industry is growing at a rapid rate because since the crash and recession of 2008-2009, banks have pretty much dried up their funding for small businesses. Other owners just don't want to go through the months of red tape that the SBA requires to consider a loan. But for alternative lending companies like us, we see that you have cash flowing and see you as an attractive lending risk. And if someone has a rough credit history, we help them through the process to help them leverage what they have now to get them a loan. The value of this type of lending is the fact a business owner can access cash immediately when in need.

3. Investment Real Estate Mortgage Fund

This is a service we offer to another kind of small business owner, the real estate investor who holds properties in multiple states and is looking for a single blanket mortgage solution. This program is designed to help residential investors looking to access cash quickly that has no limit on cash out, non-recourse, and no limit to the number of borrower notes. It offers investors five and ten year mortgages on portfolios of residential rental properties with a minimum of five units. The Investment Fund can either refinance your existing portfolio or finance the purchase or portfolios of rental investments currently under lease.

Instead of dealing with the troubles inherent in seeking SBA loans and small business loans from financial institutions, this program addresses the problems investors have dealing with traditional loans via the Federal National Mortgage Association (aka "Fannie Mae") and the

Federal Home Loan Mortgage Corporation (aka "Freddie Mac"), the government institutions specializing in secondary mortgages. This product has proven a game changer for real estate investors in the residential space.

Fannie and Freddie require you to show all your personal debt in formulating a debt to income ratio, and also limit the number of investor homes that borrowers can have on their credit. They have historically tight rules and regulations that require you to operate as an individual investor and not through a company. If something goes wrong, the borrower is 100 percent liable. Fannie and Freddie also have 'due on sale' requirements, which means that borrowers are not able to sell the equity in a corporate entity that owns the property. So the investor is not able to access the cash with the equity they have incorporated into the property. All of these housing and real estate investors have equity but when they sell their properties, they have to repay them via a due on sale requirement. The Fannie and Freddie problems go on and on. If you have multiple mortgages with different interest rates, you have a lot of payments coming out on your properties, which is an obvious cash flow drain.

The Investment Real Estate Mortgage Fund lowers that threshold with three main points that counter Fannie and Freddie. We don't limit the cash out on the properties. We don't limit the number of notes a borrower can hold, and the non-recourse element means that an investor is not personally liable if there is a failure on the mortgage. In non-recourse lending, we offer lending products up to 75 loan to value (LTV) percentage. We offer loans from $500,000 to $50 million. The single blanket mortgage covers all the properties in your portfolio and the current rate of 5.25% is significantly less than those on most of the loans Fannie and Freddie are issuing for investment properties these days.

FINAL WORDS OF ADVICE ON MARKETING YOUR SMALL BUSINESS

We started Bentley Capital Ventures because we were getting phone calls from business owners seeking help who couldn't find financing. We found everything, from having the ability to finance their next construction project, financing their new oil rig, or purchasing the next truck in their fleet. Companies like ours are quickly filling a hole in the marketplace in an economy where traditional banks (and yes, the SBA, Fannie and Freddie) are becoming more stringent in their loan policies. We strongly advise business owners that if they need financing in a hurry, they should avoid SBA loans because the process is lengthy and their approval rates are low. We're happy to provide a place where they feel comfortable applying for a loan even if they've had bankruptcies. As long as their cash is flowing and the bankruptcy has been seasoned (dismissed) for a year, we can do it.

But our job doesn't stop once we help them accomplish their goals via alternative lending options. If they need it, we're also there to help them with marketing materials to help them expand their reach. We want to loan you money to start you and keep you going, but we are also interested in helping you acquire more customers and increase your average customer value.

Old school ways of thinking might help in small communities, but most successful businesses these days are using online marketing to take their game to the next level. Helping our clients leverage their online space, we have tools and knowledge that can help businesses generate hundreds of leads per day.

We tell them to invest a percentage of their revenue getting more exposure via Search Engine Optimization This allows users to consume content that is relevant and have the ability to find exactly what they are looking for . Social media is also a crucial tool these days to get one's brand awareness out there. We use it ourselves. We have over 13,000 likes on Facebook and every time we have a message we want our subscribers to see, we can get it instantly in front of tens of thousands of business owners. Our Internet connections have allowed us to fund businesses in any industry and across state lines. We fund businesses in California every day even though we are based in Tampa. Another big thing that business owners should be taking advantage of online is "retargeting" clients. If a customer Googles "restaurants" and yours pops up the first time, there are ways to ensure that the next time they search, your name and site will pop up. For many businesses we help, the online world allows you to acquire hundreds of leads in 24 hours for less than $100.

This marketing service is all part of our overall goal: striving to provide business owners with the ability to grow their businesses without headaches. The addition of capital for growth plus proven marketing strategies allows business owners to truly succeed in their business.

It's the opposite of what happens on ABC's "Shark Tank." The guys on that show offer you money but require a piece of your business in return. Companies like ours are here saying that we don't want in on your business, but we will lend you the cash if you need more. Our M.O. is wanting business owners to have access to cash so they can grow their businesses. If they are indeed the backbone and cornerstone of our economy, they deserve no less.

About Herschel and Nick Bentley

Herschel Bentley has been in the credit and lending business for over 30 years. A serial entrepreneur and nationally-recognized speaker and expert on credit, Herschel's passion is helping people obtain the personal and business objectives they have regardless of credit history. He has been profiled in news outlets like *Forbes magazine*, *USA Today*, *Boston Herald*, CNBC, and CBS *Moneywatch* along with 27 other major outlets. He has been interviewed on the Michael Gerber show, who authored the best seller "E-Myth". Herschel touts his best accomplishment, and the thing he is most proud of, is his marriage to his wife Jennifer for 34 years.

Nick Bentley has extensive knowledge and experience in over 30 areas of structured finance. From multi-million dollar bridge loans, to $5000 start-up loans, ensuring business owners can access capital for growth is his life's passion. As Managing Partner of Bentley Capital Ventures he is dedicated to helping business owners in every facet of business from growth and development to the expansion phase. It's through the forming of strategic relationships with both institutional and non-institutional investors alike, that hundreds of business owners have benefited – who otherwise were left abandoned by the big banks.

Herschel and Nick, father and son, formed Bentley Capital Ventures with a mission to assist all businesses with alternative financing to the rigors of traditional bank loans. They believe that when a business has the capital to grow, no matter if it's equipment needs, new personnel, or ramping up the marketing, that the business has an opportunity to flourish. When that happens the business will grow, new jobs will be added and the overall economy improves.

CHAPTER 13

THE WALL STREET SYSTEM AND WHY IT WILL FAIL MOST RETIREES

BY JIM HEAFNER

Dave Butler had worked hard his whole life and retirement was nearing. He had been a good husband and father, putting his kids through the colleges of their choice, and still managed to build up a nest egg so he and Sally would have a comfortable retirement.

Dave's broker was a family friend. They knew him to be honest and caring. He put Dave's money in highly rated mutual funds, a 60/40 stock/bond mix that had averaged 8%.

Dave and Sally agreed that their one million dollars in savings was more than enough to retire on. Their Social Security income totaled $49,120 per year. They would need to withdraw only $40,000 from savings each year to provide the $89,000 total pre-tax income they wanted. They had heard the conventional wisdom that a 4% withdrawal rate was a pretty safe rate. They believed if they could average 8%, and withdraw only 4%, or $40,000 a year (adjusted for inflation), their money would easily last their lifetime, leaving their million-dollar nest egg to little Mikey and Suzie.

As it happened, their first several years of retirement were all they hoped. They cruised Alaska, the Greek Isles, and the Rhine. But after only four years of retirement, Dave and Sally got a very uncomfortable feeling. Their nest egg wasn't $1 million anymore; it had shrunk to

$730,000. How did this happen and what did it mean for their future? Would their account recover or continue falling? They begrudgingly slashed their travel plans and money spent on their grandkids, but their savings continued to shrink.

Twenty years later, Dave and Sally's nest egg was gone. Now, their only income was Social Security. It wasn't enough, but that was all they had. As much as they dreaded asking their children for help, they had nowhere else to turn.

WHAT WENT WRONG?

It turns out Dave and Sally had averaged 10% a year over those 20 years, so the market did its job. And they did their job. They had stuck to their plan to withdraw only 4%, or $40,000 each year, increasing at a 3% inflation rate. Their now-retired, trusted broker had told them they had enough to retire; that their plan would work. How could it not?

Just like Dave and Sally, the biggest need most people have is the certainty that they will have "enough" – enough income to lead the lifestyle they want without fear. Unfortunately, like Dave and Sally, most Americans use brokers, not fiduciaries. While that broker may really care about you, he (or she) is an employee of a firm, required to sell the products that make the firm the most money; not to create a plan for your success. Think about it: Does Walmart choose suppliers that give it the biggest or smallest profit margins? It's the same with big brokerage houses in the financial industry. In all likelihood you are dealing with a broker who is focused on making the most money for himself and his employer (in order to keep his job), not an investment advisor, who is a fiduciary, who must act in your best interest, over his own or his firm's.

A broker will typically place you in mutual funds that ride the market up and down, often referred to as a "buy-and-hold" strategy. This "hands off" approach may work well for a young person with years to retirement. Unfortunately, however, while a "buy-and-hold" position may average 8-10%, it cannot escape volatility and losses. What we have learned is that the most critical element of success in retirement is not high returns … it's avoiding losses!

The greatest risk to a retirement portfolio is *Sequence of Returns* risk. Sequence of Returns risk is the likelihood of running out of money, due to a few bad years occurring early in retirement. It is the timing, the order of returns, i.e., when bad years occur—not your average return—that determines retirement success. Even though you may average 10% and withdraw only 4%, a few bad years early on in retirement may doom your nest egg to exhaust before you do. It is so insidious because the symptoms of Sequence of Returns risk are rarely visible until it is too late to recover. Sequence of Returns is clearly identified as the biggest risk to retirement income by the research of Wharton, Harvard, Boston College, etc.[1,2]

So, if this is undeniably true, why didn't Dave and Sally's broker address it? How could your broker sell you (and all his clients) a "buy-and-hold" portfolio of stocks and bonds, if he knew it could likely lead to your failure?

Your broker may be unaware of Sequence of Returns risk. The "research" provided by his employer will likely omit this risk, focusing on what's good about what they sell, not what's bad. When you don't have a solution for a problem, it is human nature to ignore it.

"You'll have some ups and downs, but in the long term, your fund will be worth more many years down the road," your broker will tell you. "Hang in there!" and "You're in it for the long haul!" Valuable encouragement, and perhaps accurate for a young person, but totally irrelevant to your success once you are into retirement.

Although a "buy-and-hold" approach can be an effective growth strategy over a long time frame, it is rarely a good withdrawal strategy. Where the DOW is in 30 years, or what you've averaged over those years is secondary to avoiding losses early on in your retirement. That's why it is so important that you invest to first, minimize losses, and second, maximize growth. Because, once you need regular withdrawals from your nest egg, a few bad years can be devastating. What happened to Dave and Sally happened because their broker did not protect them from losses. And no one told them how important that is.

WHY HAVEN'T YOU HEARD OF THIS?

Over my years of working with clients and teaching financial workshops and adult education classes, I have never met anyone who had been introduced to the real enemy. Because they have seen the market crash and recover, many view volatility as a minor inconvenience. They don't realize that once you retire, the rules change. The goal now is to avoid losses, because the real enemy is the possibility of having several bad years early in retirement.

Sequence of Returns is a subject you must address with your financial advisor. Most probably, he will tell you not to worry because you are diversified. He might even shift your holdings more to bonds and less to stocks as you age. But doing so still leaves you in a buy-and-hold position, with no way to dodge losses. If you ask about actively managed accounts, your broker may tell you that they perform no better than non-managed accounts. And generally, this is true. It takes not only research, but also freedom from a rigid company product offering to find the few private wealth managers in America who minimize losses and provide competitive returns. There are private wealth managers showing strong returns without ever a loss, including in 2001, 2002, 2008 and 2009! The first step is to identify the enemy (Sequence of Returns) and develop a plan that can minimize losses. Today's technology even allows a stop/loss order to shield you from unexpected backward movements, in case your manager fails you.

What else might have contributed to Dave and Sally's bad experience? While Sequence of Returns was the ultimate cause, surely fees paid over the years reduced their chances of success. The biggest investment "fees" for most people are not actual fees but…

a) investment management inefficiencies, and

b) taxes paid on growth and/or withdrawals

Few brokers provide tax- and investment-efficient financial plans. Few provide any tax planning at all. CPA's are counted on to do that.

But guess what? They almost never do. When is the last time your CPA laid out a tax plan for you? The default tax plan is "tax-defer as much as possible for as long as possible." This advice is based on the assumption that you will be in a lower tax bracket in retirement. But, is that true for you? Will you spend less in retirement or will you maintain your lifestyle? Could taxes rise, causing your current income to be taxed at a higher bracket? If you have large tax-deferred accounts, like IRA's, might your Required Minimum Distributions, once you're 70 ½, force you into a higher bracket? Is it possible that you will be in a higher tax bracket in the future? If so, what is your plan to minimize taxes?

YOU GET TO CHOOSE HOW YOUR MONEY WILL BE TAXED

Consider that you can grow money in four categories of taxation:

1. Taxable

2. Tax-deferred

3. Income-tax-free

4. Income- and estate-tax-free

What accounts grow tax-deferred? Retirement plans like IRA's and 401(k)'s and all deferred annuities. What grows income-tax-free? Municipal Bonds, Roth IRA's and Life Insurance. What grows income- and estate-tax-free? Irrevocable Trusts, such as Irrevocable Life Insurance Trusts (ILITs). Most people choose to grow most of their wealth in tax-deferred plans like 401(k)'s and IRA's, because they have never understood the importance of growing money tax-free in Roth IRA's or in Life Insurance.

What is best for you depends on your income needs, your assets, your goals for your money, and what happens with tax law. If your goal is to pass on an account to your children, life insurance is likely to provide the most money, income-tax-free. A Roth IRA will pass tax-free to your beneficiaries and highly appreciated stocks may also pass on income-tax-free, via a "step-up in basis" on the inherited asset. It's important to discuss with your financial advisor how you can utilize these different categories of taxation to most effectively reduce taxes, because a good tax plan can allow for more after-tax growth and income.

THE WALL STREET SYSTEM

Consider that your broker and his broker/dealer (employer) are part of the Wall Street system, doing what makes the most money for them; not for you. Consider that much of the financial media, TV, magazines, websites are owned or supported by the financial industry. Their job is to ensure their financial health; not yours.

The Wall Street system typically relies on mutual funds as a significant part of the investment solution. The plan is often to diversify and hope for the best. A challenge to mutual funds is that they rarely out-perform indexed funds and exchange-traded funds (ETF). In other words, you can often buy a low-cost, unmanaged index fund or ETF and beat mutual funds. Why?

1. Unlike ETF's, mutual funds aren't sold into the market, but are redeemed by the fund, so all the money can't be invested. Some must be held in cash to redeem shares. This often results in lower performance.

2. If cash is inadequate, mutual funds must sell stocks or bonds to redeem shares, resulting in short- or long-term capital gains which are taxed to you. This is not the case with ETF's.

3. A study of mutual funds shows average fees are between 3.14% and 4.14%3. Besides the fund fee, there may be trading charges, 12b-1 fees, reinvestment fees, etc. Index funds can offer lower fees.

Mutual funds are the classic "buy-and-hold" tool, riding the market up and down. Can you name one mutual fund that didn't lose money in 2008/2009? I can't! Yet there are private wealth managers who have averaged 7% - 9% for decades and have never lost money!

For years, bonds have been the income choice for the wealthy and retirees. The promise of a competitive yield and return of premium at maturity has strong appeal, especially once income, not growth, is a priority. But what happens if you need to sell your bond before maturity? What will you get? Whatever the market will pay!

As of this writing, we have been in a 30-year interest rate decline. We're beginning to see rising interest rates, and expect that trend to continue. If so, bond prices will fall, so that selling a bond before maturity is likely to result in a loss. Of course, if you hold a bond to maturity you will receive your principal back, unless the bond issuer has experienced financial troubles.

A critical distinction, and one commonly missed by investors, is the difference between bonds and bond funds. Odds are you don't own bonds; you own mutual funds that hold bonds. What is the difference? Unlike bonds, bond funds have no maturity; no date at which you are repaid your principal. The only way out of a bond fund is to redeem it at current market value, which, if interest rates rise over the next 5 or 10 years, is likely to be less than you paid for it.

While most brokers push mutual funds holding stocks and bonds, many do not acknowledge the risks stocks face due to volatility, and the risks bond funds face in a rising interest rate market. So what else is there to help you accomplish your goals? The answer for many of us lies in income guarantees and defensive growth, provided by the insurance industry and by private wealth managers who actively manage your money to minimize risk.

For most retirees, income is king. If that is true for you, shouldn't there be something in your plan to make income predictable and shielded from interest rate changes and market volatility? Studies on retirement, done by independent academic research institutions, not affiliated with Wall Street, tell us that retirement success is greatly improved by ensuring income for life[2]. Knowing that income is available each month to pay the bills gives you confidence and control to lead retirement the way you want. It also takes the pressure off of the balance of your funds. Why? Once select assets are dedicated to providing dependable lifelong income, other investments are not required to generate monthly income. They can be accessed when the market is up, not down.

SUMMARY

Retirement planning is more than picking good investments. To increase the likelihood of success, work with a fiduciary. A comprehensive plan should be designed to address:

1) funding predictable income over your lifetime

2) reducing risk for any money that might be spent in your lifetime, and

3) tax minimization and investment efficiency.

Non-biased research[2] tells us that plans providing guaranteed lifetime income and reduced volatility provide greater confidence and financial success in retirement.

References:

1. Low Bond Yield and Safe Portfolio Withdrawal Rates

2. Investing Your Lump-Sum at Retirement

3. "The Real Cost of Owning Mutual Funds." Ty A. Bernicke, Forbes 4/4/2014

About Jim

Jim Heafner is an Investment Specialist and President of Heafner Financial Solutions, Inc. He graduated with honors and received his MBA from UNC-Chapel Hill. Jim is a proven entrepreneur, having founded, grown and sold America's largest specialty fitness retail chain. He has been nominated for Charlotte's "Entrepreneur of the Year," and his companies have made the *Business Journal's* "Fast 50," honoring the 50 fastest-growing companies in central North and South Carolina, and *Inc. Magazine's* "Fast 500," honoring the 500 fastest-growing companies in the United States. Jim believes in complete financial planning and the importance that tax planning plays in the overall result. He is an "Ed Slott Elite IRA Advisor" and has qualified for the Million Dollar Round Table every year. Jim is a sought-after financial authority, featured in *The Wall Street Journal, Fox Business, US News and World Report, Worth Magazine, New York Post, Fiscal Times,* and MSN.com.

A believer in the value of physical as well as financial fitness, Jim is an active athlete committed to regular cardio and strength workouts. Skiing and tennis, biking and scuba are his favorites. Jim lives in Charlotte, North Carolina, with his wife, retired publisher Liz Neely Heafner, and their four adopted dogs.

Heafner Financial Solutions, Inc. is a member of the Better Business Bureau and the National Ethics Association. You can find more information at www.HeafnerFinancial.com

You may email Jim directly at Jim@HeafnerFinancial.com

CHAPTER 14

WHAT YOU NEED TO KNOW ABOUT SOCIAL SECURITY

BY ERNIE ROMER

Growing up as an "Army brat," I have lived in various places in the world. I was born in Germany and graduated from high school while there, returning to the United States in 1980. I was faced with a choice at that time. I had an appointment to West Point, but I also had a college basketball scholarship. After growing up Army, I opted to take the college route and moved to Michigan. After studying finance, I spent a short period of time in the finance department of an auto dealership before settling into a career in financial services where I have been for the past twenty-five years. Beginning as a wealth manager in the banking industry, I eventually opened my own firm and now serve my clients as a Registered Investment Advisor.

Over twenty years ago, I had the great fortune to meet an individual who became one of my first clients and remains a great friend of mine today. When I first met him, Eric Hipple was the quarterback for the Detroit Lions. Eric became very influential in my life, as it was through my business relationship with him that I was able to gain entrance to the Detroit Lions organization and work with many people there as well as the Detroit Tigers and Detroit Pistons. Without going into detail, I was able to help some individuals avoid some investments that were not in their best interest. As it turned out, my advice saved many of them literally hundreds of thousands of dollars collectively, and caused me to earn the respect and trust of many within the organization. As an added bonus, my connections within the ranks of the NFL have afforded me the good fortune of being able to attend every Super Bowl for the past twenty years and the opportunity to often stay in the same hotel with the players and coaching staff.

My friend, Eric Hipple, is an individual that has experienced the greatest highs and the most profound lows possible during his life. He was selected by the Detroit Lions in the fourth round of the 1980 NFL Draft and played in nine NFL seasons for the Lions. The year he was drafted, as a result of an injury to the starting quarterback, his first NFL start was on Monday Night Football with the late Howard Cosell announcing. In that game against the Chicago Bears, he passed for 336 yards and 4 touchdowns and ran for 2 more scores in the Lions 48-17 win. That game went into the record books as the best debut by a quarterback on Monday Night Football, and his jersey hangs in the Football Hall of Fame as a result; a record that will likely never be broken.

In 2009, Eric wrote a book about his rise and fall in life entitled, *Real Men Do Cry*. In the book he discusses the highlights of his great NFL career as well as his failure in business after his football career. Many people may not realize that a lot of professional sports players, after making a lot of money at the peak of their profession, end up in other businesses or financial ventures in which they lose much of their wealth and often go bankrupt. Unfortunately, Eric also suffered the great tragedy of his son committing suicide at the age of 15. We were already close, but when that happened, we became even closer and I did my best to be his friend and offer the emotional support he needed at that time in his life.

Today Eric represents the University of Michigan Depression Clinic and speaks all over the country at schools and military bases talking about depression and mental illness. Whenever I do a seminar, I always bring Eric in to talk to my guests at the end of the program. He talks briefly about his life and how important it was for him to have a solid financial plan in place and how that helped sustain him especially through the most difficult times in his life.

He also conveys to the audience that most of the time when you see players appear for something, they get paid for their appearance. But, he assures the attendees, "I'm not being paid to be here. I'm here simply to tell you that you need to do something about your financial future.

Whether you do it with Ernie, or someone else, make sure you have a sound financial strategy in place to help sustain you in your retirement or when life sends trouble in your direction." He goes on to say, "Ernie has played such an important part in my life and financial well being that I have written about him in my book." I consider that to be a huge endorsement from my good friend and very much appreciated. But, his words are also a call to action for everyone to make sure they have a solid financial strategy in place.

In these same seminars, I enlist the expertise of a Social Security professional who retired from the Social Security Administration after over 40 years of service. He has a long history of speaking for many pension groups in California on this subject while he was employed and has done over 3,000 public seminars related to Social Security. He is definitely an authority when it comes to this topic. He has heard every question imaginable and has dealt with any scenario a person can throw at him. I feel very fortunate to have him as a resource because I know that if don't have an answer for a client's particular situation as it relates to Social Security, I have a direct source to call to get the correct answer.

Social Security is something that needs to be investigated long before you are ready to retire. There are numerous questions that you should ask and much information that needs to be gathered to determine the most effective and efficient Social Security option for you. There are literally thousands of considerations when planning for your Social Security benefit. This is not a decision to be taken lightly or entered into impetuously. It is not a one size fits all proposition and involves much more than just "signing up" to receive your benefit.

Not many will recognize the name of Ida May Fuller, but she received the first monthly Social Security check ever, issued on January 31, 1940 at the age of 65. The check was in the amount of $22.50. She went on to live to the age of 100 and collected a total of $22,888.92. Of course, today's Social Security checks are typically much larger, but Ida May became a historical figure that day. Many changes have taken place to Social Security over the past 70 years of its existence and it has become a very complex system that takes expertise to navigate.

I can't overstress the importance of getting your Social Security benefits information right the first time. If not done properly, it can cost you tens of thousands of dollars over your lifetime. Unfortunately, most people get their information and advice from family and friends rather than a trusted qualified advisor. Uncle Jimmy says, "Take Social Security as soon as you can; you may drop dead tomorrow, so why wait?" Your neighbor says he waited until full retirement age to take his. Your co-worker told you his aunt took hers at age 64. So who is right? The answer really depends on your circumstances and your plans.

The biggest question facing anyone who is nearing the age of 62 is, "Should I apply for Social Security benefits now (this is the earliest you can claim benefits) and take the money as soon as I can?" With this option, you will collect less each month than if you had waited until your full retirement age when you would have received your full benefit. Full retirement ranges from 66 to 67 years of age, depending on the year you were born. If you have stopped working and you do not have other financial resources this may be your only choice. However, if you are still working in your primary occupation, you really have to check with Social Security to see how your benefits will be affected should you start taking Social Security early. You may be surprised to learn that some or all of your benefit may be withheld.

The answer as to when you should apply for Social Security needs to be addressed in your overall financial plan. The right strategy is determined on a number of factors. Will you continue to work either part-time or full-time? How is your health? What is your financial condition? Are you married and if so, what is your spouse's age? What are your spouse's benefits? Do you have longevity in your family? The list of questions goes on and on.

There are also many things people don't know about Social Security. For example, do you know how divorce affects Social Security benefits? You may receive spousal benefits based on your ex-spouses work record, as long as your marriage lasted at least 10 years and you are currently unmarried. You can apply for that benefit as early as age 62. If you have been divorced for at least two years, your ex-spouse does not need to apply for his benefits in order for you to get yours. However, he must be at least 62 years of age and eligible for benefits. Most people have no idea that provision is available.

I have a business associate who had a 63-year-old female client in

California for whom he was doing a financial review. This client was in a relationship with her boyfriend for about 18 years and she told my colleague that they were thinking about finally getting married and she was wondering if she would lose anything by getting married at this point in her life. In passing she said she was married to a doctor for 12 years, but got divorced and had never remarried and this would be her second marriage. My colleague explained that she probably would be eligible for benefits based on her first husband's Social Security earnings. He said her mouth just fell open; she was unaware that this was even an option for her. I was later told that her benefit was around $ 1,500.00 a month and that she chose not to get married, but is still in her committed 18 year relationship and collecting her ex-husbands benefit. This is also why I tell clients to start looking at retirement and Social Security planning at least 5 years before they are considering either one.

As you can see, Social Security can be very complex and there are many factors that need to be considered when incorporating your Social Security benefit into your retirement plan. The subject of taxation on your Social Security benefits even brings another layer of complexity when you are trying to decide to take early retirement benefits or wait to full retirement age. It is very important to consider the potential taxes you may have to pay on your Social Security benefits. If you have other additional sources of income such as, pensions, income from your investment portfolio, certificates of deposit, tax-free income from municipal bonds, etc., these also must be factored into your overall income and tax liability.

Over the years Social Security benefits have increased and the guidelines for income levels have also risen. Today more and more retirees are learning that some or all of their Social Security benefits are subject to taxation. It would be very wise to consult with your tax advisor and your financial consultant for guidance in formulating and implementing the right plan and strategy for you.

The Social Security program has been around for over 70 years and has changed and been amended, but the overall goal and objective of Social Security has not. It is an important supplement for retirees and with proper planning every retiree can obtain all the benefits due them.

It is extremely important to have a Social Security analysis done to evaluate your particular situation. Everyone is different. It's not as simple as just going to the Social Security Administration office to have them tell you the amount of your eligible benefit. A qualified financial advisor is your best choice to help you personalize your analysis and incorporate that into your overall financial strategy. Since there are literally thousands of potential variables in this decision, I recommend that you not try to do the analysis on your own. Sometimes it's necessary to get expert advice and I believe this is one of those instances.

If you were to walk into my office, you would not see awards and accolades hanging on my walls. I have received many top producer awards and various other recognitions throughout the years. However, not only do I not display those things, I don't even keep them. Why? It's simply because I don't like anything that promotes sales. I strongly believe people should base their decision to work with an advisor not on their sales activity and awards, but on the quality of the information they provide. The only thing I have on my wall regarding recognition is a plaque saying, "Lifetime Member National Eagle Scout Association."

I became an Eagle Scout through the Boy Scouts of America at the age of 13 while living in Germany. Underneath that plaque is a 15" x 18" picture of me receiving my Eagle Scout award from General Alexander Haig who was, at that time, the Supreme Allied Commander in Europe and also served as Secretary of State under President Reagan and as White House Chief of Staff under Presidents Nixon and Ford. Related to that event, I had the opportunity to spend a week with General Haig in Brussels, Belgium. There he took me to the site of The Battle of Waterloo where Napoleon was defeated in 1815. As we walked the fields he gave me a lesson in the historical battle that was fought on the very ground my feet were touching, giving me an unbelievable sense of history. I'm more proud of my Eagle Scout accomplishment than anything else I ever did in life. Not only because of what it took to accomplish, but even more importantly, because it's about integrity.

I strongly believe that helping people with their financial strategy and decisions regarding Social Security must be based on integrity. The decisions you need to make regarding your financial future are too important to be handled by a salesman. I encourage you to find an advisor that will supply you with the information you need to make informed decisions and one that will act with the utmost integrity. Anything less could be very costly. You have worked hard for your money; make sure you find an advisor that will work hard for you.

About Ernie

Ernie Romer has been helping his clients navigate the complex world of personal finance management for over 28 years. He advises clients and corporations in a broad spectrum of retirement issues, most importantly focusing on trust-based client and customer relationships. As a bank top wealth management advisor for over 17 years, he understands the balance of safety, preservation, and growth concerns that clients experience as they are preparing for and going through retirement. He has been a featured speaker at the Presidents Circle conferences as well as the National Bank Pinnacle conferences around the country. He was nationally recognized continually as the top management advisor for Comerica Bank and First of America Bank. Ernie opened his own practice 11 years ago after working in the bank industry for over 17 years. Ernie is the CEO of Core Cap Solutions, a company that provides and prepares clients for retirement and then helps them throughout their retirement years. He is a noted authority on Social Security planning and analysis. Ernie has been quoted in numerous news articles, including *The Wall Street Journal* and the *Detroit News*. He counts the Detroit Lions, Detroit Pistons and the Detroit Tigers as current and former clients. Ernie is married to his wife, Trish, for 21 years and has four children. He is active in a variety of civic and cultural organizations, including Habitat for Humanity and Boy Scouts of America, National Eagle Scout Association as well as his church. Ernie is a Registered Investment Advisor and holds the following securities licenses: Series7, Series 63, Series 66, as well as Life, Health, and Disability licenses.

CHAPTER 15

THE BEST STORY WINS: FOUR WINNING WAYS TO SOUP UP YOUR BRAND STORY

BY NICK NANTON AND JW DICKS

When it comes to competition, it seems like common sense: whoever is the best at what they do wins, correct?

Well, actually, *in*correct. Think about how many contests you've witnessed – such as employees jockeying for promotions, candidates campaigning for government offices, even attorneys battling it out in criminal trials – where the outcome seemed completely unfair to you and many other people. As a matter of fact, the results may have seemed to signify that facts didn't matter.

Of course, that's not always the case. In many instances, the results of a competition are completely fact-based, such as sporting events and academic exams. But when competitions are left to people's individual judgments, when there is no clear benchmark to base a decision on, anything can happen – and frequently does!

The question then becomes – what are people using to make their judgments when it's not a black and white numbers game? What causes them to lean one way or the other when they have to choose which person to back?

The answer to that question was recently confirmed to us once again when a client came to us and told us he was getting killed in his particular market by a competitor. We asked, "Why? Is your competition really that much better?"

"No," he said, "but he's got a better *story*."

We're big on storytelling – or as we like to call it, StorySelling – because we know, when it comes to business success, *whoever has the best story wins.* That's why having a strong story in place is essential to powering up a personal brand.

In this chapter, we'll prove it – and we'll also give you some very profitable advice on how to be sure your brand story hits the number one spot in your particular industry!

AND THE OSCAR GOES TO...

One of the most highly-anticipated and publicized "contests" is the annual Academy Awards in Hollywood. And the most coveted prizes are the Best Actor and the Best Actress statuettes – because, let's face it, most of us go to the movies to see movie *stars*, which is why the first question we usually ask about one is, "Who's in it?"

Now, of course, you would think that the only criteria for winning a best acting award is who actually gave the best performance. That criteria, however, is far from being clear, since all the nominated actors competing against each other are playing very different roles that require very different talents.

That's why many actors disparage the Oscars, saying they would only be fair if each nominee had to play the exact same part, and the Academy could judge which one played it best. Instead, it's left with having to decide contests like the one it faced in 2013: Did Daniel Day-Lewis play Lincoln better than Denzel Washington played a pilot with a drinking problem or than Bradley Cooper played a manic-depressive?

So how *do* these things get decided? Again, it's *who has the best story.*

Dr. Todd Winther blogged on a disability website a few weeks before the 2012 Oscar ceremony took place and predicted, "Based on past history, Meryl Streep is assured of winning the Best Actress Oscar this year for her portrayal of Margaret Thatcher in *The Iron Lady.*"

Guess what? That's *exactly* what happened – but what past history was Winther referring to? He was merely citing the statistical fact that actors who portray real-life characters with some kind of physical or mental disability usually win the Oscar. In this case, Meryl Streep played the former English Prime Minister Margaret Thatcher, who suffered from dementia in her later years.

Why would this matter? Because it makes for *the most powerful story*. Just two years before, Colin Firth won his Oscar for portraying an English monarch with a severe stuttering problem in *The King's Speech* - a different kind of British head of state, but the same kind of situation.

In other words, audiences get so caught up in narratives about real-life people with either a lot of power or a lot of talent (think Jamie Foxx in *Ray*) who must deal with physical or mental limitations, that *voters reward the actor for the power of the story more than the actual performance.*

STORYSELLING THROUGHOUT SOCIETY

Now, there are numerous other high-profile examples of this kind of StorySelling (whether intentional or not) working their magic. For instance, in a political campaign, one candidate will generally have a story that resonates more strongly with the voters than the other. That candidate will win, even if he has significant scandals in his or her past.

Take the recent case of Mark Sanford, who, when he was governor of South Carolina, had a very public affair with an Argentine woman and a very messy divorce from his wife. Two years later, he prevailed over his opponent when he ran for Congress, because his conservative StorySelling mattered more than his personal peccadillos. (And this isn't unique to conservatives – remember how many extramarital scandals Bill Clinton weathered?)

Then there's the matter of the O.J. Simpson trial back in the '90's. *Every single fact* pointed to Simpson's guilt in the murders of his wife and a friend of hers – and yet, he was found innocent, because his defense team *told the best story* – and it was the story the jury wanted to believe.

Why do stories many times trump facts? Well, there are many significant scientific findings that explain this phenomenon (you can check out our new book on StorySelling to find out more), but, suffice it to say that our brains are conditioned to listen more to *stories* than facts – it's how we process the world around us so it makes sense to us.

Now, that doesn't mean that we can get away with misrepresenting ourselves and our businesses. Besides the issue of the importance of personal integrity, telling an untrue story does catch up to you over the long haul and generally blows your brand story to smithereens. If Mark Sanford, for example, started voting as a liberal instead of a conservative, he would violate his brand story – and the constituents who put him into office would end up hopping mad!

What it does mean, however, is that when you create a brand story that's authentic *and* uses proven, effective story-telling tools, you set yourself up for success.

HOW TO CREATE "THE GREATEST STORY EVER SOLD"

As we noted, StorySelling is really a science – and if your brand story ticks off one or more of the right boxes, you're able to make it both influential and profitable. Your brand will gain power, your audience will grow and conversions to sales will become much easier.

In the remainder of the chapter, we're going to offer you some of the most powerful ingredients you can add to your brand to make sure it outstrips your competition's. Without further ado, here are our 4 Winning Ways to give your brand story the edge in the marketplace.

WINNING WAY #1:
REFLECT INCREDIBLE ACHIEVEMENT

Donald Trump, of course, can give us all a master class in personal branding (and he probably will, but it'll cost you!). His StorySelling is all about his own mammoth personal success, which allows him to have the best of everything, including gold-plated furnishings. This, in turn, makes others believe he has the secret to *their* success as well as his own – so they're eager to buy his books, watch his TV shows and attend his seminars in order to find out more about what that secret is all about (and put it to work for themselves).

When you're the living embodiment of incredible achievement, people are naturally attracted to you, because that achievement is *inspiring* to them and they want to share in your reflected glory. Also, they feel that, because you've accomplished great things, you, like Donald Trump, have secrets to impart to them. Obviously, this type of StorySelling works best when you're selling coaching and informational products that are centered around concepts you teach, but it can also work from a product/marketing standpoint too. Think of how many star athletes are used to sell sneakers, grooming products, etc. — even though it's obvious that's not where their expertise lies!

Of course, incredible achievement can be reflected in many other ways as well. You may have an amazing rags-to-riches story that will inspire your followers, or you may have overcome a physical disability or other overwhelming circumstances that might have prevented others from achieving what you did. These are also important to weave into your brand story, because it distinguishes you from your competitors and also raises your profile sky-high.

WINNING WAY #2:
GIVE YOUR AUDIENCE WHAT THEY WANT

Remember Mr. Goodwrench? General Motors, one of America's most time-honored brands, used that advertising gimmick as a way to reassure customers that their cars would receive repairs and maintenance from people who were nice and competent at their jobs. "Goodwrench" was a name, albeit an imaginary one, that conjured up both those qualities. Mr. BadWrench might fix your car, but he might also be mean or rip you off. Mr. GoodSpatula, of course, isn't a guy you'd let near your car, but maybe you'd let him make you an omelet.

Anyway, Mr. Goodwrench was a GM advertising mainstay for almost 40 years, before he was sent to the scrap heap two or three years ago – so he obviously made for a winning long-term brand story. That's because, even though he was a mythical creature, Mr. Goodwrench made GM customers feel as though they would get what they want out of the guy.

Now, you probably don't want to legally change your name to Mr. GreatCoach or Ms. RealEstateRiches...but there's no reason why you can't create a brand story that matches up with what your potential customers want out of you. Zappos built a billion dollar business out of providing incredible customer service; even though you could buy the shoes they sold pretty much anywhere else, they worked so hard to fulfill their customers' needs that their brand story took off and their revenues followed suit.

So think about the NUMBER ONE thing prospective buyers might want from you – and work out a way to make that a vital part of your brand story. It creates an irresistible incentive for your leads to check you out further.

WINNING WAY #3:
MAGNIFY A MAGNETIC PERSONALITY

Back in 1988, the top two comedians in the U.S. couldn't have been more different. One was Jeff Foxworthy, the "You Might Be a Redneck" guy who to this day still has a giant career as TV host and stand-up comedian. The other was Andrew "Dice" Clay, an incredibly controversial "Jersey Guy" who based his routine on X-rated sexual material; although his star has diminished considerably, his acting and comedy careers are still going strong and he earned acclaim for his role in the recent Woody Allen movie, *Blue Jasmine*.

Again, these two guys were worlds apart in their approach. One had a large, dedicated rural Southern audience, the other had a huge urban following, particularly in New York and New Jersey. What they had in common, however, was much more important and much more integral to their brand story: their *personalities*. Both of them took existing aspects of who they were and blew them up big enough to fill up a stage - as well as the seats in front of that stage.

This is another trait common to the StorySelling of such familiar personal brand legends as Richard Branson and the aforementioned Donald Trump; they take the aspects of their personalities that people find the most exciting, focus on them and make them larger than life in the process. Nobody wants to see Richard Branson in a long, boring business meeting, although he undoubtedly participates in them. Nobody wants to see Donald Trump act concerned that he won't succeed at something, even though, privately, the man probably does fret a bit from time-to-time like we all do. So people rarely, if ever, see those sides of these two business titans – they make sure of it!

The important thing to remember about this particular Winning Way is that you should *build on an existing part of your personality*. You'll come across as a lot more authentic if you're leveraging a part of yourself that's already there instead of creating an outrageous character from whole cloth.

WINNING WAY #4:
LEAD WITH YOUR EDGE

Okay, so you want to establish your brand story as the best. Well, then... simply make being the best your brand story.

Brands as diverse as Jaguar, Ritz-Carlton and Neiman-Marcus all make it a point to position themselves as superior to the vast majority of their competition; yes, they can sometimes come across as snobby for that reason, but, on the other hand, they exert a strong attraction to those who can afford to patronize them. Since these brands are perceived as superior, those who buy from them also feel superior as well!

Of course, if you take the luxury brand approach in your StorySelling, your products and services also have to be premium quality; otherwise there's a distinct disconnect between what you're saying and what you're selling. Ultimately, as in any instance when your StorySelling isn't authentic, that will cause a breakdown of your brand's narrative.

Another thing to note is that, in order to implement this particular Winning Way, you don't have to go the luxury brand route; you can also focus on some essential element of your business that's better than your competitors. Apple's brand story has always practiced this Winning Way as an integral part of its brand story, because it markets itself as an overall superior choice to the competition (which is usually Microsoft).

One of their most successful stabs at this kind of StorySelling came in a series of simple and impactful TV ads that were so effective in delivering their message, the campaign continued for three years. The commercials featured actor Justin Long, representing an Apple Mac computer, squaring off against comedian John Hodgman, representing a Windows PC. Each touted the benefits of his product, with the Mac, naturally, always coming out the winner. Both personalities accurately reflected the consumers' view of the brands, making it feel both authentic and credible.

Positioning your brand as better than the competition is nothing new; it's essential to most marketing. However, when you incorporate some of the Winning Ways we've discussed in this chapter into your brand story, you continually reinforce that superiority with customers and prospects alike as a matter of course. Whoever has the best story wins, whether it's in business, politics or the Oscars – so make sure you're the one who always walks away with the biggest prize.

About Nick

An Emmy Award-Winning Director and Producer, Nick Nanton, Esq., is known as the Top Agent to Celebrity Experts around the world for his role in developing and marketing business and professional experts, through personal branding, media, marketing and PR. Nick is recognized as the nation's leading expert on personal branding as Fast Company Magazine's Expert Blogger on the subject and lectures regularly on the topic at major universities around the world. His book *Celebrity Branding You®*, while an easy and informative read, has also been used as a text book at the University level.

The CEO and Chief StoryTeller at The Dicks + Nanton Celebrity Branding Agency, an international agency with more than 1800 clients in 33 countries, Nick is an award winning director, producer and songwriter who has worked on everything from large scale events to television shows with the likes of Steve Forbes, Brian Tracy, Jack Canfield (*The Secret, Chicken Soup for the Soul* Series), Michael E. Gerber, Tom Hopkins, Dan Kennedy and many more.

Nick is recognized as one of the top thought-leaders in the business world and has co-authored 30 best-selling books alongside Brian Tracy, Jack Canfield, Dan Kennedy, Dr. Ivan Misner (Founder of BNI), Jay Conrad Levinson (Author of the Guerilla Marketing Series), Super Agent Leigh Steinberg and many others, including the breakthrough hit *Celebrity Branding You!®*.

Nick has led the marketing and PR campaigns that have driven more than 1000 authors to Best-Seller status. Nick has been seen in *USA Today, The Wall Street Journal, Newsweek, BusinessWeek, Inc. Magazine, The New York Times, Entrepreneur® Magazine, Forbes,* FastCompany.com and has appeared on ABC, NBC, CBS, and FOX television affiliates around the country, as well as CNN, FOX News, CNBC, and MSNBC from coast to coast.

Nick is a member of the Florida Bar, holds a JD from the University Of Florida Levin College Of Law, as well as a BSBA in Finance from the University of Florida's Warrington College of Business. Nick is a voting member of The National Academy of Recording Arts & Sciences (NARAS, Home to The GRAMMYs), a member of The National Academy of Television Arts & Sciences (Home to the Emmy Awards), co-founder of the National Academy of Best-Selling Authors, a 16-time Telly Award winner, and spends his spare time working with Young Life, Downtown Credo Orlando, Entrepreneurs International and rooting for the Florida Gators with his wife Kristina and their three children, Brock, Bowen and Addison.

Learn more at www.NickNanton.com and:
www.CelebrityBrandingAgency.com

About JW

JW Dicks, Esq., is America's foremost authority on using personal branding for business development. He has created some of the most successful brand and marketing campaigns for business and professional clients to make them the credible celebrity experts in their field and build multi-million dollar businesses using their recognized status.

JW Dicks has started, bought, built, and sold a large number of businesses over his 39-year career and developed a loyal international following as a business attorney, author, speaker, consultant, and business experts' coach. He not only practices what he preaches by using his strategies to build his own businesses, he also applies those same concepts to help clients grow their business or professional practice the ways he does.

JW has been extensively quoted in such national media as *USA Today,* the *Wall Street Journal, Newsweek, Inc.*, Forbes.com, CNBC.com, and *Fortune Small Business*. His television appearances include ABC, NBC, CBS and FOX affiliate stations around the country. He is the resident branding expert for *Fast Company's* internationally syndicated blog and is the publisher of *Celebrity Expert Insider*, a monthly newsletter targeting business and brand building strategies.

JW has written over 22 books, including numerous best-sellers, and has been inducted into the National Academy of Best-Selling Authors. JW is married to Linda, his wife of 39 years, and they have two daughters, two granddaughters and two Yorkies. JW is a 6th generation Floridian and splits his time between his home in Orlando and beach house on the Florida west coast.

CHAPTER 16

APPROACH SUCCESS AS A TEAM

BY BRIAN SMITH

When I was in my 20's, success was a solo effort. I thought of success in terms of "I" and "me" – what I wanted, who could help me, what I could accomplish, and what I had to do.

You get the picture…it was all about me!

Then in 1995 I was introduced to the A-Team philosophy of forming a tight group of people who work together towards a common goal. In the A-Team, instead of putting yourself first, you focus your energy and attention on the other members and they do the same for you.

It promised extraordinary results and excited me right away. Deep down I felt that it was the missing ingredient to long term success and prosperity, but I was afraid to put my life in someone else's hands! It meant that I had to shift my attention from "I/me" to "you/them."

Eventually the philosophy seemed so right to me that I surrendered and nervously gave it a try. And as I gave more and more of myself, my relationships flourished and I had more fun. My income improved exponentially and my savings increased. Key relationships and clients expressed their loyalty and kindness to me.

Today I still have a long way to go. I can always give more and be more considerate of others. There is still room to grow and surrender to the process. It's an incredible human journey that never has to end, providing me and the people I care deeply about with rewards forever! It may not be easy for you to let go of "me" and "I" – I know because it wasn't easy for me – but I can testify that it's worth it!

These are the 13 A-Team principles that I've collected over the past 19 years – principles that I've used to get the most success for the key relationships in my life:

#1. SET A DEFINITE GOAL

First, set a definite, specific goal. Make sure it's a big goal that you can really sink your teeth into – a goal that is worth your time and attention.

What does this have to do with relationships and why is it first?

To achieve any big, worthwhile goal, first it will require the help and cooperation of other key people. By concentrating on a definite goal, you begin to attract the right people to you while opening your eyes to the many ways you can help them.

Don't worry if there is not much detail about your goal in the beginning. As you work on it, more detail will come. The people and resources you need will start to appear and you'll see how you can help them in return.

#2. CHOOSE THE RIGHT PEOPLE

Choose the right people to help you get where you want to go. Think of it as a team and you're in charge of picking the best teammates. Find people that have the talents, resources, experience, desire and character you need to accomplish your goal. Look for people you respect and work well with.

This is a critical step that can make or break you!

Demand high standards and don't allow someone into your inner circle unless they meet your strict criteria. They have to possess the character and qualities necessary to get the job done by bringing something of tremendous value to the relationship. Not everyone will be a fit and that's ok!

#3. FIND OUT WHAT'S IMPORTANT TO THE OTHER PERSON

You will need the help, cooperation, advice and resources of other people and those relationships have to be a two-way street. If you are always asking for help, always receiving but never giving, then you are not doing your part. You have to give too, and give generously.

But you have to give the other person what they want, not what you want them to have. Which is why you have to find out what's important to them. What are their biggest goals? What really excites them? What keeps them up at night? What are the thoughts, dreams and goals that dominate their mind?

These are deeper, more meaningful things they will not share with just anyone, so you're going to have to work at it to find out what's important to the other person.

#4. GIVE NOW TO GET LATER

Don't wait for the other person to help you. Instead step up and give first. Show that you're serious about building a mutually beneficial relationship. By giving first you show confidence in the other person and faith in your growing relationship.

What can you give? Your time, talent, experience, and resources.

Remember – don't push your agenda first. Put your needs aside to prove you sincerely want the other person to benefit as much, maybe even more, than you. If you have a clear, noble goal in mind, and you've picked the right people, giving first will pay off for everyone.

#5. BE COMMITTED

Every relationship, even the best ones, will have ups and downs, misunderstandings, shortcomings, mistakes and flaws. But you have to be committed to the other person and your common goals, especially during those tough times.

When approached with the right attitude, tough times make the relationship special. They are your opportunity to show that you will be there through thick and thin, and that you don't run and hide from hardship.

It's easy to get along when everything is going well but the real test comes during trouble and conflict. It's going to happen at some point so go ahead and decide upfront that you are committed to the relationship; that you will stand united in the face of adversity.

#6. QUALITY OVER QUANTITY

Nowadays there seems to be a trend to see how many Facebook friends or Twitter followers a person can get. But most of these relationships are shallow at best, and their quantity can never be a substitute for quality.

It is much more rewarding – personally, emotionally, professionally and financially – to have fewer, more significant relationships. The quality of the relationship is often determined by what you talk about. Get to know the other person and let your guard down so they get to know you too. Be genuine, never fake or phony.

These things take time so be patient and watch your relationship grow.

#7. STOP HIDING BEHIND TECHNOLOGY

Email, text and Skype are great tools for efficiency, but they can't take the place of sitting down one-to-one to tackle a challenge head-on.

Don't depend on technology as your main communication in key relationships. Don't make technology your crutch! Instead, grab a cup of coffee together, treat them to lunch or dinner, drop by their office, or just call and chat for 5 minutes with no set agenda.

Sure, you're busy and these things take time but that's the point! You have to prove that you're 100% in the relationship and that you make time for the other person. If you can't prove it, then it's not real!

#8. DEVELOP YOUR CHARACTER AND PERSONALITY

One of the most amazing things about human beings is our ability to change. If you want to improve your character and personality, paint a picture in your mind of the person you want to become. Imagine yourself in tough situations and how you would like to respond. Imagine how you want to treat others and the successful accomplishment of your goals. Notice the people you've helped and the people who have helped you along the way.

Now examine your own character and personality. What areas must be improved so that you can be your best for yourself, your family, and your key relationships?

Although this type of self-examination can bruise the ego, don't hold back. If you find that you need a lot of self-improvement, be encouraged because recognizing these weaknesses and deciding to do something about them are your first steps!

#9. KEEP YOUR PROMISES

If you want a relationship to grow stronger, you have to keep your promises. The secrets to keeping a promise are to deliver clear communication, check to make sure everyone is on the same page, and set realistic expectations. Don't get lazy by being confusing and vague. Deliver your message with precise words, a pleasant tone of voice, and suitable facial expressions.

What do you do if a key relationship asks you to do the impossible? There might be a temptation to say "yes" but if you can't deliver, then you have to say "no." It's better to know what you're capable of and deliver consistently than to over-promise and under-deliver.

You will never have relationships that are rewarding for both sides, if you cannot keep your promises. Earn a reputation for keeping your promises.

#10. TAKE RESPONSIBILITY FOR THE RESULTS IN THE RELATIONSHIP

If the relationship is not producing the results you want for yourself and the other person, don't blame others. Take responsibility and look to yourself to make the necessary changes.

What could you have done differently to get the results you wanted? What actions can you take now to get things back on track? What actions must you take to get us closer to our common goals?

If there was a misunderstanding, take responsibility for the misunderstanding, apologize, seek to understand the other person, back up and try again, but this time with a different approach. Sometimes you realize that you have chosen the wrong strategic partner, employer, employee, or plan. That's ok! Take responsibility for your choices then take responsibility to change.

The sooner you stop blaming others, the more capable you become. You will inspire others by your example and be of greater benefit and service to your key relationships.

#11. WORK IN HARMONY

Constant bickering, nagging, discouragement and faultfinding limit you and your relationships. This doesn't mean that every relationship will be picture-perfect 100% of the time. Of course, there will be disagreements, problems and conflicts. It's natural and a small amount is to be expected and tolerated.

What makes the difference is how you and the other person approach these issues. Do you truly want to understand the other person's point of view or do you just want your side of the story to be heard? Are you capable of putting your emotions aside so that you can listen? Remember, a winning relationship is a two-way street.

Once you have heard their opinion, you owe them your sincere, genuine advice and honest evaluation. Be respectful, use a pleasant tone of voice and control your facial expressions. Focus on the important things and let the little things slide, as long as they don't affect the results. It takes effort to work in harmony but the rewards are worth it!

#12. MAKE YOUR KEY RELATIONSHIPS BETTER BY BEING AROUND YOU

It's been said that basketball Hall of Famer Michael Jordan made his teammates better just by being around him.

You too can make your key relationships better by being around you. Hold them accountable and push them to be their best. Give them a larger-than-life reputation to live up to by praising their accomplishments and good qualities. An honorable reputation gives them the strength and determination to keep going when the going is tough.

Are your key relationships inspired and enthusiastic when they are with you?...Or discouraged and indifferent? When you accomplish something together, give them all of the credit. Be generous with your praise and cautious with your critique.

Your attitude towards yourself and others can inspire greatness in your relationships!

#13. SHOW GRATITUDE

It's true that every worthwhile accomplishment in life is a team effort and no well-intentioned person will help you for long without receiving the gratitude and recognition they are due. To get anywhere meaningful in life, you have to take time along the way to thank the people who helped you get there.

How many different ways can you show thanks?

Sometimes a sincere phone call or thank you note is all you need to give. Or maybe a personal gift, something that's important to the other person, is right for the occasion. You could stop by their office to personally thank them, or invite them to dinner, a show or sporting event.

What's important is that you give thanks, do it often and quickly, and you do it in ways that are meaningful and relevant to the other person. Honest, sincere gratitude is proof that you care and appreciate them.

About Brian

Brian Smith is Vice President of Mortgage Lending for the nation's largest private mortgage lender, and a Mortgage Loan Originator licensed by the state of California through the Nationwide Multistate Licensing System.

For most families, their home is life's biggest purchase, and since 2006, Brian has helped more than 2,000 families to buy or refinance their homes. And because the home is where families share so many good memories, he considers it a tremendous responsibility and an honor to be part of something with such great importance to their daily lives and financial goals.

With the ultimate customer experience in mind, Brian invented his Premier 13 Point WOW! Service that treats his clients and real estate partners to the highest possible level of service, eliminating the stress and worry of traditional home buying, while keeping them informed every step of the way.

CHAPTER 17

SHOW ME THE ~~MONEY~~ PEOPLE

BY CLAY DUGAS, ESQ.

As the son of a prominent small town attorney, I had my sights set on practicing law since I was a young boy. After my father finished serving in the Texas state legislature, I moved with my family back to Orange, Texas when I was 8 years old. There my dad continued to practice law as he had done prior to his election. I'm sure growing up in the home of an attorney played a significant role in the direction my life would take.

I went to four undergraduate schools and then law school while I was married with two children. At the age of 24, I graduated from law school on a Saturday. On Sunday I was pulling a U-Haul trailer from Waco, Texas back to Orange, Texas and was in my dad's law office ready to work on Monday morning and have been practicing law ever since.

In my father's criminal defense practice, we encountered some high profile cases. One in particular was a case of a man who was accused of burglarizing a house and raping a single mother and her two children. He was convicted and sentenced to fifty years in prison. Fifty days later, the authorities found the person that actually committed and confessed to this horrendous crime. Certainly, that was an eye opening moment for me from the standpoint of how dramatic a jury trial can be.

The first case that I tried was a false imprisonment and malicious prosecution case against a very large grocery conglomerate. They offered us $5,000 to settle the case, but we chose to go to trial and we were able to obtain a $135,000 verdict in favor of our client. That was a record verdict for false imprisonment at that time in the state of Texas.

After practicing law with my father for some time, I decided to go in a different direction and opened my own law office. I joined with another lawyer and we tried many high profile criminal cases together, including three capital murder representations. In one case, we were able to get an acquittal with five eyewitnesses to the crime. We also had a case on which a documentary was made, *The Thin Blue Line*, based on the capital murder trial of David Ray Harris.

In 1986 I decided to change the focus of my practice to personal injury cases. I really enjoyed the work, and was glad to be able to help my clients that needed someone to do battle on their behalf in a court of law. But, I must confess, I was lured in by the significant financial reward in this area of law. However, when tort reform came around in 2005 there was a dramatic change in my practice. There were monetary caps placed on various damages surrounding personal injury law—which resulted in a 60% decrease in my firm's overall income. Also, by this time I had become quite spoiled, and I was letting other people do my work. I came to a place in my practice where I was no longer enjoying my work. So, not only was I facing a significant decline in my income, but I was also growing disinterested with my job.

Life has a way of getting our attention at times and causing us to become contemplative about our future. This seemed to be my time. My circumstances prompted me to begin to rethink my law practice and I asked myself, "What got me to where I am today?" I also began observing that other attorneys were struggling and some were even going out of business in Texas. Dramatic situations were occurring—such as lawyers I worked with embezzling money and even committing suicide.

During my reassessment I had started looking at some motivational materials and began subscribing to Success Magazine. Each magazine came with a CD every month. I listened to the CD that came with the most current issue and it was talking about obtaining success in a holistic way, not just financially, but also spiritually, physically, and relationally. It was a 360-degree approach to success.

One of the things that stood out to me was a comment by Zig Ziglar when he said, "You can get everything in life you want if you will just help other people get what they want." The magazine and CD was promoting the fact that if you take care of your customers and clients the money will follow. It was like a light just came on. It caused me to realize I had my priorities backwards. Somewhere throughout my career, my motivation became more self-absorbed and I was focusing on the money and not on the client.

So, I started making a concerted effort to focus on my clients. I began giving them my cell number. If they had surgery, I made sure I called them to see how they were doing. I would even call them after hours and on weekends to check on them. I also made sure they knew I was available for them to call me. I simply let them know I really cared about them. Once I started doing that, I really became more invested in what I was doing and it became less of a job and more of a calling and personal mission. Interestingly, after I started to change the way I viewed my clients and my approach to them, it wasn't long before my practice began to increase.

Fortunately, I've had opportunities to make a difference in people's lives in a non-financial way. I had a young mom whose three-year-old daughter claimed to be sexually molested in a day care. In this particular jurisdiction, one of the police officers happened to be related to the individual against whom the allegation was made and did not do anything in regard to the accusation. The mother understandably was very disturbed about the incident as well as the inaction of law enforcement. She came to me to determine if anything could be done to obtain a just outcome. The owner of the day care settled for negligence in hiring the molester. We were then able to have the case tried in front of a jury and obtained a jury verdict convicting the individual of molesting this child. When everything was concluded, the most important issue was that justice was served on someone that perpetrated a crime on an innocent life. The mother of the child couldn't have been more happy and thankful for the outcome of the trial. She later said to me, "I'm sure it won't surprise you that I cannot recall the specific date I met you. But I do know that I had a broken little girl, a broken heart, and no one to fight for us. Thank you for being that person. When my daughter is older and the story is told you will be one of the many heroes. Thank you for not letting me give up. No matter what the verdict our God is still just." There is great satisfaction in knowing I was able to make a difference in that family's life.

In another case, one of my best friend's brother's wife was involved in an automobile accident in which she was literally incinerated inside her wrecked vehicle. The young woman who caused the accident was intoxicated at the time of the accident and only had minimal insurance coverage on the vehicle. She had been on probation, but continued to use drugs and never accepted responsibility. The woman who died had two beautiful adult daughters that were now left without their mother. The oldest daughter was due to deliver her mother's first grandchild shortly after this tragedy. It was a very heart-wrenching trial that uncharacteristically brought me to tears at several points during the proceeding. However, we were able to get the young lady who was at fault to get on the witness stand and sincerely apologize. All the family really wanted was an apology. That was an important milestone. It wasn't a monetary milestone, but a milestone that enabled the family to begin to heal and process the tragedy they experienced. And, it was a milestone for me because I was able to have a part in the emotional healing of a family torn by such tragedy.

I don't think it is simply coincidence that my practice has grown since I began genuinely caring more about my clients and less about the money. In fact, my practice tripled in 2012, and increased again by 50% in 2013 as the result of my putting people first. I'm doing well and believe I am being blessed because I am making an effort to put people first instead of money. I now tell lawyers who work for me, "You can't try a case for me until you go to the client's house and sit with them in their environment and understand them, because that desk in your office is a huge barrier to communication and expression." It is very important to have that client connection if we are going to represent them and their specific needs.

We sometimes even give money back to our clients when we feel it is the right thing to do. One of the last things we do when a case is closed is to give the client a financial statement and if the balance sheet looks disproportionate, we give money back to the client. We don't do it all of the time and we evaluate each situation on a case-by-case basis. But, if it's something that will make a significant difference to the client, it is not unusual for us to give them additional money for which we are not contractually obligated. If it's the right thing to do, we do it.

When I first started as an attorney over three decades ago, I was a "Joe Friday" kind of guy. I was looking for "just the facts." I didn't let my clients get off the main storyline because my time was valuable. My dad even taught me how to stand up to get the client out of the office. He would tell me, "If you stand up and walk toward the door, the client will also stand and follow you to the door and leave." Along the way I read something from a prominent Houston lawyer that said, "If you want to be a better lawyer, spend more time with the client." I now practice that advice. Once you understand the client, who they are and what they're about, it goes a long way to help you sell their case, believe in their case and in them. I'm no longer the "Joe Friday" guy I was years ago.

It's actually pretty easy to follow the herd and be part of the 8 to 5 group that doesn't take calls after 5 p.m. and, of course, never on weekends. It's more convenient to not have much interface with the client. There are many attorneys that slip into that mode without even realizing it. But, when you experience how rewarding it is to engage with clients and find out their uniqueness and their stories, you won't ever want to go back to the 8 to 5 group again. I've heard some amazing stories from my clients and I'm a better person for it.

I have had the good fortune of having many successes in life as well as many accolades. I'm a member of the Million Dollar Advocates Forum and the Multi-Million Dollar Advocates Forum. I have been recognized as a Texas Super Lawyer now for six straight years, and I was chosen by my peers and clients to appear in the 2014 20th edition of Best Lawyers in America. While I am very appreciative of these honors, I must say that they pale in comparison to the honor it is to be concerned about my clients, understand their needs and struggles, and help them receive the justice they deserve. After over three decades in this business, I absolutely love my job!

Based on my own experience, I would like to encourage you with these final thoughts regarding what I consider to be six powerful principles that will lead you to great success:

1. **Feed your mind the right things** – The information you feed your mind will eventually control your decision-making and your choices, so make sure you are putting the right information in your mind.

2. **Be authentic** – For me, that means especially in the courtroom. In the courtroom I am a conduit for information and I have to be a believable and authentic person to be an effective conduit. You can also be authentic in your profession; you're clients and customers will notice.

3. **Caring is an action** – You can't just talk it, you have to do it. And, the more you do it, the more you will love it.

4. **Always put your client first and the money will follow** – I have found this to be true in a very profound way. Remember the earlier quote from Zig Ziglar, "You can get everything in life you want if you will just help other people get what they want."

5. **Don't be afraid to change the way you are doing things** – I came to a point in my career when I had to change if I was ever going to find satisfaction in my work again. Change can definitely be a good thing.

6. **Don't be afraid to grow** – If you aren't growing, you are falling behind. Growth can sometimes be painful, but the benefits are well worth it.

I have finally come to a place in my career, after some very interesting cases, trials, successes, and failures, where it's not about the number of cases won or the size of the verdict, it's about getting justice for the client. Helping my client is more meaningful to me now than the amount of monetary award. What is it, besides money, that should be meaningful in your profession? If you look for it, you'll find it. You can start by putting your client or customer first and the money will take care of itself.

About Clay

Clay Dugas is an experienced, board-certified personal injury and trial lawyer. With more than 150 jury trials taken to verdict, Mr. Dugas is not afraid to stand up for the rights of his clients. He has successfully obtained over 35 settlements and verdicts that exceeded $1 million. Based in Beaumont, Texas, Mr. Dugas' practice, Clay Dugas and Associates, accepts cases from all over the United States.

Mr. Dugas is Board Certified in Personal Injury Trial Law. The Martindale-Hubbell Law Directory awarded Mr. Dugas an AV rating, which means very high to preeminent legal ability and very high ethical standards. Quoting from Martindale-Hubbell, The AV Peer Review Rating shows that a lawyer has reached the height of professional excellence and is recognized for the highest levels of skill and integrity.

Clay is a member of the Million Dollar Advocates Forum, the Multi-Million Dollar Advocates Forum, Texas Trial Lawyers Associate, and the American Association for Justice. He was recognized as a Texas Super Lawyer in 2008, 2009, 2010, 2011, 2012 and 2013. Clay was chosen by his peers and clients in the 2014, 20th edition of Best Lawyers in America.

In addition to his awards and honors, Mr. Dugas is a member of various associations in the legal community. Among his memberships are the Texas Bar Association, the American Association for Justice, the Texas Trial Lawyers Association, and the Million Dollar Advocates Forum. His reputation speaks to his passion and dedication to his craft and his clients in Texas and across the nation.

You can connect with Clay at:
lclay@claydugas.com
www.twitter.com/ClayDugas
www.facebook.com/ClayDugasAssociates

CHAPTER 18

USING TECHNOLOGY TO WIN

BY DAVID LEE

I guess you could say I'm a marketing automation pioneer. I've been involved in marketing automation and technology for years. I've been fortunate enough to work with thousands of businesses along the way, and helped create the industry it is today. My background and experience has uniquely prepared me for my "mission" as a marketing automation pioneer.

It all started in high school—my love for technology, that is. My love for mullets was a totally different story (after all, it was 1986).

My father was an investment banker, which at the time, was a high touch business that required a lot of personal communication. Because of this, he would keep all of his contacts in a very extensive Rolodex. Back then everything was manual. Every time he met with a client, he would take their business card, punch a hole in it, and put it in the Rolodex. Like clockwork.

I was taking a course in high school to learn how to build databases. One day, my father approached my brother and me and asked if he could "hire" us to build him a database that would manage his contacts for him. I thought, "hey, it's extra money…why not?"

So, we went to work, and built what ended up being an efficient, systematic way for him to manage his contacts. This database was suddenly a tool that became part of his everyday life.

Because we used the technology that was available to us, we provided my dad with an on-demand system. All of a sudden, he had a process for entering, searching for, and categorizing his contacts.

A decade and a half later when I was in business school, one of the books we had to read was called *The E-Myth*, by Michael Gerber. The premise of the book is all about systematizing your business. He talks about how just because you are a great accountant, a great baker, a great dentist, or a great fitness professional, doesn't mean you are a great business owner and manager of your business.

In order to be successful you have to systematize the different areas of your business. This concept suddenly started to make sense. To be a successful entrepreneur is something much greater than being good at something you love. Just because you're good at what you do, doesn't automatically mean that you're great at doing, managing, and leading.

It's important to put systems in place where it's done the same way every single time. The idea of a business on paper may be easy. But when you get into the details it can be hard, which is why you have to create systems. And use technology to do it.

USE TECHNOLOGY TO WIN BY CREATING SYSTEMS

In about 1987 (I was still in high school), we had a few guest speakers come to present to us in my computer class. They were talking to us about this new service called Prodigy (one of the first Internet service providers).

So, the speakers were basically showing us how you can connect this thing with a modem to look up stuff (I don't even think they called it the Internet). I was kind of bored, not going to lie.

"So, with Prodigy, you can download news, information, weather, and ski reports," said the guest speaker.

What? Did they just say ski reports? Okay, now I'm listening.

Now, back then, if you wanted to access ski reports, you had to call up the resorts and listen to their pre-recorded weather reports. I remember thinking, "if this is for real, my life is changed." So, the entire rest of the day was spent thinking of what I could say to convince my parents to allow me to sign up for this "Prodigy" thing.

Later that night, I came home from school and told my parents about this awesome new thing I learned about in school, called Prodigy. To sell it to them, I told them I would do research and use it for reports. I wouldn't have to go to the library anymore. And, to my surprise, they agreed. Little did they know, I really wanted to use it for downloading nightly ski reports for Lake Tahoe.

Looking back on it now, it was painfully slow. Seriously, it was a joke. But back then it was awesome. I had real time access to information and details, which was unlike anything I had ever had before.

Now, obviously today the Internet is a staple. We would be surprised if we ever came across someone who didn't use, or know about the Internet and its capabilities. But, there are certain tools that are made available to us that we can use to access real time data.

Take Google Analytics for example. At SixthDivision, we use this tool to filter everything down to very specific criteria. We have unparalleled access to information about people or target markets like never before. We can see their browsing behavior and engagement with our website. We can even see where they're located.

Today's technology enhances our knowledge and our ability to drill down on real time data.

USE TECHNOLOGY TO WIN BY ACCESSING REAL TIME DATA

I had a friend in high school whose dad worked for a software company. The company had been contracted by a law firm to transcribe law depositions. Now, there happened to be a multi-million dollar case on discrimination that they picked up to transcribe. Basically, the attorneys wanted to be able to have the deposition in an electronic format, so they could cross reference things easily, do quick searches, and find holes and flaws in the testimonials.

They needed some help with the case, so my friend and I were working as transcribers. For an entire summer, we would ride our mountain bikes down to this office and did nothing but transcribe law depositions, so every word could easily be accessed in an electronic format.

They wanted to be able to organize their data in a way that would allow them to access anything they needed to access quickly, without having to sort through thousands of pages to find one specific statement. They wanted speed...and efficiency.

Think back to the first job you got. Or maybe the second job. How did you get that job? And where did you find out about it? Odds are you most likely found out about your first, or second job, by word-of-mouth, or an ad in the newspaper. Or maybe, you just happened to drop in to your former place of employment to see if they were hiring.

Fast forward to today's world. Now, we have the Internet to do the work for us (or at least part of the work). With sites like Careerbuilder, Jobing, Monster, and Craigslist, you not only can post job descriptions, but also can search thousands of resumes that are on file.

Not too long ago at SixthDivision, we were in the process of looking to hire an Office Manager. And we had 200 resumes within 4 hours. Why? Because we used technology to get the word out that we were hiring.

It literally saved us hours and hours of searching for candidates. We were able to sort through all of the resumes we collected, and narrow it down to those who looked good on paper. We then assigned a project to those candidates to truly test their skillset. They submitted their projects via email, which also saved tons of time.

At the end of it all, we ended up with an incredible employee who loves what we do, that we wouldn't have been able to find without the help of technology.

USE TECHNOLOGY TO WIN BY IMPLEMENTING AN ELEMENT OF SPEED

In 2005, a former business school classmate and a dear friend of mine contacted me and wanted to get my take on a new company that he was forming. It was a CRM tool that they named Infusionsoft.

After spending time looking at the software that they were creating and how it would help entrepreneurs win in their business, I knew I wanted to become part of what was being created. This software helped businesses get organized, it simplified things, and most importantly, it automated. It automated processes and systems within the business, and created a scenario where the small business owner could win. It was called automation. And, I knew that it was my calling.

One of the core problems that Infusionsoft fixed is an issue faced by every single business that I've worked with. The problem is that many businesses absolutely stink at following up. They stink at tracking leads, and following up with leads and customers. It's the truth. And, as entrepreneurs, we're not the only ones who have issues with follow-up. Our employees are even worse, because they're typically not as committed to the business as we are.

If the follow-up failure could be fixed, it would be a huge opportunity for each business. They would finally be able to seal the cracks and eliminate leads falling into a black hole.

What Infusionsoft does in a nutshell is it automates the follow-up process. So, if a new lead comes in, it's automatically assigned, it's automatically put through an educational drip campaign, and the leads become better qualified and better prepared.

This automated nurture marketing has led to higher conversion rates, faster deal velocity, and increased revenue and growth for businesses... and that's just one process.

There are all kinds of systems within the business that can be automated. For example: purchase fulfillment, new patient welcome, notifying internal staff what needs to be done, billing and collections, communications with partners, affiliates, and referral partners...all of these things can be automated.

Infusionsoft quickly became my technology buddy because I could see how much it could automate in a business, and I started to see the results immediately.

We use Infusionsoft in our own business. We use it in our marketing, lead nurture, sales, and fulfillment processes, and that's how we were able to grow (and continue to grow) so quickly.

USE TECHNOLOGY TO WIN BY
IMPLEMENTING AUTOMATION

Now, there are a few cautions I want to make you aware of. Innovative technology can be life changing, but some people can go overboard.

Caution #1: Don't get caught up in the technology. Don't let your focus shift from the business and the fundamentals. There's a fine line between the technology working the way it should, and the technology taking over. You can play all day long and get nothing done. Don't let the tool dictate your business.

Caution #2: If you have a crappy process and you automate it, you get a lot more crap. So, take the time to really get your process dialed in before you automate it, otherwise it's just going to compound your pre-existing problems.

The same thing applies with the cleanliness of your data. If you have bad data to start with (whether you're not collecting email addresses, addresses or phone numbers, or not tracking lead sources like you should), implementing isn't going to fix it. You have to get your data right.

Caution #3: Make sure you're focusing on what's important.

When I was in kindergarten, I woke up one morning to find our house had been toilet papered. We went racing out to the front lawn to check it out, and my dad yelled, "stop!" So I stopped and he came over, and pulled me back.

The reason he was so worried was because there was a tripwire on our lawn. If I had run across the black filament, it would have set off a scream box that you couldn't turn off.

So, as you set up your own automation and tripwires in your business, just make sure you're setting up the right stuff. You don't want to set off the shriek box. Focus on things that are going to generate additional revenue, save you time, and give you piece of mind.

Caution #4: If you're going to go down this path of automation, don't do it yourself. Hire an expert who has done this before. It will make your journey much less painful, and much more successful. I've seen too many implementations fail from lack of knowledge of how to implement properly.

And finally...

<u>Caution #5:</u> Don't be afraid. Many of these technologies are proven now. Fortunately, you don't have to be the pioneer creating new technology. You can be the pioneer adopting these things and implementing them in your business to create new success.

About David

Dave Lee is an entrepreneur, optimist, and marketing automation pioneer. He was raised to believe that anything is achievable; therefore, his unique ability is to call his shot and "will" it to happen through strategy, execution, and undeterred persistence.

Dave used this ability to grow Infusionsoft from infancy to over $17 million in recurring annual revenue while creating the marketing automation for small businesses category. He then helped LeadMD, a marketing automation consulting company for medium and large businesses, grow from a startup to over $3 million during an 18-month period.

In late 2011, having driven growth and success for other organizations, Dave decided to return to his entrepreneurial roots and co-founded SixthDivision and PlusThis alongside business partner, Brad Martineau. The companies help small businesses implement and take advantage of marketing automation principles and technologies. As CEO of SixthDivision, he grew the business to over $1 million in sales during its first year of operation.

In March 2014, Lee stepped down as CEO of SixthDivision to focus his efforts on growing PlusThis, a software company that builds products to enhance sales and marketing automation within entrepreneurial businesses.

Dave graduated from the Marriott School of Management, Brigham Young University, with a Master's degree in Business Administration with emphasis on Technology Marketing. In 2008, he was named a Warrillow Marketer of the Year finalist. Additionally, he helped Infusionsoft achieve the prestigious Inc. 500 award three years in a row (2007, 2008, 2009). Most recently, Dave has been featured on NBC, ABC, CBS, and Fox television affiliates speaking on marketing automation and small business success, and was quoted in *Forbes Magazine* as one of America's PremierExperts™. He has also been featured in CNBC, Reuters, MarketWatch, and Yahoo Finance, among other notable news outlets throughout the country.

Dave has been happily married for nearly two decades, and has three young boys who keep him on his toes. When he's not helping businesses succeed or spending time with family, he fills his life with service, heli-skiing, wakesurfing, kiteboarding, doing what's right, and getting things done.

You can connect with Dave at:
Dave@PlusThis.com
linkedin.com/in/davelee123

CHAPTER 19

THE GAME CHANGER

BY ANDY HO

CHANGE IS INEVITABLE

Whether you realize it or not, managing and implementing changes is the key to every business. However, change does not take just money and time, it requires emotion. If someone does not feel strongly about something, you can bet it won't happen! That is why each change needs a champion - someone who can get going when the going gets tough. Someone who can attach his energy and time to the change, and stay committed to make it happen.

Since joining the financial services industry 15 years ago, I have spent many of those years in a senior management role in insurance, securities and independent financial advisory (IFA) firms. I have always been regarded as the game changer in the industry, transforming companies from Losses to Profitability. My key motivation is being able to make an impact by improving the industry and people's lives by setting a new benchmark for how business should be done professionally – with the consumers' interests at heart.

IF YOU DON'T CHANGE, THE MARKET WILL MAKE YOU IRRELEVANT.

The way we have worked in the past is not sufficient for today – or tomorrow. It is mandatory that we change. If we don't, as our industry morphs, it will place a greater value on work habits that we have not developed, styles we have shunned, and strategic thinking we are not capable of doing.

It doesn't matter how smart, how charming or how innovative you are, if you don't change the way you work to match what is needed, none of that will matter. The companies that fail have incredible people in them. But that doesn't stop the company from nose-diving to failure. We have all seen brilliant people fail at business – all because they were unwilling to change.

Typically, there are four main possible outcomes:

1) You don't change the way you work. Others do, as does the company. The company grows and your skills are marginalized along with your paycheck.

2) You don't change the way you work and neither do your peers in the company. The company is incapable of following the trends and the company suffers a less than pleasant fate.

3) You upgrade the way you work but your peers do not. You find a company that is ready to move in the right direction. You join them and sadly watch your former company stumble along.

4) You upgrade the way you work, become a champion and influence your peers to the do the same. That culture drives the company in the new direction.

When the subprime issues hit the market in 2008, I was the managing director in one of the largest IFA companies in Singapore. While the whole industry was putting the blame on the situation and felt lost, I got the entire company to come together, implemented and acquired marketing and operating systems at a fraction of the cost, and helped advisers to increase their productivity by changing the whole advisory landscape. When no one else in the market consoled clients and ensured that they were taken care of, we took the opportunity to do just that. During that period between 2008 and 2011, we grew the company's profitability, and productivity of the financial advisers, by at least 5000%, advancing it from the #6 largest to the #1 financial advisory firm in Singapore.

As with the individual, structural change in an organisation is key to the success of an organisation. The path to structural change may not be simple, but it should be clear. Key factors include: how your company views itself, how it makes decisions and how it deploys resources. These factors are all inextricably linked to your company's business model.

For example, you might decide to shift from a decentralized finance or marketing function that primarily resides within business units to a centralized function based at corporate headquarters. However, such a shift should not be made arbitrarily, but only if it is consistent with your business model.

Several signs may indicate that it is time for your company to rethink its business model. In general, your business model needs to be revisited if:

1. It does not support your company's go-to-market strategy.
2. It does not allow your company to adjust to market changes, such as price deflation, competitive pressures, or cost pressures.
3. It no longer supports your overall corporate strategy.
4. It becomes too expensive to maintain or support, or places your company at a competitive disadvantage.
5. Shared services do not yield expected savings.

Along the way in my career, I was involved in an external consultancy project, helping financial institutions in the region to make significant changes to their distribution channel, resulting in more than 100% growth in that channel.

In 2011-2012, as a driver of change and progress, I was tasked to revamp the entire operations of the IFA branch in Hong Kong. Not only did I change the management team, but also the entire business model, and our offering to the clients. The Hong Kong market is very competitive and operating costs are high. Through major reconstruction of the business model by changing the business model from B2B to B2C, we started working with business partners to bring in the mass of affluent and high-net-worth clients, turning the P & L from red to black within 6 months. We also brought in more than $300 million in sales within a year of implementation of these changes.

One important lesson to takeaway is that the key to revamping and changing your business model involves the stakeholders of the company. Everyone in the company plays a major role in turning the company around, and it is therefore important to ensure that your stakeholders are aligned with the company's direction towards growth.

When implementing changes to your company, the seven steps below act as a guide for you to achieve the results you want:

Step 1: Create Urgency
For change to occur, it helps if the whole company really wants it. Develop a sense of urgency around the need for change. This may help you spark the initial motivation to get things moving.

Step 2: Form a Powerful Coalition
Convince people that change is necessary. This often takes strong leadership and visible support from key people within your organization. Managing change isn't enough – you have to lead it.

Step 3: Create a Vision for Change
When you first start thinking about change, there will probably be many great ideas and solutions floating around. Link these concepts to an overall vision that people can grasp easily and remember.

Step 4: Communicate the Vision
What you do with your vision after you create it will determine your success. Your message will probably have strong competition from other day-to-day communications within the company, so you need to communicate it frequently and powerfully, and embed it within everything that you do.

Step 5: Remove Obstacles
If you follow these steps and reach this point in the change process, you've been talking about your vision and building buy-in from all levels of the organization.

Step 6: Create Short-Term Wins
Nothing motivates more than success. Give your company a taste of victory early in the change process. Within a short time frame, you'll want to have some "quick wins" that your staff can see. Without this, critics and negative thinkers might hurt your progress.

Step 7: Anchor the Changes in Corporate Culture

Finally, to make any change stick, it should become part of the core of your organization. Your corporate culture often determines what gets done, so the values behind your vision must show in day-to-day work. Make continuous efforts to ensure that the change is seen in every aspect of your organization. This will help give that change a solid place in your organization's culture.

CASE STUDY: CHANGING THE ENTIRE OFFERING IN THE INDUSTRY

In 2013, I was approached by one of the largest insurers in the world to set up an alternative distribution channel. Together with my team, we thus set up IAM Advisory Group to help build and grow this channel. Recognizing that today's consumers require assistance in many areas that affect their financial abilities, I made four major changes to the business model for this channel as compared to the rest of the industry:

1. The Advisory Process

The issue with financial planning is that financial advisors tend to focus only on the numbers—budgeting, investments, taxes, estate planning, or insurance–without exploring the broader context of a client's life.

In addition, most people approach advisors with similarly preconceived ideas. They put their questions in financial terms: I want to "grow my portfolio," "save for retirement," simply "get organized" or "get the best retirement products." The assumption is that advisors are essentially financial wise men or engineers. Given the right input, they can figure out the best way to invest, pay down debt, reduce taxes, or just manage things better.

So we see the need to have a more holistic standpoint. Our philosophy is founded on the idea that every human being strives to live a life of meaning and purpose. A financial advisor's task must therefore begin with a discovery of each client's unique aspirations.

2. The Services

Traditionally, financial advisers focus on helping clients look for a financial tool that will best suit their retirement needs. At IAM, we understand that wealth is only one tool for success and happiness; thus IAM assembles an entire toolbox to ensure our clients have the right tools to successfully build and manage their lives. Through our panel of partners, we assist and advise clients on other aspects of their lives, beyond just their finances. We adopt a stringent selection of partners to ensure that our panel can uphold the unique client experience for which we are known. Our life-planning solutions help clients in different stages of their lives.

Sometimes, what clients need is just someone to offer them good advice, help them solve their problems and add value to their lives. IAM Advisory Group works with a panel of unique partners such as:

- career coaches and headhunters to provide solutions for our client's career problems
- children education specialists for DNA mapping to provide clients with a better understanding of their children's potential
- a wills and trusts firm to help clients better understand legacy creation

…giving our clients specialized incentives through our tie-in partners.

3. The Compensation

Most financial advisers in the market are compensated purely through the commissions they receive. With regulations rolling out non-sales KPI, the compensation structure is bound to change. At IAM, we went a step further to encourage our associates to be more client-centric and ensure that clients are well-serviced.

Debunking the common commission-based compensation scheme, we introduced our Revenue Sharing Model. This gave our consultants the opportunity to be remunerated much more competitively, and in a way that is more equitable with their efforts.

"You are paid the way you should be paid." The more productive and successful you are, the more you share in the company's revenue. First, our associates can partake up to 95% of the company's revenue, and secondly, they earn more if they are more productive and compliant.

By selecting the right people who live by the philosophy of giving clients added value, our associates can earn more with a smaller clientele base, and can focus their time and energy on servicing their existing clients.

In this way, clients will be happy to refer potential clients to the adviser and this positive cycle will continue.

4. The Support

Traditionally, financial advisers are left on their own to carry out their own practices and many tend to fail. Not only do they fail in their career, but also they tarnish their company's brand, as more often than not, these advisers do not provide decent service or advice to their clients. It is only with the determination and dedication of our people that we can serve our clients, generate long-term value for our shareholders and contribute to the broader public.

At IAM, we set up our marketing and training modules to ensure that our associates are able to give clients great advice while ensuring that the clients are well-served. At the same time, we also help the associates to pursue their personal branding and develop effective programs to reach out to clients and their targeted prospects. Our proprietary training and mentoring system ensures that the associates are able to earn an income not lower than six digits a year, and at the same time, ensure that clients are served well and are able to make progress in their life.

"If you do not change, the market will, and you will be irrelevant."

About Andy

Andy Ho has spent 15 years in the financial industry – many of those in a senior management role in insurance, securities and as an independent financial advisor with an IFA firm. He started off his career in the financial industry as a financial adviser and within 4 years he was in a senior management position in a financial advisory firm. He pays tribute for his success to his mentor (Mr. Jack Cheong) and other coaches that he has met in his career.

Today, Andy has established his presence in the region as a consultant to leading financial advisory institutions and distribution networks in the region. He lent his competence and expertise to both local and regional firms, greatly facilitating the growth of these companies through educating and systemizing the process of the firm to deliver created value to the end consumer. Below are some of the projects he has been involved in while holding a senior management position in the largest financial advisory firm in Singapore.

The projects include:

- 4th largest insurance company in Singapore – Increased sales performance by 250% within six months since they established their agency sales force.

- 366 branches of the 2nd largest bank in Malaysia – Enhanced performance by 400% in just six months with our bancassurance training.

- 708 branches of 4th largest bank in Indonesia – Peaked performance at 300% within six months since we provided bancassurance training.

- Largest FA in Singapore – Record of over 5000% increase in revenue to become the largest financial advisory within 5 years with our assistance

- Hong Kong – Financial advisory operations established by our management team translated to over HKD300 million worth of business within the 1st years operations.

Andy believes that the financial advisory landscape in Singapore should be more client-centric. In order to achieve that, advisers will need to change their approach and marketing effort. With that belief in mind, he started IAM Advisory Group – a company that helps advisers double their income by bringing values to their clients. In order for advisers to double their income, they need to increase their value in the value-chain and ensure that clients are delighted with their service and advice. He believes in bringing in a WIN-WIN scenario into a perceived WIN-LOSE world. A win-win scenario is possible when there is an abundance mindset and those people with the same mindset are selected to play the game together.

Andy is also known for developing leaders in his company. In his words, "A company is just a legal entity and its people are the reason why companies rise and fall. At every step of our employees' careers, we invest in them, and ensure their interests remain focused on the long term and are closely aligned with those of our clients and shareholders." His goal is to maximize individual potential, increase commercial effectiveness, reinforce the firm's culture, expand their people's professional opportunities, and help them contribute positively to their greater communities.

CHAPTER 20

POWERED BY PRINCIPLES

BY BRANDON COX

Some people have the great fortune of being born into wealth while others get to experience the tremendous blessing of starting from scratch. My story happens to be the latter. Having lived on both spectrums of the wealth scale, I've gleaned tremendous experience in my quest, ranging from desperation to euphoria, and of course, every other emotion in between.

If anyone told me when I graduated from high school, that by the age of 32 I would be the CEO of an oil and gas company, have my own radio show, be a best-selling author, and share a speaking stage with Steve Forbes, I would have told them they were crazy. I had great ambitions to be successful, but the incredible blessings I have experienced have been beyond anything I ever imagined.

I grew up in a poor family in a small Kansas town of 1,800 people. We didn't even have a traffic light. There was a single grocery store and only 132 people in the entire high school. Needless to say, everyone knew everyone else's business in that tightly-knit group.

My parents divorced when I was five years old and we were on welfare. I remember going to the grocery store with my dad and asking him, "Why do we pay for groceries with stamps?" He responded, "It's just our way of using money." I'll never forget that.

Being an avid high school athlete, I went on to play football at the University of Kansas and my dad was my biggest fan at those events.

However, my dad was tragically killed in an automobile accident. When that happened, I determined I was leaving college and the state of Kansas. So, at the age of 19, with no cash on hand, but a $3,200 limit on a credit card, I moved to Phoenix, Arizona.

When I arrived I didn't know anyone, but I knew exactly what I wanted to do. I knew from the age of 5 that I wanted to be in the real estate business. Something about real estate just intrigued me. The first 4 days, I slept in my truck and obtained a gym membership where I would shower and press my clothes. I quickly acquired my real estate license and began in the re-sale market. Thankfully, I learned how to live off of $6,000 a year while I was in college, because the first months after moving to Phoenix were financially very challenging.

I started doing some real estate deals and thought I was doing pretty good – making about $50,000 my first year. Then I heard about new home sales and began to specialize in that. While I was selling new homes I also began rehabbing existing properties and selling them. I got to a point where I no longer needed to sell new homes because I was making a good sum of money fixing and flipping houses. During 2008 to 2009 when everyone else was losing their properties, I was buying and flipping properties. At the peak, I was doing about 30 houses a month. I knew that it was just a cycle and that I was in the right place at the right time.

During this time I also started cutting my teeth on the radio and building relationships. I was working 110 to 120 hours a week for almost 2 years. I was constantly trying to find the next deal, managing construction crews, and handling the listings on the properties. At one point, I realized I wasn't doing this to make money anymore. My bills were paid and I had plenty of money, but I felt very empty. I knew I couldn't keep up that pace for much longer. So, I started seeking other real estate opportunities where I could make money but not have to work so many hours.

While looking at commercial real estate opportunities, I came across 1031 exchanges into oil and gas properties. I found out that the IRS looks at oil and gas fields as real estate and there are opportunities to write off up to 85% of your investment in the very first year. For people that have a substantial income, that's great news. After careful evaluation, I set out to get involved in this market.

I was contacted about an oil company in Texas that had a project going and the caller suggested I "try it out." I flew to Texas and met with the person in charge of the project. After evaluation, I told him I would give him $50,000 just to "test the waters." Within 4 months several of my friends also invested collectively $1.2 million in the same project. However, after 7 or 8 months I found that we were not having success in the field because of what the project manager termed "delay after delay." I was able to uncover that he was really using the money to fund other projects. When I found out what was happening, I felt horrible because I had relationships with these investors and I didn't want them to suffer financial loss. I didn't do anything wrong. I didn't force them to invest. But I felt personally responsible.

My response to this situation is a great segue into the Power Principles I have learned and incorporated into my life and business. Let me share them with you.

HELP OTHERS ACHIEVE THEIR GOALS

Armed with a plan to make sure my friends who invested in the Texas project didn't lose money, I personally invested in a few projects in Kansas and was able to gain a few million dollars in equity in those projects. I then transferred the Texas project investments of my friends to the Kansas project in which I had more control. I gave them $2 million of my equity interest in the Kansas projects to make them whole. In fact, not only did I make them whole, but also just about doubled their money. I gave up $2 million in assets to help these people simply because I thought that was the right thing to do.

I tell people that I got into the oil business by losing $2 million. You see, it goes back to a philosophy that is a core principle for me when I do business with other people. I can't just talk about it, I have to walk the walk; I have to do it and show others that I can be trusted. It's like the great Zig Ziglar said, "You can have everything in life you want, if you will just help other people get what they want."

FAITH APPLIES TO BUSINESS

Often people will ask me how I became successful. My response is very simple, "Faith." It's the number one contributing factor to my success in the business world. When I establish a goal, I start chipping away at it little by little. Eventually, some doors begin to open up. There will be people that call that luck or a coincidence, but I call it faith.

Some people think faith in business is taboo. I'm here to say, "It is OK!" I strongly believe that the power of prayer, combined with my faith, will make me aware of the great things that are happening to me, for me and around me, every single moment. Not just in the business sense, but in a personal way as well. I have determined that the reason I'm here is to serve others and help build God's kingdom. I try to bring that atmosphere into the office and let each person know that their role is just as important as my role and that they are very valuable.

Interestingly, people usually try to do the exact opposite. Many business people make a point to keep their relationship with God out of their business because they think it will taint their business relationships and be considered tabu. Once you realize it's OK to have confidence in your faith publicly, you begin to attract people that actually respect that.

God has never let me down; He's never made a mistake or broken a promise. Sometimes I have my plan and God has His plan. I will guarantee you that only one of them will get executed. Every good thing that comes from my business comes directly from Him. I have seen miracles happen. I call them miracles because I don't know how else to describe them.

HIRE THE BEST AND SURROUND YOURSELF WITH THE BEST

Be a part of something that is greater than yourself. Successful business people have to surround themselves with others they trust because they can't do it all themselves. You want to surround yourself with the most talented people possible. But, usually the most talented people want to do their own thing. You can't force them to do something you want to do. You have to find people with similar vision and drive who can fill in the gaps where you may have weaknesses, lack knowledge or time.

DON'T EXPECT THINGS TO ALWAYS GO AS EXPECTED BECAUSE THEY RARELY GO AS PLANNED

When things don't happen as you expected – and 99% of the time they don't – you have to have a foundation to fall back on and understand that all things happen for a reason. There is a lesson to be learned in what happened. We just have to be alert and aware of the lesson. Many times it's because God has another door He wants us to go through, not necessarily the door we intended to go through. And, it always ends up being better than we initially planned. A door of opportunity will always be there if you don't give up.

Take the aforementioned Texas project as an example. That project didn't go as I intended. But, those circumstances caused me to look at other opportunities that I may not have explored if the Texas project went well. As a result, I have made connections with people that have boosted the success of my business considerably.

Sometimes you take a step of faith with only the belief there will be something there to step on. It keeps you grounded and humble and gives you the ability to show grace toward other people. Faith can definitely be scary at first, but eventually you get to the place where it feels OK to walk by faith.

UNCLE RICHARD'S POWER PRINCIPLES

In the 1980's, my Uncle Richard opened a plastics company that became very successful in the 80's and 90's. The selling price of his company revealed the great success he had in that industry. I never had any financial support from my parents at any level and this was one person that I trusted to give me solid advice. I've always been self-taught and try to learn from the experiences of others. So, seeing his accomplishments, when I was just 19 years old I asked him what he could share with me regarding the keys to his success. He said, "Let me think about that and I'll get back to you." Sometime later I received a letter in the mail from him. He said, "Brandon, I've thought about what you asked me and I believe this sums it up the best." He enclosed an article that I still have taped to my computer to this day. It was "Investors Business Daily's 10 Secrets to Success." Investor's Business Daily, a national financial newspaper, took many years interviewing world-class business leaders and visionaries and crystallized their list of success principles into the following 10 Secrets of Success. I have read these principles countless times and practice them in my business. I believe they are worth your consideration.

1. HOW YOU THINK IS EVERYTHING – Always be positive. Think success, not failure. Be aware of a negative environment.

2. DECIDE UPON YOUR TRUE DREAMS AND GOALS – Write down your specific goals and develop a plan to reach them.

3. TAKE ACTION – Goals are nothing without action. Don't be afraid to get started. Just do it.

4. NEVER STOP LEARNING – Go back to school or read books. Get training and acquire skills.

5. BE PERSISTENT AND WORK HARD – Success is a marathon, not a sprint. Never give up.

6. LEARN TO ANALYZE DETAILS – Get all the facts and all the input. Learn from your mistakes.

7. FOCUS YOUR TIME AND MONEY – Don't let other people or things distract you.

8. DON'T BE AFRAID TO INNOVATE – Be different. Following the herd is a sure way to mediocrity.

9. DEAL AND COMMUNICATE WITH PEOPLE EFFECTIVELY – No person is an island. Learn to understand and motivate others.

10. BE HONEST AND DEPENDABLE – Take responsibility. Otherwise, principles 1 – 9 won't matter.

THE SKYLAR EFFECT

My 11-year-old daughter, Skylar, a special-needs child with Down syndrome, has had a profound effect on my life and has taught me very important principles that I use in my personal life as well as in business. She is my inspiration. She's a big part of who I am and how I operate. If you have children, you know children have a way of changing your perspective on life in a positive way.

She has a way of bringing out the best in people. Often people that are having a bad day will interact with her and it changes their perspective. She sees the good in people across the board. It causes me to think, "How can I have a similar effect on people? How can I influence them in such a way that it turns their bad day into a good day?"

In a nutshell, here are the main components of the "Skylar Effect" in my life and business. You may find wisdom in them as well.

Be patient with others. Be compassionate. Be kind. Accept people for who they are. Be nice to people. Don't judge them. Be there to help others through the issues with which they are struggling. Turn someone's bad day into a good day. Let things run their course. Don't be a prima donna. Don't complain when things don't go as expected. Instead, view it as an opportunity. Love your neighbor. Be grateful for even the smallest accomplishments.

It's amazing what can be accomplished simply by practicing some very basic principles of respecting and honoring others. Volumes have been written about business success, but nothing can quite compare to the simple, yet very powerful, principle of treating others the way you would want to be treated. I challenge you to help someone achieve their goals and watch how far you progress as a result.

About Brandon

Brandon E. Cox is the Founder and CEO of Pipeline Oil & Gas. Brandon leverages a background in the oil and gas industry and finance to identify, acquire and develop underperforming and underdeveloped oil and gas properties. His proven track record and model for turning oil and gas projects into income-producing assets increases the market cap for Pipeline Oil & Gas and its clients.

As CEO and Founder, Brandon Cox secures the development of capital for projects involving natural gas pipelines and the drilling and reworking of oil wells. He has assembled a seasoned leadership team of geologists, field operations and financial professionals who oversee successful operations in Kansas, Texas, Louisiana and Mississippi. He is also a licensed and bonded oil and gas well operator in the state of Kansas, where he currently manages over 75 wells.

Prior to founding Pipeline Oil & Gas, Brandon Cox was President of Cox Capital, LLC, helping to fund and manage over $200 million in real estate development.

For the past four years, Brandon has been the host of *Crude Awakenings*, a #1 financial news talk radio show on Money Radio 1510 AM. In addition, Brandon Cox is featured in the March 2014 issue of Forbes. He has also recently been acknowledged by America's PremierExperts® as one of the nation's leading experts in the oil and gas field.

Brandon E. Cox -
CEO & Founder- Pipeline Oil & Gas
Phoenix, Arizona
www.PipelineOilandGas.com

CHAPTER 21

THE POWER OF A POSITIVE MINDSET

BY AARON PITMAN

I wasn't always a positive person. Being pushed around as "the short, balding, acne ridden kid" made me pretty angry. I hated being shoved into lockers, I hated being terrible at sports, and I hated not fitting in.

At the same time, though, I was driven to prove myself. When I was first introduced to entrepreneurship, I loved it because I knew that I would be the determining factor in my success or failure. I felt that I had control for the first time in my life, and that for once my incredibly short height wasn't dictating my ability to succeed. So I started my first business selling toilet paper and household cleaning supplies and began to work really hard. I spent my first few years just scraping by and getting more and more frustrated that things just didn't seem to be going my way, again. I was still angry, still not forming the friendships and relationships I truly desired, and my bank account was still empty at the end of every month.

I had been attending leadership conferences and trying to practice the success principles I was being taught, but I still wasn't getting optimal results. Then one day at a conference I heard the speaker say, "Your thoughts and beliefs and actions got you to where you are today, so are you happy? If not, you need to make a change." I wasn't happy. I wasn't where I wanted to be. I was lonely and frustrated. I was very egotistical and had recently been told that people didn't enjoy being around me, which was very hurtful and reminded me of my past. I had a lot of built up anger and my attitude was horrible. It was at that moment that I decided I was finally sick of who I was. I wanted to change; I wanted to be someone that others liked and wanted to be friends with, and I wanted to reach the goals I had set for my business.

What I realized was that I needed to change my mindset if I wanted to find success. I learned that my anger and pessimism would only hinder me on my journey. I needed to focus on the upside of things, but I wasn't sure how to do that or where to start. So I became a student. I read every business and personal development book that I could get my hands on, and I asked questions. I found people that had what I wanted, everything from great relationships to business success to sustaining wealth, and I asked them how they did it. I discovered the concept of positive affirmations and I began stating them out loud daily. I embraced a fully positive lifestyle; from sunup to sundown I spent my time with positive people, reading positive books and articles, and constantly repeating my positive affirmations to remove the negativity from my mind. I became annoyingly positive, so much so that within just a few months, my friends and clients started calling me "Mr. Positivity".

The truth is, the conditioning that most of us have from our childhood and educational years tends to be inherently negative. After years and years of trying to fit in with the crowd and society around us, we tend to get a hardened "too cool for school" attitude that only hinders our potential and performance. Or we take it to the opposite extreme and put so much pressure on ourselves to be the very best that we become incredibly critical of everything we do, never allowing ourselves to celebrate our accomplishments. This doesn't do us any good when we are then striving for success and trying to start new businesses or career paths. It's one thing to recognize and learn from your failures, it's another to condemn yourself and get stuck in a rut of negativity.

Fact: Life is a world of ups and downs. You can't let a bad day drag down your entire month. You can't let a bad month impact your year, because soon it won't just be one bad year; it'll be five. If your mindset is negative, then only negative things will happen; if your mindset is confident that better times are coming, great things will happen. What you think shapes how you feel, which dictates what you do, which determines what you get, which results in what you become. And here's the hard truth: If you don't buy into a bulletproof mindset of positivity, you won't make it to your desired level of success in whatever career or entrepreneurial venture you choose.

SHIFT TO A POSITIVE MINDSET

Previously, I was radiating negative energy. I created arguments and my friends could only handle being around me for limited amounts of time. I found opportunities to push buttons, and I was pretty unpleasant. Once I became a more positive person, my energy changed – and so did my attractiveness to others. My friends enjoyed spending longer periods of time with me and my girlfriend (now wife) and I deepened our relationship. I was amazed at the massive affect my new positive mindset was having in such a short time on my entire life.

As I continued to pursue positivity, my confidence also shifted. I became much more outgoing and willing to network and talk with anyone. I was more enjoyable to be around, and with that came new friends and business partners. People began seeking me out for business opportunities instead of me being the one to bang their doors down. I connected with the right people and within a year I was able to broker 60 million dollars in real estate, netting me a large commission. With that success and new capital, I went on to start various other businesses and got into the Internet, Digital Media, and Domain Name Industry, where I currently spend most of my time today.

Since then, I have been able to build a multi-million dollar company that owns, grows, and develops a portfolio of websites in some of the world's most premier categories. The little company we started back in 2009 is now a respected authority in lead-generation, digital marketing, and turning website rankings into revenue. None of this would have been possible at the young age of twenty-six if I hadn't worked on myself to become a student of personal development and positivity. The changes I made in my mindset ultimately led to the success I have today.

When my first six-figure investor approached me, he said, "I'm not investing in this project – I'm investing in you." And that is exactly how each investor, partner, and prospective client is thinking about you as a business leader. They are choosing to do business with YOU. You could have the best opportunity in the world, but if people see you as negative, short tempered or dishonest, you won't be able to find a single investor.

195

On the other hand, if you are upbeat, fun and positive, you will have return business and people that specifically choose you because of how pleasant you are to work with.

There are three things you can do right now to create a bulletproof mindset and become more attractive. They might sound hokey or seem uncomfortable at first, but all of us can benefit from more positivity and subsequently more success in our lives. Make these three habits part of your daily life, and I promise that you will have a prosperous and successful future.

1. **Write down ten affirmations that you aspire to achieve** on a piece of paper. The idea is to figure out what you want or have not achieved yet, and write these goals down as if they've already happened: "I am an incredible entrepreneur," "I deserve all of my success," "I have beautiful, deep, and lasting relationships." These goals can be personal, business and/or career, or even health-related. Pick the most important things specific to your definition of success and incorporate them into positive affirmations.

   When I decided to use affirmations for the first time, I honestly thought it was weird. I felt awkward and I thought to myself, "There is no way this is going to work." But I really wanted my life to change. So the first affirmations I used were sayings like, "I am creative," "I am caring," "I am wealthy," "I attract abundance into my life today," and "I deserve success and I require results." And that last one is still repeated amongst my closest friends in a mocking voice because of how often I would walk around saying it out loud. Effectively, it sort of became my trademark. It may have been weird and a little funny to some, but it worked and my affirmations became my reality.

   So trust me and try this: upon waking in the morning, read all of your affirmations out loud with pride and confidence. Really believe in what you're saying. Write them down and post them in areas you visit frequently. For example, write them on notecards and put them in your car, on your mirror, in your planner, on your refrigerator, and at your office. Each time you see them, envision them happening in your life. Try this for 30 days, and see how your mindset becomes more positive and upbeat.

2. **Take a few hours to write out your perfect day** if money and time were not obstacles. Be as descriptive as you can, from sunup till sundown. Where would you wake up? When would you wake up? Who would be next to you? What would you eat? What activities would you do? What car would you drive? This will expand your vision and erase your limitations. Read the entire thing out loud daily for 30 days. Envision it, make it yours, and watch your life change.

I firmly believe that thoughts become reality. Your thoughts will lead you to take the correct actions to achieve your goals. When I did this exercise, I was nowhere near where I wanted to be. One might even think that what I had written on my "Perfect Day" was never going to be a reality for me. But about two years later, after a lot of hard work followed by action and daily recitation of my "Perfect Day" and positive affirmations, I was living most of the "Perfect Day" I had described. (My wife wouldn't let me move away from family to the beach, but short of that, everything else came true!) So dream big and design your life.

3. **Surround yourself with positive people.** Like it or not, the people around you have a big impact on your life. Entrepreneur, author, and motivational speaker Jim Rohn says, "You are the average of the five people you spend the most time with." They will impact everything from how much money you make, to your attitude, to how far you get in your career.

As I was making my transition to a positive mindset, I started to realize that many of the people around me were what I typically call "toxic relationships." They weren't encouraging me to achieve my dreams, and were even trying to deter me from working towards success. I had to make the hard decision to cut people out of parts of my life. For instance, I stopped spending as much time with my parents because they simply did not understand the path of entrepreneurship that I had chosen. Now that may sound harsh and very difficult for some people, and don't get me wrong I absolutely love my parents, but they are not entrepreneurs and just couldn't imagine the pursuit I was after. Sometimes family members can be your most supportive cheerleaders, and other times they can be your biggest critics. If you feel like a family member or close friend may be hindering your journey to success, you may need to make the hard decision to distance yourself from them for a little while.

Once I stopped associating with people who were unsupportive or negative and started spending time with people who wanted to find success, my own personal success soared. I sought out people I could learn from and who had similar goals and interests as I did. I was willing to try anything to learn and succeed. When I passed expensive and exotic cars in parking lots, I would approach the owners, ask to buy them lunch, and pick their brains. That proved to be invaluable in that most of the people I approached had accomplished incredible things and were able to guide me in the right direction. Knowledge is everywhere; you just have to take the steps to find it.

FIND YOUR SUCCESS

As you finish this chapter, I know you may still be thinking that some of this is weird. I'm sure it's uncomfortable to stand in front of a mirror and talk to yourself while stating your affirmations. I understand, because I thought that too. But I was so desperate for change that I forced myself out of my comfort zone and tried it anyway. I started asking myself whether success or comfort was more important to me. The final choice wasn't hard to make, and let me tell you, it paid off.

Clients and customers want to invest in – and do business with – people who have good energy and people they feel they can trust. Having a bright outlook will attract people to you, and it will earn you the reputation and foundation you need to be successful. It's not something you can fake, and it's not something you can learn in a day; it's something you have to set your mind to. And if you do, it can and will change your entire life.

About Aaron

Aaron Pitman is a highly regarded Internet entrepreneur, business builder, manager and senior executive. He is an expert at teaching small business owners, executives, and sales representatives on **how to become more productive and increase revenue through digital marketing**. He is considered a pioneer in the Domain Name Industry and is the Founder of RA Domain Capital, an Internet media company that owns and grows a portfolio of web businesses in some of the world's most premier categories.

Aaron has built multiple 7-figure Businesses in the areas of Digital Marketing, Distressed Internet Investments, Real Estate and Product Placement Consulting. As a consultant, Aaron has worked with dozens of businesses and specializes in online marketing, business development, lead-generation, business growth, strategic acquisitions, exit strategies and turning website rankings into revenue.

Aaron has been featured in numerous publications such as *Fast Company, Forbes, Mashable, INC, Yahoo, Small Business Trends, Under30CEO, Life Hack, Upstart, The Huffington Post,* and more. He was voted Top 10 Digital Entrepreneurs of 2012 by MO.com. Aaron also sits on the Young Entrepreneur Council for the most successful entrepreneurs in America under 35 years of age. He is often quoted as a creative thinker, idea man, innovator, investor, and dealmaker. Aaron loves to support charities advocating for Autism and International Orphan Care. Aaron and his wife Rachel reside in Mason, Ohio with son Noah and dog Simba. He welcomes anyone to visit him directly at: aaronpitman.com.

CHAPTER 22

SECURING YOUR FINANCES IN RETIREMENT

BY GARY SCHEER, RFC, CSA

When I began my financial services career in the early 1980's, most retirees used the "three legged stool "approach to retirement funding. They had a company funded pension, social security and their own savings. The first two legs provided a guaranteed income for life. The third leg allowed people to enjoy the fruits of their labor and some of the niceties of life. Defined Contribution 401(k) plans were added to employee benefit programs as a way for higher level executives to put away more of their money on a tax deductible basis. Middle management and lower level workers were encouraged to contribute to these plans as well. 403(b) plans have many characteristics of 401(k)'s but are available only for employees of nonprofit employers.

During the course of the 1980's and early 90's nearly all organizations with the exception of government and municipal employers, significantly reduced or eliminated their defined benefit pension plans . These were substituted with full blown 401(k) and other limited benefit pension programs. This move forever changed the retirement planning landscape for American workers. They now had a two legged or even a one-and-one-half legged stool from which to launch a retirement that could last 20, 30 or as many as 40 years.

There are four stages in the life of every saver and investor. This is based on one's appetite for risk, income requirements and investment time horizon. As we get older and approach our retirement years, it is important to adjust the level of risk in our investment portfolios. With few exceptions, people in the 20's, 30's, 40's and early 50's are in the accumulation phase of their investment lives. Upon amassing a nest egg, those in their late 50's, 60's and 70's transition into the preservation stage. When people draw down their investment accounts for income, they are in the distribution phase. Finally, when we are approaching the end of our lives, we are in the transfer phase. The goal at this point is to pass on the remainder of our assets with minimal intrusion by the Federal and State government.

The focus of this chapter is on the preservation and distribution phases. As was stated earlier, traditional defined benefit pension plans and social security provided income security by generating a guaranteed income for the life of the individual and spouse depending on the chosen pension distribution election.

Having served the financial and retirement planning needs of families, business owners and professionals for over three decades, I've learned that the greatest fear of most retirees is outliving their money. They want to maintain their independence for as long as possible and not be a burden on their children.

Social scientists estimate that the average retiree will incur as much as $250,000 in unreimbursed medical expenses during retirement. Even many retirees who an average individual would consider well off are concerned about how these costs may cause them to one day have to choose between food and medicine.

With the demise of traditional pensions, employers have transferred the responsibility of managing the growth of and risk of their workers' retirement portfolio square onto the backs of their employees. After spending much of their adult lives managing growing retirement assets during the accumulation stage, newly-minted retirees now have to manage their nest eggs and convert their principal balance into a reliable "paycheck" that will carry them and their spouse, if they're married, for the rest of their lives. They have to change their thinking about saving and investing and focus on how to sustain a predicable income that can withstand the eroding effects of ever-increasing taxation and inflation.

At the time of this writing, the challenge for most of these people is how do to this in an era of high stock market volatility, historically low interest rates, depressed real estate values and life spans that are ever increasing due to medical advances. Ironically, wealth distribution is more complex than wealth accumulation. Once a retiree "turns on" the income stream, they are immediately exposed to new layers of risk. It is no longer enough to say you're going to earn X% on your portfolio and withdraw Y% for income. Retirees need to protect their income from behavioral risk, sequence of return risk, longevity risk, taxes, and inflation and so on.

A popular retirement income planning strategy that has been promoted for years by Wall Street is known as the 4% rule. Based on studies of stock and bond returns since 1926, financial planners had settled on a benchmark for how much a retiree could spend each year without fear of running out of cash. It turned out that a person who invested half in stocks and half in bonds could spend 4% of his or her wealth in the first year, adjust that dollar amount for inflation in subsequent years, and still have money 30 years later. UP until recently, this worked in every historical 30 year period, as well as in most computer simulations based on the historical rate of return. In past rising markets, even drawing as much as 5% worked more often than not.

According to Dr. When Pfau, professor of retirement income at the American College for Financial Services, without strong stock and bond returns to help refresh one's nest egg as one spends from it, those old numbers can no longer be relied on. In times of below average interest rates on 10-year Treasury securities and deep dips in stock market values during recent downturns, Dr. Pfau suggests that the probability that a 4% withdrawal rate will continue to work in the future is much lower. His new safe starting point is a 3% drawdown. That means that if you've saved $1 million, you're living on only $30,000 a year before Social Security, and any other sources of income you might have.. When inflation is factored into the equation, the result is a 2.2% real return before income taxes; a sobering number indeed.

In a study with Dr. Michael Finke, Associate Professor of Personal Financial Planning at Texas Tech' and David Blanchett, Director of Research at Morningstar Investment Management, Dr. Pfau found that with returns in that range, taking an inflation adjusted $40,000 per year out of a $1 million portfolio will drain your assets about 57% of the time, depending on the pattern of good and bad years. More bad years early in the distribution phase mean your investment will be more likely to run out. This realization has caused many retirement planners and academicians to claim that the 4% rule is dead.

Now that you know the bad news, what solutions exist for current and future retirees? Some of these may seem obvious.

1. **Save more money** – if you can. This is a worthy strategy for people who are not close to retirement, since they have more time on their side.

2. **Use Diversification to stretch your cash.** Spreading out your assets among more asset classes will decrease volatility and tend to prolong the life of one's portfolio.

3. **Stay Flexible.** Most retirees with whom I've counseled have drawn down the greatest percentage of their nest egg in the first years of retirement. They tend to relish the opportunities and excitement for travel and other recreational pursuits while they have optimal health and energy. Their spending tends to lessen on a non-inflation adjusted basis as time goes on.

Since these methods require discipline and sacrifice, retirees and their families have been demanding more systematic methods for predictable, guaranteed income for life. One solution to this challenge is known as **Sequential Income Planning**. This involves providing a steady income stream by separating assets into distinct "buckets". If you've ever been to a tree farm and noticed how the growth of the trees is staggered-some of the trees are ready to harvest now, while the rest are given time to grow to maturity—then you understand the concept behind the buckets.

Bucketing has great appeal as a distribution strategy because it offers an organized, systemized process for getting one's retirement savings from a 401(k), IRA, stock portfolio, etc. into his wallet in a way that minimizes taxes, and protects against market volatility while leveraging the market as a hedge against inflation. The buckets designated for the first few years of retirement should hold very stable, secure investments, so retirees know their immediate income needs are covered. The buckets designed for later years, meanwhile, hold potentially riskier investments meant to generate portfolio growth over a longer period of time. There are many versions of the bucket strategy, and some are so complex that they require the help of a financial advisor. But do-it-yourselfers can implement basic elements of the strategy in their own portfolios.

FILLING THE BUCKETS

To start, consider the amount of money you will likely spend annually in the first five years of retirement. Then, after factoring in Social Security, pensions and any other steady sources of income, decide on how much to draw from your portfolio each year to cover expenses.

Money to cover the first five years' worth of spending should be invested in extremely safe holdings. You might place money in a money market fund to deliver income for the first year, for example and buy certificates of deposit (CD's) that will mature in years two, three, four and five. Short term, high-quality bond funds, a "ladder" of Treasury bonds, maturing each year, or a single premium immolate annuity (SPIA), could also go in this bucket.

"Structured Cash Flows" may be very suitable for funding one's initial bucket. Structured Cash Flows represent a fixed income stream such as secondary market annuities or pre-owned pensions income sold at a discount in exchange for a lump sum. A discounted cash flow may provide a higher rate of return than traditional income products such as annuities, bonds and Certificates of Deposit.

Many advisors design the second bucket to cover another five years' worth of living expenses and fill it with slightly riskier investments. Appropriate holding might include high quality intermediate term bond funds, global bond funds and a small allocation in a well-diversified portfolio of stocks. After your first five years of retirement, you can use the money to replenish the your first bucket – for example, buy another five year ladder of Certificates of Deposit, Treasury bonds, a single premium immediate annuity or structured cash flow.

To keep your plan relatively simple, you can design the third bucket to hold the remainder of your portfolio. In this segment, it's appropriate to go after some growth with moderate risk. This could include a diversified portfolio of stocks, fixed indexed annuities and alternative investments.

A fixed indexed annuity links interest earnings to a variety of stock or bond indices such as the S&P 500 and the 10-year Treasury bond. When the market goes up, the individual can participate in some of the gains; when the market goes down, there is a no loss guarantee. In addition, many of these vehicles offer income riders that provide a guaranteed income for life and potentially the life of one's spouse, if married. Inflation options to increase income over time may be available in these plans as well. Alternative Investments do not have any correlation to the stock market. These include real estate limited partnerships, commodities such as gold, silver and copper, and diamonds. While a do-it-yourself bucket approach may use only three basic segments, some advisors divide a client's retirement into as many as six or more five-year buckets, each with its own investment mix and targeted return.

If you've read this far, you may now understand why I believe that wealth distribution planning is much more complex than planning for wealth accumulation. In order to put the odds in your favor and enjoy a retirement with income security and peace of mind, It may be wise to consult a financial professional specializing in income planning to help maximize the abundant planning opportunities available to today's retirees.

About Gary

Gary Scheer, RFC, CSA is the Founder and Managing Member of Gary Scheer, LLC. and a graduate of Purdue University. Recognized as one of the top retirement experts in the nation, Gary Scheer has helped thousands of individuals and families in New York, New Jersey and across the nation prepare for a secure, successful retirement since 1982. Specializing in Retirement Income Planning, Advanced Financial and Estate Planning Strategies, and Creative Tax Reduction Methodologies, Gary works with people who are in or nearing retirement to find solutions to help them enjoy their retirement years. With a background in traditional financial planning, Gary has pioneered strategies that protect his clients from volatile and risky financial investments while helping them grow their retirement income.

In addition to giving presentations on estate planning, wealth preservation, asset protection, IRA planning and other topics in the Northern New Jersey area, Gary hosts *Gary Scheer's Safe Money & Retirement Show.* Gary's show has been on the air for more than seven years and is heard in New York, New Jersey and Pennsylvania. Gary offers a unique On Demand Seminar entitled: *How Big Is Your Retirement Shortfall.* Lasting just under 15 minutes, people can view the seminar 24 hours per day, 7 days per week on their computer, tablet or mobile phone from the convenience of their home or office.

In addition to his memberships with the Estate Planning Council of Northern New Jersey, National Association of Insurance and Financial Advisors and the elite Top of The Table, Gary has earned the Registered Financial Consultant and Certified Senior Advisor Designations. He is currently a candidate for the Certified Financial Planner designation. Gary was featured among *America's Select Financial Advisors* in 2013, has been quoted in the *Austin News* and has appeared on News 12 NJ, Verizon's FIOS1 News, WPIX 11 NY, and Time Warner Cable's NY1 News.

As a complement to his professional achievements, Gary is a past President and former Treasurer of a local private school board. In these capacities, he has been consulted on issues ranging from employee benefits to fundraising and investments. Additionally, Gary has played trumpet with the acclaimed Livingston Symphony Orchestra, in Livingston, New Jersey for over 20 years. Gary and his wife Susan reside in Northern New Jersey and are the proud parents of three adult children.

You can connect with Gary at:
Gary@GaryScheer.com
www.garyscheer.com
www.garyscheerpresents.com
www.twitter.com/GaryRScheer
www.linkedin.com/pub/garyscheer/5/2a5/34

CHAPTER 23

FIVE STRATEGIES TO ENJOY A SUCCESSFUL RETIREMENT

BY DAVID HOYT, CLU, ChFC

It seems like only ten minutes ago when I walked across the stage floor to greet our principal, Mr. Wayne Kincaid, and received my high school diploma. Then it was on to college, drafted and served during the Vietnam War, met my wife, Sue and began a career in the financial services industry. And now here I sit, some 40 years later with Sue, with three grown children and five not-so-grown grandchildren.

Maybe that sounds like you. You are coming to the end of a successful journey through your career path, the kids are raised and hopefully pointed in the right direction, and now you are ready to enjoy a peace-filled and worry-free retirement.

As for me, I am certainly old enough to retire, but still young enough to enjoy helping my clients—and you—have a successful retirement. So what brought me to where I am today?

As a youngster, I came from a good home, but without any extra money. Out of necessity, I would do all the work necessary on my bicycles and later my cars. I learned to tune-up motors, change generators, radiators and brakes. On one of my cars, I learned how to re-install the drive shaft I sometimes would leave on the road behind me. Those were the days we call "good-ole'?"

Today, I would not think of doing any of the work on my car. It requires too much sophisticated technology, tools I don't have, and most of all, a specialist with the knowledge and experience I don't have.

Your retirement planning works that way, too. I have 40 years specializing in strategies and the financial instruments that help my clients meet their most important financial goals—namely growing and protecting assets while developing a strategy that maximizes income. I have the education and the experience specifically for these financial matters.

Many of my clients—perhaps like you—have the time, the talent, and the motivation to do much of their own planning. But, none of us knows what we don't know. Just like I have specialists who work on my car, we need specialists to help us with one of our most important decisions we will ever face, getting the most from our retirement dollars!

Here are five strategies my clients have utilized that you may want to consider for your worry-free retirement. These concepts are intended to help make your money last longer, provide protection from unforeseen financial setbacks, and provide a degree of financial certainty in the event of health-related calamities. Sometimes, just one of these strategies can help accomplish more than just one of your financial goals. Here they are:

1. **Consider postponing lifetime income until your age or your health is an asset.** Income can be purchased in the same way you purchase a hamburger from McDonald's. When I go to my favorite McDs, I order a McDouble and give the order-taker a buck and some change in return for the sandwich.

   Likewise, you can take *cash* to an insurance company and exchange it for lifetime income. But, just as hamburgers are not priced the same from one restaurant to another, neither is income. So you want to shop companies—or have a retirement specialist do it for you—in order to get the most income for your cash.

   Here are the factors that determine how much income you can buy with your money:

   • Your age. By the very fact the income is going to last your lifetime, your age is an important factor given the younger you are, the longer you will likely live. Conversely, as you get older, your cash will buy more income as your life expectancy is shorter. By the way, life expectancy is simply an actuarial calculation for a specific time in the future when half the individuals at your current age will have deceased. They don't know who, just how many!

• Your spouse's age. If you are married, and you and your spouse have agreed upon a survivor option that meets your needs, your spouse's age is also used in determining your lifetime income amount. Since the income is being paid out for the lives of two people, income will cost more.

• Your health. There are a few companies that will consider this factor. If your health condition affects your mortality, your life expectancy is for fewer years than someone your age who is healthy. Some companies will issue you a lifetime income as if you were older than you are, thus giving you more income for your cash.

• Interest rates. The insurance company can pay you more income given your age and health when interest rates are higher because the insurance company can earn more on your dollars. One strategy this will affect is when you convert cash to income. If you think interest rates are going up in the future, you may want to factor that into when you purchase lifetime income.

• A factor that is seldom discussed is whether the insurance company quoting you the income is competitive in that very specific market place. The more the company is trying to compete to get that business, the more income your money will likely purchase. This is one reason to be working with someone who knows this market, is independent and able to shop the marketplace, and knows who is competitive. I do this for my clients.

What if the income is being offered from a pension? Do the same rules apply? Yes! Therefore, before you take the income offer from your pension, determine the cash option, and have it shopped to be sure you are getting the most income available to you.

2. If you haven't already taken Social Security, consider postponing taking it as long as possible.

This is a hot topic, a controversial topic, and one in which smart people take different sides of the argument. Given the limited space here, I cannot possibly satisfy what should be your quest to get it right for you and your spouse. Nearly half of all people retiring early take Social Security at age 62. But, should they?

There are three key elements that determine your Social Security amount:

First, it is your earnings history that determines the monthly benefit to which you are entitled. Second is the age at which you initially file for benefits. And third is the potential delayed retirement credits to which you are entitled should you elect to wait beyond your full retirement age, up to age 70, to begin collecting benefits. The potential to earn delayed retirement credits—which can add up to as much as 8% per year in addition to the cost of living adjustments each year—may add up to a substantial increase in your monthly benefit amount.

Let's look at a hypothetical case study:

You and your wife are currently age 62, and are considering taking Social Security now, the earliest age at which you can collect a Social Security retirement benefit. Your normal retirement ages are 66 (persons born in 1952 have a Full Retirement Age of 66), and you are eligible for a $2,000 monthly benefit while your wife is eligible for $1,200.

So if you choose to begin now, you will receive a reduced benefit of what you would get at your full retirement age. Let's say you receive approximately $1,500 monthly and your spouse receives about $900 monthly at your ages of 62. Historically, the cost of living adjustment is about 2.5 to 3% per year.

If you can find the income you need from an alternative source, such as your 401(k), instead of taking it from your Social Security, you can use an election few know about. It is called the "file and suspend" election. The goal here is to postpone taking

Social Security until the benefit is at its maximum. The spouse with the least benefit, in our example the wife, elects at age 66 the spousal benefit under your work record while you will not actually be receiving your benefit so as to earn delayed credits on your benefit to age 70.

At age 70, you both switch to your own benefits, having enjoyed the benefit of delayed retirement credits of approximately 8% per year making your adjusted benefit $2,640 and your spouse's benefit $1,584—not including any applicable cost of living adjustments.

By using this technique, at age 85, your combined Social Security benefit will total $1,162,000 or roughly $300,000 more than taking Social Security early.

That's not all. If you predecease your spouse, you are leaving her a much larger benefit. And one more thing: Your Social Security benefit is probably your only income that will likely increase each year. You want the income that will go up with inflation to be as large a number as you can have.

I'm not discussing the political football Social Security has become or whether it is likely to be here for the next generation. But it is here now, and you want to plan using it to your advantage.

3. Match your financial goal with the financial instrument that best accomplishes your goal.

One of the mistakes I see made as one nears or is in retirement is not matching one's goal—including sometimes not even having a defined goal—to the proper tool to achieve the goal. Most of us would not choose a hedge trimmer to cut our lawn. We could, but it would take forever and probably not be the end result we wanted.

Similarly, you shouldn't use short-term instruments like CDs, for long-term goals. That's a mistake I often see. There is nothing wrong with having money in the bank; in fact, it is desirable. But bank instruments are meant to provide you liquidity—access to your money—not growth. The money you have in the bank should be money for which you are willing to sacrifice earnings to have liquidity. But, you don't have to sacrifice earnings for safety.

So nearly 20 years ago, the insurance industry came up with a hybrid instrument that has principal protection and guaranteed interest while still benefiting its clients with reasonable rates of return. They are called fixed index annuities.

With these instruments, you can choose between a fixed interest rate, currently around 3% (1st quarter of 2014), or have your interest earnings credited based on distinct Index Account Options and the annual performance of these indices. The Interest Credits will not mirror the actual performance of the index itself, but rather the index closes (daily, monthly, annually, etc.) are used as a basis for determining what the Interest Credits will be. With these instruments, you can benefit when the index goes up without any risk of loss when it goes down.

Who should own these instruments? If you don't want market risk, you don't want to pay tax on money as it accumulates (you pay tax only when you withdraw earnings), or you want to benefit from market trends without the risk of loss, these instruments might be for you.

Choosing the right accumulation vehicles through retirement can be difficult, but having some of your money free of market risk, yet with long-term growth opportunity can be a good choice.

4. **A Split-Annuity Strategy can provide tax-free income and tax-deferred savings.** If you are in your 50s or 60s, or if you are very healthy and in your 70s, a split-annuity concept can be a great way to add to your income while building additional wealth for the near future.

Let's say you and your spouse are each age 62, and have $500,000 to provide both of you an immediate income. Traditionally, people would look to buy lifetime income from an insurance company, or if they have other assets and are risk tolerant, maybe they would purchase bonds for the income. But you don't like the risk of bonds, and currently Treasuries are paying next to nothing, so you purchase a lifetime income. It will pay you around $22,000 a year until you are both deceased.

However, you might consider a split-annuity strategy. Let's take $200,000 and purchase a ten-year immediate annuity. This means for ten years, you receive about $22,000 a year of which about 92% of that is tax-free. Then you take the other $300,000 and purchase a fixed index annuity with the goal of growing that back to the original $500,000 in ten years. By definition, this money is growing tax-deferred so the money left in the annuity is earning interest also, sometimes referred to as triple compounding.

At the end of the ten years, you have the $300,000 plus the tax-deferred interest it earned during the ten years. Now you are at an age where the *mortality credits* (your age determines in part how much lifetime income you can purchase) work in your favor. Now your principal and interest can be used to purchase lifetime income.

I have used as an example splitting the annuities with 60% of the money going to the deferred annuity and 40% going to the immediate annuity. The way the split is actually designed depends upon your income goal, the interest rate that can be earned or assumed, and the number of years for which the strategy is designed. A retirement specialist who is familiar with this technique could put together a strategy that would work for you, or you could contact me for a proposal.

5. This Alternative to a Long-Term Care Insurance Policy can accomplish multiple goals.

Traditional long-term care insurance policies are expensive and difficult to qualify if you have waited too long to purchase. "Too long" is relative to the assets you have to purchase a policy and how good your health is.

Some of my clients have liked the option of "hitting two targets with one arrow." A handful of life insurance companies have created what is often referred to as "living benefit riders" for their life insurance policies. In essence, these riders allow the policyholder to accelerate the death benefit to use for reason like nursing homes, assisted living, home health care and even catastrophic illnesses requiring surgery.

Usually, if one qualifies, 2% of the death benefit can be used each and every month until the death benefit is exhausted. Let's say you have one of these policies for $250,000 of death benefit. You need home health care and you qualify by the terms of the contract for the accelerated benefit. Two percent of $250,000 is $5,000. This is the amount you would receive each month you need the care. Do the math and you will see in fifty months your death benefit will have expired and the benefit would terminate, thus the term *accelerated death benefit rider*.

If you pass away before the entire death benefit is paid out, then your beneficiary receives the remainder as a death benefit. If for some reason, you determine you no longer need either, then the policy can be surrendered for its equity or cash value often times equal to at least the minimum you put into it.

These are five popular and safe strategies for the conservative "investor." They are intended to help your money accomplish more for you, meet multiple goals, and allow you to enjoy a worry-free retirement.

So who can help you with these kinds of strategies? I would suggest you seek a Chartered Life Underwriter (CLU), or a Chartered Financial Consultant (ChFC) for any of these strategies I have discussed here. A Certified Financial Planner (CFP) is also a good choice. Now enjoy your retirement!

About David

David Hoyt has been in the financial services since 1972. He earned his Chartered Life Underwriter (CLU) designation in 1987 and his Chartered Financial Consultant (ChFC) designation in 1989 from the American College of Bryn Mawr, Pennsylvania.

He was founder of Hoyt Brokerage Company, a national marketing organization providing financial instruments to consumers through a network of financial planners, brokers and insurance agents. He is founder and owner of Hoyt Financial Group, specializing in serving its clients with strategies and financial instruments to help them grow and protect their incomes and assets.

David welcomes inquiries from anyone interested in learning about the safe-alternative strategies he teaches. He believes every retired person should have some of his/her money free from the worry associated with volatility of the stock markets. He believes that there are risks associated with retirement that must be mitigated, and that is his value to his clients.

He hosted the radio talk show, *Financial Facts with David Hoyt.* He is author of the book, *Life Lessons from Beyond.* He is a member of the Society of Financial Services Professionals, National Association of Insurance and Financial Advisors and member of the Retirement Income Industry Association.

David is married to Sue and together they have three children and five grandchildren. Besides spending time with them, he and Sue enjoy traveling, hiking, fishing and golf.

He can be reached at: HoytFinancialGroup.com, or: dave@hoytfinancialgroup.com or call him at: (317) 882-3676.

CHAPTER 24

THE RETIREMENT JOURNEY

BY GREG PARADY

Several years ago, my brother Luke, a world-class rock climber since the age of 15, asked me to join him on a climb to the summit of Longs Peak in Colorado. The hike was described to me as a 7½ mile trek to the summit of a 14,000-foot mountaintop. I accepted his challenge (and challenge it was). Refusing to be shown up by my younger sibling, I spent six months training for this hike. I ate all the right food, jogged several miles a day, and trained on a gym treadmill as often as possible. The treadmill in my mind was a critical part of the training process, because living in Florida, I was otherwise unable to mimic the incline that the mountain would present to me.

So I went to the gym and worked my way up all the machine settings until it maxed out at a 45-degree angle. This was my routine for months. Since I live at sea level, I had to acclimate my body to the thin air and high altitude of the Rocky Mountains, so I arrived in Colorado a full month prior to our scheduled adventure. During this time I learned how to fly fish in the rivers and streams of Estes Park. In hindsight, I would have preferred the solitude of fishing at the bottom of the mountain rather than try to climb to the top of it.

The day of the climb arrived and we departed prepared with headlamps, backpacks of water and hydration gels, multiple layers of clothing and rain gear. You name it and we brought it! We began our journey at midnight. Initially my training served me well, but the altitude proved to be a bigger challenge than I could anticipate. Because we had to stop so often to drink water and to breathe, we averaged less than one mile per hour, a humbling experience because I have always taken pride in my health and athleticism.

At 5:30 a.m., after 5½ hours of walking, stumbling, and resting in the dark, I witnessed the most beautiful sunrise I had ever seen. This was one of the most amazing and breathtaking experiences of my life. After nine hours, we finally reached the summit and words cannot describe the beauty or the tremendous feeling of personal achievement. Not a cloud in the sky and easily the greatest physical accomplishment of my life.

We weren't alone either. There were at least 100 other hikers who had taken the same challenge, reached the summit, and were now enjoying themselves. Many sat on the rocks eating lunch and taking in the views. However, I only got to relish the sights and bask in my self-congratulatory accomplishment for 12 minutes. As soon as we reached the summit, my brother began to talk about our descent. He'd say, "Okay, snap some photos and let's get going!" Did I mention he's my little brother and I rarely listen to him?

But this time my brother was adamant we begin our descent and before I understood why, he was back on the trail. As I followed him begrudgingly, I realized I had never put the treadmill on a DECLINE setting. I had only trained for climbing UP the mountain. My focus on getting to the top had over shadowed my now obvious realization— what goes up must come down. It never crossed my mind to train the muscles that I would now need to navigate the descent. In many ways, it is much harder to climb down a steep mountain than to climb up.

There was also a definite reason we began our journey at midnight, as well as for Luke's prodding to begin the return trip. I didn't get to argue with him this time because his quick pace showed he was on a mission to get back. After being 5 to 10 minutes behind him for what seemed like forever, I finally caught up at 12,000 feet when he stopped to rehydrate and enjoy an energy bar. I inhaled enough air to question his mad retreat and he told me a story I will never forget. He said there were unknown risks to our trip, and you wouldn't know them unless you have been on the mountain before. He relayed his experience:

"I was on this mountain two years ago and was about 200 feet from the top when we were caught in a sudden lightning and hail storm. I wasn't on this trail though. I was totally exposed on the mountain face climbing with some friends." (My brother is a rock climber, not a hiker. He does the crazy stuff.) *"The lightning came out of nowhere around noon and was cracking and thundering all around us. I thought it was all over. Like most climbs I set a goal to reach the top and that day was no different. My only goal was to reach the peak. I didn't know then that the peak of this summit is like a magnet for electricity, so when it warms up around noon there is often a thunderstorm that is attracted to the same spot almost daily."* (Sure enough, I saw huge black clouds enveloping the summit we had briefly enjoyed earlier.)

"The success of this trip, or any trip, isn't measured by reaching the top; success is measured by how well you navigate the challenges facing you once you've reached the top. The people that are up there right now are in danger, and they're making decisions under extreme stress, they're tired and weak from the climb and they're all panicking to get down from there. And it's never a good idea to make big decisions under extremes duress.

It is the **exit strategy** *that determines achievement. And you must be prepared prior to the ascent. We began this trip at midnight so that we could reach the top early enough to get out of harm's way prior to the storms."*

Who would have known that the single biggest reason that our trip was successful was the starting time? Only someone who had been there before would know the risks. I learned a lot about my brother that day. How did those other people manage the descent? I learned a lot about myself too. But the greatest lesson I learned was about life, and how it pertains to my career and my passion as an insurance professional. Most people only do one-half of the planning. They think climbing to the top of the "retirement mountain" is the goal. They do not think about the storms that could arise or know all the potential dangers and obstacles one faces once they have reached the top and are in retirement.

Just as I prepared for the task that day, so have retirees planned, sacrificed, saved, invested, and utilized resources to help them get to the top of their own retirement mountain. I now call that the "accumulation" phase of life. Once you've reached the top of the mountain it's important for retirees to have sound exit strategies to get them down the mountain safely so they can reap the benefits of their years of hard work and careful planning.

I call the descent the "distribution" or "preservation" phase of life. Since I only work with people that are nearing or have already reached the summit, I am well-versed in the financial challenges that retirees can face and how to address them.

For almost 18 years we have successfully designed strategies using annuities and life insurance for more than 1,500 families who want to feel confident in their retirement income strategy. An exit strategy must be customized to fit your goals. It takes you from where you are today, (the top of the mountain) to where you want to be tomorrow. Some examples of retirement exit strategies include: transitioning from accumulation to distribution, moving tax-deferred assets to a tax-favorable position and looking at ways to protect assets from negative market volatility. There's a big difference between growing wealth during your working years and enjoying the wealth you've already accumulated in your retirement years. Do you have an exit strategy for your IRAs and other tax-deferred assets? Paying too much in taxes can have a significant impact on your retirement.

Let's face it—once you've reached the top, we have to strategize on the best route for you to begin coming down. Since you are not working anymore, the mistakes and risks can have a bigger impact on your future. If you trip at the bottom of the mountain, you may only fall a short distance. But when you stumble at the top, the fall could have greater consequences.

This is a chapter from my book where I spotlight the challenges of creating and protecting assets and income now that you have reached the top of the retirement mountain.* We believe that annuities and life insurance offer attractive benefits and guarantees to help transition from the top of the retirement mountain to the descent. Knowing *how to choose and when to use* annuities in retirement can provide security for people who want to spend more time enjoying life and less time worrying about the financial challenges ahead.

About Greg

As Chief Executive Officer of Parady Financial Group, Inc., Greg Parady leads a team of outstanding advisors that include Certified Financial planners (CFP), Certified public accountants (CPA) and annuity/life insurance agents in order to provide his clients with incomparable financial services.

Greg began his career in financial services in 1996 in Portland, Maine. In 2001 he moved to Florida and founded Parady Financial Group. From the beginning Greg has focused his practice on addressing the complexities associated with wealth preservation and wealth distribution for conservative-minded retirees. He is generally considered by his peers to be a pioneer in the field of income planning by maximizing the living benefits of annuities and life insurance.

At the age of 22, Greg qualified for the *Million Dollar Round Table*, MDRT, and is currently a *Top of the Table* qualifier. This prestigious association is made up of the world's best annuity/life insurance and financial services professionals and is internationally recognized as the standard of sales excellence. He is also nationally recognized for his dynamic public speaking talents and unique ability to explain complex financial issues in a way that is easily understood by people of all educational backgrounds.

In Greg's book, *Not Your Parent's Retirement**, he touches on the subjects found in his chapter here - along with a multitude of other informative retirement planning strategies. Greg's book is due to be released in the summer of 2014.

Greg is well known for his philanthropy, and fundraising efforts within the community. He loves spending time with his wife, Jenni and their young son Bennett. He also enjoys gourmet cooking, traveling, fly fishing and spending time at his second home in the mountains of Colorado.

CHAPTER 25

ONE DAY I'LL SUCCEED!

BY DARYL G. BANK

In 2005, my partners and I started an investment company to help community banks develop investment divisions. While working with one community bank, we were exposed to rampant fraud and deception.

We made two decisions:

1 - We had to disassociate and distance our firm, and

2 - We had to report the fraud.

We chose to report the fraud anonymously to avoid being associated. We did so confidentially through two major investors and a writer in the community paper. Additionally, we sent numerous anonymous letters to government regulators as well as law enforcement.

In early 2008 we departed the bank. Bank management assumed, rightfully, we were leaking internal information that aided in the disclosure of the fraud. The bank reacted by trying to discredit us. By besmirching and discrediting us, our accusations would be discredited. The bank president/CEO launched his first attack. He spun a web of criminal accusations, everything from embezzlement to misappropriation, whatever he could dream up to cast the light of doubt over me and my partners. Friends of mine in the business reached out to warn that the FBI was called in to investigate. Even though I knew I was completely innocent of all these accusations, no one wants the FBI looking at you; this is not a good feeling.

Living under a cloud of suspicion will affect you to your core. As a businessman, all you really have is your reputation, and in my world, this was being threatened. For the first time in my life, I couldn't sleep. When I did sleep, I awoke in a cold sweat with wild visions of the FBI breaking in the door to my home or barging into my office and leading me away in handcuffs. It was the worse thing I have ever had to endure. While my wife was extremely supportive and knew exactly what was going on, I often found myself not bringing my concerns and fears to her, in order not to scare her more than she already was.

While my partners were all in the fight with me, I often found myself not wanting to discuss the situation with them, as every conversation drained me and made the entire nightmare more and more real. While my parents were right there to help in any way, I often found myself keeping things to myself, as not to worry them. Even though I was surrounded by people who loved me and supported me—in so many ways I felt alone.

Time droned slowly by and the FBI never came, never called, not a peep. Perhaps they looked into the accusations and found no merit, perhaps they already knew exactly who the guilty parties were—whatever it was, they didn't come. This had to anger my accuser. He remembered one thing I had told him during my tenure at his bank "…if you ever want to bring down a person in the financial industry, sick FINRA on them." Even if you are innocent of all accusations, they could bring a guy to his knees emotionally and financially. Two years later, after an endless, very expensive fight with FINRA our firm was almost broke. Several partners were on the brink of bankruptcy. We lost numerous financial managers and clients that wanted to avoid the drama. We were in the unenviable position of rebuilding our business and reputation.

When you go through a struggle as I had, and you come out on the other side, you learn some important things. You learn how strong you can be. I knew that I could now handle anything that life had to throw at me. You learn who your supporters are. I knew I had a core group of people behind me – my wife, partners, inner circle clients that I also call friends, my family – that would always be there to help, support, listen, love me; no matter what. You also learn, unfortunately, that some people you counted as friends will run for the hills when the going gets tough. This was my biggest disappointment in this entire ordeal.

The Bank was shut down by the FDIC. Several executives are in federal prison and it is expected more will be indicted.

Since 2010, we have rebuilt the firm into a thriving boutique financial firm. We have 300 financial managers in over 40 states. I believe all experiences are learning experiences. All things happen for a reason. It might not be for your reason nor might you understand the reason at that time. The experience of managing a thriving firm…taken to the brink of failure…turning that company around…reinventing and expanding that firm—these experiences of building and rebuilding our firm, as well as working with some of the finest financial professionals across the country, have taught us several keys to success over the last ten years. I have learned those Secrets to our Success. The things we learned about ourselves and why we are unstoppable are:

1. YOU HAVE TO WANT IT

You have to want success. You have to want it bad, really bad.

2. HAVE FAITH

You have to have faith. You have to have faith in yourself and your vision. Even when those around you don't see it, they don't believe it. Others won't join you, worse they may leave you. There will be those that won't see what you see. They won't have the vision. Never, never lose faith. As Henry Ford said "The man who thinks he can and the man who thinks he can't are both right."

3. TRUST

Surround yourself with people you trust and that trust you. Not yes men. In fact, I intentionally surround myself with different views and opinions. However, I implicitly trust each of them. I learned that from Lawrence Smith, CEO of Resource Bank.

4. TEAM

There are winners, losers, and those of us that won't settle for either. Attract winners. Attract people that are motivated and won't settle. Surround yourself with people that refuse to accept where they are or what life has given them. Find winners to attach yourself to. People that want success as much as they want to live.

That trust with my team extends to unstoppable loyalty.

5. FAIL-2-LEARN

Be willing to fail. Be willing to do something wrong. Don't be afraid to take a chance. All of the things I do right each day is possible because I've done it wrong at least once. Learn from every obstacle. Learn from every setback. When you make a mistake, don't look at it as a negative. See it as one more way not to do it in the future. Be willing to fail. Learn from your failures. *Fail in order to learn.*

6. NEVER QUIT

I have failed, but I have never quit. Life has knocked me down... hard... real hard. Each time, I get up and move forward. Sure there are times you want to quit. I have wanted to. Quitting is easy. Use that pain to move forward. Let that pain push you forward and achieve your dream. Life will judge you by your last action. If you get knocked down and stay there, there lies your legacy. Be willing to fall and get back up. You will never get there—get to where you want to be—if you quit. Every single successful person has a path littered with knockdowns. *It takes no effort to give up.*

7. SUCCESS DOES NOT FIND YOU

You have to find success. No one brings it to you. Opportunity does not knock. There is not a perfect moment, time or situation. You have to create your opportunities. You have to develop the situation. You have to make this your moment. If you want something greater, do something about it... go get it. If you are not where you want to be, look at you. You are where you are because of you. Keep doing exactly what you are doing and I assure you, your life will be the same. *If you want a change, then change.*

8. MOTIVATION

Motivation is not understood. In fact I don't think you can motivate anyone. Either you are motivated or you are not. Motivation is really the difference between a need and a want. NEED contains its own motivation—suffering/survival. WANT contains nothing—it's a reward/desire--you lose nothing. You will always live up to a need, but you won't always live up to a want. You want motivation? *Turn what you want into what you need.*

9. INSPIRATION

I don't believe one can be motivated, however, they can be inspired. In fact inspiration can be contagious. *We have grown our company by inspiring. Our vision has been infectious.*

10. WORK HARD

Name your favorite athlete. They make it look easy. Behind every successful play is hours and hours of work. Nothing in life is easy. It takes a lot of hard work. Be willing to work your butt off.

When I graduated High School, the top half of the class was made possible by people like me. I have never been the smartest or brightest. I had to work hard through college, graduate school and life. That's the only real talent I have, the ability to work hard. I have a nauseating work ethic. My business partners know when we enter the arena of business together, I won't quit or tap out. I will only be carried out. *You can accomplish your dreams with hard work.*

11. ACCOUNTABILTY AND COMMITMENT

You are not committed or accountable to you. You are committed to others.

12. ONE DAY

When are you going to achieve success? When are you going to change? Go on that diet? Be a better husband, father, son?

That day is coming. When everything will be totally different.

The day it all changes:

- you start working out
- you spend time with the kids
- you go on that diet
- you hold your wife till the sun comes up

…One day.

"One day" is the day after you die. Only you won't be here for it. Stop waiting for one day. It will be here soon enough.

13. COACHING TRAINING

Remember the athlete I asked you to think about? Who's your favorite musician? Everyday they practice and train. They are coached constantly. Some have several coaches. But most walk through business and life doing it by the seat of their pants. *Get a coach...several coaches. Never stop learning.*

14. GIVE BACK

Several years ago I had a client, Robert Dean. Robert retired young from a major retailer. Robert's resume was several pages of volunteer work with the State, City and numerous non-profits. I asked Robert why he spread himself so thin. Robert shared his vision that as citizens, we take. From birth, we take from the community, libraries, schools, museum, police, fire, etc. We have a duty to give back. In fact we should give back more than we take. I will never forget Robert's advice. *I continue working to give back more than I took.*

What's at stake? Everyday is at stake. Your life and your greatness! Live everyday like your life depends on it.

One day it will!

About Daryl

Daryl G. Bank is the Managing Partner of Dominion Investment Group. For more than fifteen years, Daryl Bank has served client's financial interest through research, attentiveness, and a common-sense approach to successful relationships. This extensive experience, throughout various stock and bond market cycles, enables him to help clients structure their portfolios to meet their specific financial objectives.

Daryl was born in Norfolk, Virginia. After graduating from Indian River High School, and Old Dominion University, he pursued a Masters Degree in public policy and a Masters in Business Administration at Regent University. Daryl began his financial career at Morgan Stanley, and then joined UBS/Paine Webber in 1996. In 2003 Daryl launched Dominion Investment Group and helped Resource Bank form their investment division. From 2003-2005 Daryl opened four investment offices, formed an insurance company, as well as a property and casualty company, for Resource Bank. In 2005 Daryl joined Bank of the Commonwealth and formed their investment division. In February 2008 Daryl affiliated with Virginia Business Bank to form their wealth management division.

Daryl hosts the syndicated radio show *Getting "Your Financial House In Order."* He serves on the Boards of Dominion Trust Company, Lyric Opera Virginia, DV8 Sports, Warped Inc., and is an Advisor of Project Lifesaver International. Professionally Daryl is a member of the National Institute of Certified Estate Planners. Daryl and his wife (Catrina) live with their son (Jackson) and daughter (Vivian) in Port St. Lucie, Florida.

Contact info. for Daryl G. Bank:
Tel: (757) 226-9440
Email: dig@dominv.com

CHAPTER 26

BEYOND SURVIVAL, HOW U.S. COMPANIES CAN THRIVE IN THE CONTEXT OF GLOBALIZATION AND THE NEW ECONOMY

BY MACODOU N'DAW, CFA

According to the Small Business Administration (SBA), ninety-six percent (96%) of the world's consumers live outside the United States (U.S.) and almost two-thirds (2/3) of the world's purchasing power reside in foreign countries.

This makes the U.S. a small market, relatively speaking, despite its mighty economic power. Furthermore, population and economic growths outside the US are taking place at a faster rate. Therefore, these percentages of world consumers and purchasing power will undoubtedly continue to increase.

Globalization has knocked down many trade barriers and has made easier the movement of goods and services. Governments are also easing up the delivery of visas and work permits, especially in the computer sciences, to allow companies to recruit and retain qualified professionals. This brings savings in training costs, reduces learning curves, and facilitates the transfer of technology and the provision of technical assistance.

We also know that small businesses[1] account for 64% of the jobs created in the U.S. But, one statistic that is often overlooked is that: every year, 10-12% of jobs are created but also 10-12% of existing jobs disappear.[2] SBA statistics also indicate that only about one-third of businesses created survive past their tenth anniversary.

The obvious question one should ask is why such dismal statistics from an economic superpower with second to none on research and development (R&D), high productivity, technological supremacy, efficient markets, reliable judiciary systems, the best universities and access to abundant capital?

The answer might lie in one of the negative aspects of being an economic superpower, i.e., the reluctance or uneasiness of most US companies to explore markets outside the United States. Many US companies think that exporting or establishing a company overseas is the purview of only big companies.

This thinking might have been true in the past but is no longer the case. Things have drastically changed in the last decade and continue to do so at a frenetic pace. As it is popularly stated: "change is the only constant." This gains even more credibility with the advent of technology, the signing of more and more Free Trade Agreements, the easier access to capital both in the U.S. and internationally, the increased connectivity between countries (hence the ease of communicating around the globe), the ability to gather and to quickly disseminate market data, and lower marketing budgets through the use of the Internet and social media.

On the one hand, this has made competition stiffer and compelled companies to be visionary, not reactionary, to market trends. But on the other hand, this has facilitated the entry to new markets and the creation of joint ventures and partnerships. In this context, and given the ever-increasing globalization and free trade agreements, what should US companies do, not only to stay alive, but more importantly, to maintain profitability?

A DIFFERENT MINDSET

Despite repeated claims made by U.S. politicians and high officials

---

1 0-500 employees as defined by the SBA
2 Source: sba.gov

(mostly for electoral purposes), many of the jobs lost during the recent economic recession will not be coming back anytime soon, if ever. First, many U.S. companies, which have laid-off workers during the economic recession are producing the same output with less workers, hence a higher productivity per worker. In addition, health care costs and an increasing demand (to which more and more city councils are heeding), in living wages (as opposed to minimum wages) will further increase the cost of goods and services sold. This, in turn, makes it more cost effective for many firms to outsource their production and services overseas (China, Vietnam, India, The Philippines, etc.).

For U.S. companies, especially the small and medium-sized firms, to strive, and consistently, they will need not just to think outside the box, **but to break out of the box!** A box only reinforces self-limiting beliefs about the world outside the U.S., an incremental approach to moving out of one's comfort zone, and a strong belief that if growth cannot be achieved in the U.S., the world's top economy, then it cannot be done in emerging markets or developing countries.

As mentioned earlier, U.S. companies should not think that only big firms are capable of expanding overseas. Also, one often overlooked fact is that enrollments of foreign students in American universities, especially in engineering and business schools, continue to increase year after year, even at the leading universities.

Although some students remain in the U.S. after graduation, more and more foreign students are returning to their countries or to other emerging markets such as Argentina, Brazil, China, and Dubai. They are a source of well-qualified professionals who speak fluent English, understand the American culture, and are usually paid at a lower rate than their counterparts working in the U.S. In addition to bringing savings and better communication to the U.S. companies, these U.S.-trained professionals also provide great market intelligence when they operate in their native countries because they understand the culture.

THE GROWTH PYRAMID PARADIGM

There is, and rightfully so, a certain pride in "Made in America." But this concept, in itself, is no longer sufficient to generate sustainable growth for most U.S. companies. "Made in America" should be associated with "Made by America."

"Made in America" is nothing but the traditional approach of delivering goods and services in the U.S. local and national markets.

"Made by America," on the other hand, is the approach whereby a U.S. company is producing the goods and/or the services, but not necessarily in the U.S. But, by doing so, it is not only increasing its competitiveness, but also solidifying its presence in its own local and/ or national market(s).

A very important element is the involvement of a multi-lateral or bi-lateral institution, which will facilitate the access to a foreign market through funding (debt and/or equity), marketing intelligence in a given sector and for a given country, and provide technical assistance, political risk insurance and legal frameworks.

I have termed the marriage of these three concepts, the "Growth Pyramid Paradigm." It is a win-win-win situation for;

a) the U.S. based company. It increases the financial viability of the U.S. company in its own home market by allowing it to access new markets, generating additional revenues and benefits;

b) the multi-lateral or bi-lateral agency that facilitates the entry to the foreign market(s) while providing funding and teaching best practices; and

c) the country that receives the investments, the jobs created, and the ancillary benefits.

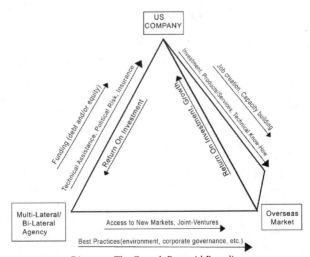

Diagram: The Growth Pyramid Paradigm

More importantly, it would result in financially-healthier U.S. companies while making them more competitive and better equipped, through market diversification, to sustain economic downturns.

CASE STUDIES

Let's illustrate the workings of the "Growth Pyramid Paradigm" with three actual examples:

Case Study #1: Telecoms Sector

A small U.S. telecom company based in Great Falls, Northern Virginia, wanted to establish the first cellular company in Africa. For more than 2 years, they were facing obstacles after obstacles.

Then, they contacted the International Finance Corporation (IFC). After successful negotiations and the writing of a feasibility study, a team consisting of a telecoms engineer, a lawyer, and an investment officer (the writer), was set up and visited Zaire for the project appraisal.

An Investment Memorandum was written and was approved by both IFC Senior Management and the IFC Board. Funding was provided as well as political risk insurance, legal frameworks, and a business model to expand to several other countries. When the company was in full gear, it was so successful that it established operations in several countries before the sponsors sold it to other investors for millions of dollars.

Case Study #2: Agribusiness Sector

Cameroon had a yearly export quota of about 170,000 tons of bananas to France but was fulfilling less than 50,000 tons. The IFC devised a strategic plan to make sure that the company could produce bananas in sufficient quantity and of sufficient quality to be able to compete in the French market.

A team comprised of a project manager and investment officer (the writer), a lawyer, an agro-engineer consultant with excellent knowledge of climatic conditions similar to those in Cameroon visited the country. After full due diligence, an Investment Memorandum was prepared and submitted to the IFC Investment Committee and to the Board of Directors that both approved the project.

First, the IFC provided funding (debt-equity) to the sponsor, then technical assistance through a Panamanian company to increase productivity and quality while reducing production costs and waste. These actions increased substantially the company's valuation, thus attracting a well-known US multi-national agribusiness firm to take a controlling interest in the company.

Consequently, the U.S. firm was able to enter the well-sought and high-priced French banana market, which it could not previously do because of a French policy of banning imports of bananas from any other country, except former French colonies like Cameroon. Even though it was a U.S. company that was reaping the benefits, it was able to operate in the French market because it was created as a Cameroonian legal entity.

Case Study #3: Mining Sector

This case study involves one of the premier multi-national companies in the gold sector, with offices in San Francisco, California. The project was located in Mali, West Africa.

IFC provided a loan while ensuring an equitable distribution of benefits, a respect of environmental laws, which triggers a welcoming attitude of the population in the remote areas where the gold was being mined. The project achieved tremendous success and served as a model on how to have a buy-in and a continuous support of the local populations versus having a confrontational approach between investors and local residents as seen in other countries.

OPPORTUNITIES ABOUND

There are hundreds of cases similar to these three examples where the "Growth Pyramid Paradigm" was used to bring feasibility studies to fruition by analyzing the project in all its forms, doing full due diligence, raising the necessary funds through direct financing or through syndication, ensuring that the proper technical assistance was formulated, an adequate legal framework was put in place, environment regulations and laws were applied, and if non-existent, guidelines with benchmarks were drafted, etc.

Also, the reader would have noticed that the three case studies were projects located in Africa. This was intentional. Despite the fact that the bulk of projects using the "Growth Pyramid Paradigm" were done in Asia and Latin America, the writer has chosen projects in Africa for two (2) reasons:

(1) to dispel the notion that Africa, which is made of 54 countries of different economic levels, is a continent where it is too difficult to do business; and

(2) to bring attention to U.S. companies that Africa is being viewed as the New Frontier because of its high economic as well as population growth, hence a nascent and juicy market. The Chinese government and firms have recognized this fact for sometime and have devised an un-matched strategic plan, which has resulted in an ever-growing presence of Chinese firms in all economic sectors and throughout Africa.

Unfortunately, the majority of the success stories involved non-U.S. companies. Globalization, free-trade agreements and the new economy have brought about a game changer. Entering new markets has become easier but competition has also become stiffer.

It is true that some very small companies, especially those in the professional services (doctors, dentists, etc.), cannot extend, or not very easily, beyond their local markets. But, many more other companies can, and should, look beyond their local and national markets. If they don't, foreign competitors will challenge them in their own markets and will win!

How many people know that about half of the fresh fruit and some 86% of the shrimp, salmon, tilapia, and other fish and shellfish that Americans eat come from other countries?[3]

Therefore, U.S. companies, especially small and medium scale businesses, would be wise to apply the "Growth Pyramid Paradigm" concept if they want to stay alive.

WHERE TO FIND ASSISTANCE?

Multi-lateral and bi-lateral Agencies are the institutions more able to help U.S. companies apply the "Growth Pyramid Paradigm." The following institutions (the list is not exhaustive) are the predominant ones, especially for U.S.-based companies:

---

3 Source: Christina Rexrode, Associated Press

The International Finance Corporation (IFC). This is the private sector arm of the International Bank for Reconstruction and Development (IBRD-World Bank). IFC operates in all emerging and developing countries. It is headquartered in Washington D.C. "The IFC helps mobilize financial resources for private enterprise, promoting accessible and competitive markets, supporting businesses and other private sector entities, and creating jobs."[4]
www.ifc.org

The Overseas Private Investment Corporation (OPIC). "This is the U.S. government's development finance institution. It helps U.S. businesses gain footholds in emerging markets, catalyzing revenues, jobs and growth opportunities both at home and abroad. OPIC achieves its mission by providing investors with financing, guarantees, and political risk insurance."[5]
www.opic.gov

The Export-Import Bank (EX-IMBANK). "This is the principal government agency responsible for aiding the export of American goods and services through a variety of loan, guarantee, and insurance products. The mission of the Bank is to create and sustain U.S. jobs by financing sales of U.S. exports to international buyers."[6]
www.exim.gov

The Asian Development Bank (ADB) "provides loans, grants, technical assistance and equity investments for projects located in the Asia and Pacific regions. The ADB promotes private sector development/operations, good governance and capacity development, knowledge solutions, partnerships."[7]
www.adb.org

The African Development Bank (AFDB) "is a multi-lateral development finance institution whose mission is to fight poverty and improve living conditions in Africa through promoting the investment of public and private capital in projects and programs that are likely to contribute to

---

4 Source: Wikipedia
5 Source: Wikipedia
6 Source: Wikipedia
7 Source: www.iadb.org
8 Source: Wikipedia

the economic and social development of the region."[8]
www.afdb.org

The Inter American Development Bank (IDB) "supports clients in the design of projects, and provides financing, technical assistance and knowledge services to support development interventions in Latin American and The Caribbean. The IDB lends to national, provincial, state, and municipal governments as well as to private sector companies."[9]
www.iadb.org

The European Investment Bank (EIB) "is the European Union's Bank. As the largest multilateral borrower and lender by volume, they provide finance and expertise for sound and sustainable investment projects, which contribute to furthering European Union policy objectives. The vast majority of its financing is through loans, but it also offers guarantees, microfinance, equity investment, It can also help with administrative and project management capacity which facilitates investment implementation."[10]
www.eib.org

The European Bank For Reconstruction and Development (EBRD) "provides project financing for banks, industries and businesses., both new ventures and investments in existing companies. They also work with publicly owned companies. The EBRD provides loan and and equity finance, guarantees, leasing facilities and trade finance."[11]
www.ebrd.com

---

9 Source: www.iadb.org
10 Source: www.eib.org
11 Source: www.ebrd.com

About Mac

Macodou (Mac) N'Daw is the CEO and Chief Consulting Officer of Business Consulting Masters, LLC, a company that teaches aspiring as well as established consultants how to get engagements on a consistent basis and how to add great value to clients.

Mac, also known as the "Business Consultant's Consultant", has more than 33 years of experience in transnational investments (debt and equity), corporate finance and restructuring, strategic analysis, syndication, and joint-ventures. During his 27-year tenure at the International Finance Corporation (IFC), the private sector arm of the World Bank, Mac consulted, supervised and advised on projects located worldwide and in various sectors—such as mining, telecoms, agribusiness, fisheries, aquaculture, etc. His last position at the IFC was Associate Director in charge of a world-wide portfolio of 105 projects totaling US$1.5 billion, with Argentina, Brazil, China, India and Ukraine holding the lion's share.

He has visited, conducted workshops, participated in seminars and delivered speeches and talks in 67 countries located on four continents (Africa, Asia, Europe, and America). Mac speaks French, English and Spanish fluently, and has a working knowledge of Portuguese.

Mac is also the owner of a real estate company (www.imacrealty.com), which invests in single families residences and apartments buildings nationwide.

Mac has been a Chartered Financial Analyst (CFA) since 1993. He holds a B.S. in Finance and Multinational Enterprise from The Wharton School (1979), a M.B.A and a M.A. in Agricultural Economics from Stanford University (1986), and attended The Harvard Business School Executive Development Program (1998).

For more information on the "Growth Pyramid Paradigm" concept, reports, articles and blogs on management consulting, please visit:

www.businessconsultingmasters.com

CHAPTER 27

UNDERSTANDING THAT SUCCESS COMES FROM WHO YOU ARE – NOT WHAT YOU DO

BY GREG ROLLETT

We are taught from an early age to go to school, get good grades and the skills and education you receive will help you to get a good job. Then you are told to go to graduate school, get your doctorate, your MBA… all to help you advance your career!

But the advice they never give you is to work on yourself, your personality, your relationships and to showcase who you are.

We focus on test scores and lab results. We then tie credential into credential and start adding letters to the back of our names. Next thing you know we are in the real world. Thrown to the wolves in the mean streets of business.

And none of those credentials matter when it's you against the world. What matters is how you relate to the person on the other end of your conversation. How you connect. How you get in tune with their emotional needs at that specific moment in time.

For all good business is done based on who we are, not necessarily what we do.

All doctors go to medical school. All pass state board exams. But not all doctors are created equal. They have different beliefs. Different values. Different systems and processes. Different styles. Different backgrounds.

Each factors into the acquisition and retention of a patient. And if you were a doctor, just relying on the fact that you have your shiny degree hanging on the wall, you are going to keep spinning around and around in circles losing clients to the new lowest price doctor with credentials.

I want you to focus on something much more important. I want you to focus on who you are. Not what you do.

And I want you to focus on the top of the food chain, not the bottom.

You see, today's affluent clientele are eager to work with people who are like them. Who relate to them. Who have an affinity or connection to their own life. They understand that most competent people with a certain skill level can perform the task at hand. What they really want is someone they know, like and trust.

They don't want an institution either. They want the person for the job.

Remember those old mafia movies where someone would always shout out, "*I got a guy?*" You want to be that guy. Someone that gets referred. Someone that gets talked about at cocktail parties. Someone who is known for being the only solution for the given situation.

Where no one else even comes up in conversation.

Different success and business mentors have made reference to this type of person before. They might be called a guru or wizard. Others might call them a savior or even an expert.

Legendary marketing and business strategist Jay Abraham has a brilliant strategy based around this theory, called the *Strategy Of Preeminence*, where you are seen as the most trusted advisor for life.

We call this person a Celebrity Expert®. That is someone who combines the marketing and the "be seen everywhere" aura of a celebrity and the knowledge and talents of an expert. You see, being famous for being famous can only get you so far. You need to apply some type of skill or knowledge in order to take that fame and put it to good use.

Thus the Celebrity Expert knows that he needs to share his story of magic powers with the world. Much like how we know the origin stories of our comic book heroes like Superman and Spider-Man, so must everyone in your market know your story.

People remember these stories. I know people that can tell me the entire Bat-Man origin story and have never read one of his comics or seen any of the movies. That is the power of a great story that is told time and time again. It's about the person. There is an emotional connection to a boy whose parents are murdered and seeks vengeance.

Showcasing flaws is also a powerful part of the equation. It's ok to be vulnerable. To pull back the veil. Too often we showcase only the good. We try to manipulate perfect lives through social media. We post status updates only when vacationing in exotic locations or eating fine foods.

But a superhero without flaws ultimately becomes boring. We lose interest. We know what the outcome is going to be. The flaws give the character life… a reason to keep tuning in every week or month. Your own success depends on selling yourself, your personality and your own unique super powers.

YOUR STORY IS THE DRIVER OF NEW SUCCESS IN TODAY'S ECONOMY

Many entrepreneurs and professionals today simply have a fear of sharing their story. They fear they are not unique or distinctive. They feel their story is plain or boring.

That is simply not the case and one of the biggest limiting beliefs to overcome. As humans we all relate on a very primitive level. …Family …Travel …Hometowns …Love …Relationships …Food.

These build the essence of your story. Where you grew up. How you grew up. The schools you went to. The sports teams you root for. Your first love. Your children. By starting on this basic level you start to create a connection that is easy for others to gravitate towards. It starts the conversation. And it continues the conversation.

It's the reason we go to the same barber for 20 years - we keep having that new conversation based on the connection we created the first time we sat in their chair.

It's the reason we go out of our way to the dentist who remembers us, has a child the same age as our own and always has a story to tell.

It's the reason we listen to certain news programs and sportscasters. The reason why we read every book from certain authors and never get into books from other authors. It's why we will watch certain movies before others - because of the story we heard about the actor or the filming of the movie - it's not just the movie itself.

We are drawn to people. And people working together provide the fastest path to success there is:

- One person sharing an idea with another person.
- An introduction or connection made.
- A partnership or joint venture opportunity.
- One person's resources being applied to another's
 ability to implement and act.

But none of this is possible without the two people getting together. And it's never the thing that gets them together. It's the two people connecting.

All too often we fall back to what we do. It's easy to talk about the details of the thing…the features…the benefits. It's harder to find stories and build context. But we remember the stories about the person. We forget facts. It's why 48% of all statistics are made up 63% of the time.

SO HOW CAN YOU FOCUS ON WHO YOU ARE AND NOT WHAT YOU DO?

By telling your story. And by using media to enhance the visibility of your story.

Every advertisement you write is a place to tell your story, not just what you do. Why do you do what you do? How did it come about? Where did your magic powers come from? What is the story about the first person that you helped?

These are all key elements to share every opportunity you can. It's why I lead every presentation, webinar, interview or video with some rendition of my background in the music industry, which led to starting my first business venture, which spawned my successful ventures today.

I do this for many reasons. The most prevalent is to have some common ground that people will want to talk to me about. It is something they will remember long after I leave the stage or the interview has ended.

They will remember that I was the marketing guy who used to be a rapper in a rock band. They will forget the facts, the tactics, the steps in whatever it is I am talking about. But they won't forget the fact that I was a musician, that I toured the country, that I survived on ramen noodles in the back of a van for weeks, or that my band mates left me hanging out to dry just weeks after I got married to my high school sweetheart.

DO YOU SEE HOW I SNUCK ALL OF THAT INTO THIS CHAPTER?

And even with everything I have written about, it is those interesting tidbits about the author that you will remember above all else. My marketing skills are implied. You assume I can write a great sales letter or ad for you. You assume that I know my stuff. That I have the necessary credentials.

And it's the same in your business. The letters at the end of your name mean nothing to the person making the buying decision. And it will stop you from being successful in today's economy. It will hold you back. It is a belief you need to get over.

Today more than ever, you get paid and hired for who you are and not what you do. And the higher up the ladder of affluence you go, which is where you should be aiming at, the truer it becomes.

I was speaking with a client recently who was working on the marketing for his company. He said that his customers were having a hard time connecting to his product. They had the best specs, the best raw materials, the best formula, the best delivery times – everything you would want from this product.

The immediate problem I saw was that there was no human connection. All of the emails came from the institution. They sounded vanilla. There were no stories, just facts.

I reminded him that we forget facts. And we forget facts fast. But we remember people and stories. I told him to talk about his life. To introduce his daily thoughts and issues into his emails, newsletters and even proposals. I told him to start telling his story about why he started the company and the first customer he helped using his products. The minute he made that adjustment, the difference was clear. The customers had someone to cling onto. They suddenly remembered who he has when the phone rang. And when his sales reps went into the field they were flooded with questions about the CEO of the company and his kids, his trips around the world and about his magic powers.

Sales spiked because of stories, not specs. The specifications were assumed at that point. They were a quick point of negotiation and reassurance as the contract was being signed.

Your business is too important to be forgotten. Especially in today's fickle economy. When price becomes a prospect's only point of reference, you lose. If you don't lose today, you will lose tomorrow. Someone will always come along cheaper and faster. But no one can replace you. Who you are. With the relationships and the connections that you have with your customers, your list, your clients.

The first step is to write down your story. Map it out. Reverse engineer the pieces that you want told and re-told. Simplify the complicated. Create emotional ties. Paint pictures with your words.

After you have your story, start inserting it using media, both online and offline. In your brochures and catalogs, do you tell your story, the story behind the products, or do you just state the facts? If it's the facts, it's time to make a change.

In your social media posts are you just pointing people back to sales pages and product pages? Or are you connecting and sharing things about you? Make the change.

Most importantly, adapt the mindset that you are the biggest asset in your business. You alone have the ability to grow, multiply and expand your operation by sharing more of you...by telling your story and having others tell the tale for you...to build your legend. And it starts today.

Your success depends on who you are, not what you do.

About Greg

Greg Rollett, @gregrollett, is a Best-Selling Author and Marketing Expert who works with experts, authors and entrepreneurs all over the world. He utilizes the power of new media, direct response and personality-driven marketing to attract more clients and to create more freedom in the businesses and lives of his clients.

After creating a successful string of his own educational products and businesses, Greg began helping others in the production and marketing of their own products and services. He now helps his clients through two distinct companies, Celebrity Expert Marketing and the ProductPros.

Greg has written for Mashable, Fast Company, Inc.com, the Huffington Post, AOL, AMEX's Open Forum and others, and continues to share his message helping experts and entrepreneurs grow their business through marketing.

Greg's client list includes Michael Gerber, Brian Tracy, Tom Hopkins, Coca-Cola, Miller Lite and Warner Brothers, along with thousands of entrepreneurs and small-business owners across the world. Greg's work has been featured on FOX News, ABC, NBC, CBS, CNN, *USA Today, Inc Magazine, The Wall Street Journal*, the *Daily Buzz* and more.

Greg loves to challenge the current business environment that constrains people to working 12-hour days during the best portions of their lives. By teaching them to leverage marketing and the power of information, Greg loves to help others create freedom in their businesses that allow them to generate income, make the world a better place, and live a radically-ambitious lifestyle in the process.

A former touring musician, Greg is highly sought after as a speaker, who has spoken all over the world on the subjects of marketing and business building.

If you would like to learn more about Greg and how he can help your business, please contact him directly at: greg@dnagency.com or by calling his office at 877.897.4611.

CHAPTER 28

BRINGING YOUR BRAND STORY TO VIRTUAL LIFE: THE 7 LESSONS OF ONLINE SUCCESSONOMICS

BY LINDSAY DICKS

SuccessOnomics. There's a course we'd all like to walk away from with a 4.0 GPA, right?

Well, If you're looking for a way to get to the head of your industry's class, just open your web browser and start schooling yourself – because the online world is essential to making the grade when it comes to your own success.

Of course, you may not agree. You may not think Facebook, Twitter and even your own website matter that much to your day-to-day business. If that's the case, then I'm sorry to say that you may never be elected President of the United States!

I'll give you a moment to deal with your disappointment – and then ask you to take a look back at the last presidential election in 2012 between incumbent Barack Obama and challenger Mitt Romney. Consider these campaign statistics, compiled three months prior to the actual vote by InternetMarketing.com:

Facebook "Likes": Obama, 27 million, Romney, 2 million

Twitter followers: Obama, 17 million, Romney, 650,000

Instagram followers: Obama, 1.1 million, Romney, 24,000

YouTube channel views: Obama 200 million, Romney 12 millions

Pinterest followers: Obama, 1.1 million, Romney...well, Mitt didn't have a Pinterest page, but *Ann* Romney's page had 7000 followers....

Even accounting for the fact that Obama had a younger group of voters than Romney, the above numerical gaps are nothing short of astounding. Obviously, the Obama team had a much more engaging and dynamic online strategy than the Romney campaign.

But, you say, how much did that strategy contribute to the President's victory? Well, ORI, a market research and strategic business intelligence firm, and The George Washington Graduate School of Political Management teamed up to do some research on just that question.

Their conclusion? *Almost a third* of those polled said social media was moderately to extremely influential in their opinions of the candidates and issues. That influence also counted when it came to the candidates' bottom lines. In terms of dollars and cents, the impact of the Internet is once again very clear: Of likely voters, *77% made their political contributions online.*

In other words, when it comes to where you should focus your marketing, my advice is to "Follow the money!" So, file into my classroom, take your seat and I'll help you do just that – because I'm about to educate you on how to engage in the most profitable kind of online story-telling.

THE IMPORTANCE OF YOUR "VIRTUAL STORY"

The overriding lesson of Online SuccessOnomics is that, in order to make it work for your business, you have to have in place a robust Internet strategy – and the centerpiece of that strategy should, of course, be your brand.

Now, the basis of your brand is your *story*. What makes your business different? What makes *you* different? How are your benefits to potential customers unique and special? All of those elements and more go into creating a narrative that attracts leads, converts them to customers and keeps them buying from you for the foreseeable future.

Elsewhere in this book, you'll learn some inside secrets from my partners at the Dicks-Nanton Celebrity Branding Agency, Nick and Jack, who reveal how to craft a story that's more compelling than your competition's. In this chapter, however, you're going to matriculate to the next level of study – and discover how to effectively *communicate* that story through today's overwhelming number of online tools.

The good news is that, even if you're a single-person entrepreneur, you can still level the playing field against the big boys by telling your brand story via the Internet *consistently and effectively* - by observing what I call "The 7 Lessons of Online SuccessOnomics." These "lessons" are all proven ways to deliver your message across a range of powerful platforms in a memorable and impressive way. So please, read on - and think about how you can use each of them to promote your own specific brand story.

LESSON ONE:
MAJOR IN UNIQUENESS

To begin with, your brand story should stand out from everyone else's – so make sure you tell that story in a different and compelling way that reflects how you want to be perceived. If you want to seem cool and cutting-edge, it's very easy to create some weird and wonderful video "Vines" (find out more about them at Vine.com) with your smartphone that can extend your brand message. If you want to communicate in a more buttoned-down professional manner, think about how you can tell your story through attention-getting LinkedIn content or informative Facebook posts.

This idea of differentiation, of course, extends to your website, which should never look like a generic cookie-cutter creation. Instead, it should reflect the 5 W's - *Who* you are, *What* your business is about, *Why* visitors should buy from you, *Where* you're known and *When* they should act (to which the answer is always, of course, NOW!).

By the way, your uniqueness should be a natural evolution from whatever your basic brand story is. Don't be different just to be different – be different in a way that makes sense for your story!

LESSON TWO:
EDUCATE WITH EVIDENCE

Anyone can tell a story. That doesn't mean the listener has to believe it! As a matter of fact, in this day and age of marketing overkill, most potential customers are more inclined to dismiss rather than believe a brand story.

Don't see that skepticism as a disadvantage – instead, leverage it to your advantage, by providing credible evidence that *your* brand story is true, and put yourself in front of the line when it comes to establishing consumer trust.

Do that by creating and posting legitimate content that supports your story. Authoritative articles and blogs, tweets and status updates that provide relatable and usable information establish you as an authority in your field and draw people to your expertise.

Of course, customer testimonials go a long way towards proving your story. Third party verification (people other than YOU saying you're great) always goes far in terms of backing up your story – especially if you have some case studies with individuals or companies that have a good, well-known reputation that you can share with potential leads.

LESSON THREE:
SHOW *AND* TELL

Many of the hottest new social media sites – Instagram, Pinterest, and Vine – as well as old standbys like Flickr and YouTube – put the accent on the visual, either through photos or short videos. With today's overcrowded social media landscape, anyone going through their Facebook or Twitter feed might zip right past your latest post – unless there's a provocative or interesting photo that motivates them to take their finger off the scroll button.

When it comes to telling your brand story, a picture can definitely be worth a thousand words. A photo of you and a happy customer – or your latest and greatest product, accompanied by a caption that entertains and sells – can make each of your statuses and posts a must-see for your following.

Think about what's visually interesting about what you do and what you offer – and also, of course, make sure it fits in with your brand story!

LESSON FOUR:
EXCEL IN PERSONAL CHEMISTRY

Interesting characters are essential to a good story – and since you're presumably the representative of your brand, it's up to you to be that interesting character!

Personal chemistry is the formula that allows you to bond with your customers and prospects. You may think it doesn't matter what you're personally interested in and what you're all about, because, after all, we're talking about your business here, not an eHarmony.com profile! The truth of the matter, however, is you *are* your business – and, as the old maxim has it, *"People buy people."*

So don't be afraid to make jokes or root for your favorite sports team (if you don't have one, the Florida Gators football team is an excellent place to start!). Or, in my case (and as some of you already know), I use Pinterest to share fashion ideas, home décor inspiration, and of course, anything and everything shoe-related!

Of course, when you're getting 'up close and personal,' you should try to avoid topics that might actively alienate some of your potential customers. Otherwise, don't be afraid to be yourself and let your personality out of the box - because nobody likes a story with a boring main character!

LESSON FIVE:
EARN YOUR DEGREE IN CONSISTENCY

Entrepreneurs and business owners are busy people – and that means, unless they have a staff person or department dedicated to doing social media, they can find it hard to *consistently* communicate their brand story.

First of all, because there are so many different social media sites available, you can find yourself jumping from one to the other – and never developing a real following on any one of them. Or, you may only post updated statuses, photos and videos every so often when you have an idea or a few extra minutes – and, because you're so hit-and-miss with those posts, you may fail to engage anyone with your brand story.

That's why you must:

(a) focus your efforts on the social media sites that attract the most people in your specific niche,

(b) regularly update content on those sites by sticking to a schedule, and

(c) make sure your messaging is *consistent* on every platform (in other words, if you act hip and cool on one site and revert to Mr. Suit and Tie on another, it's going to confuse people).

Let me elaborate a little more on the second item in that list – regularly updating content. This isn't as daunting as it might sound; it can involve something as simple as updating your status, but, if you have the time, it can be as elaborate as posting a new blog, article or video. Whatever you choose to do, make sure you're able to carve out the necessary time in your schedule to do it. Even if you have to limit yourself to just five minutes to send out a quick tweet or two, it's better than nothing. Consider it your SuccessOnomics homework!

LESSON SIX:
"ACE" YOUR VIDEO PRODUCTION

I've touched on video a couple of times already in this chapter's curriculum – but it's important enough to feature in its own specific lesson.

As I noted, "people buy people" – and video is the best way to sell yourself! A video featuring you is the next best thing to meeting in person with someone – because the viewer experiences your personality in an immediate and human way. Not only that, but video also gives you the opportunity to demonstrate your expertise, by talking about subject matter that directly relates to your business. That makes for quite a one-two punch!

Probably many of you have heard of Gary Vaynerchuk – he's been profiled in *The New York Times*, and has appeared on such national TV arenas as the CBS and ABC news, as well as on the Conan O'Brien and Ellen DeGeneres shows. Well, he became a national success story mostly because of his online videos.

He began working at his parents' retail wine business in New Jersey while still a teenager – and soon brainstormed ways to boost its revenues to unimaginable heights. First, he gained the necessary expertise; he trained himself in wine-tasting, became an expert and began advising customers on what was a good buy. He rebranded the store as "Wine Library." And he began increasing the store traffic and sales because people sought out his advice and liked his reboot of the business.

But he wanted to take his brand story beyond the borders of New Jersey, so he started selling wine online and – most importantly - began recording a video wine blog, called Winelibrary TV, in 2006. He promoted the video blog and his website endlessly, through YouTube, Facebook and Twitter, until he got Wine Library to the point where sales had increased to 60 million a year – over ten times what it had been making. In the process, Gary also turned himself into an incredibly successful self-help and business advice guru!

That's what the power of video can do when used properly. There's only one major word of caution I have to share when it comes to videos – and that's when their production quality is poor. That can be very damaging to your brand. These days, almost everyone has access to quality equipment, so there is no excuse for posting a video that looks like it was shot on a cellphone 10 years ago and makes you resemble a hostage victim. If you're going to use video to tell your story, which I highly recommend, you have to be sure that you do it right!

LESSON SEVEN:
GRADUATE TO NEW GROWTH

Finally, if you've mastered the first six lessons in this chapter, never feel as though your education is complete. You should always be evolving your brand story and how you tell it online.

A common element in every good story is *growth*. Characters in great stories face challenges, overcome them, and often transform themselves in the process. So don't be afraid to let your audience see you grow. Sure, you don't want to post on Twitter every time something goes wrong with your business… but you can use social media to celebrate your victories and to let people see how you and your business are evolving. And by the way, your slip-ups can be endearing too – sometimes laughing at yourself creates an even stronger bond with your audience.

Also, the Internet landscape keeps changing rapidly. Three or four years ago, nobody had ever heard of Pinterest; now it has, as of this writing, over 70 million users (and, by the way, over 80% of them are women, if that's the demo you're after!). So always look for what the Next Big Thing might be, when it comes to online marketing – and see if it could be a big thing for your branding!

Did I hear the bell? I guess class is over for now – but I encourage you to keep learning on your own (or with my help, if you need it!). As I noted, the online marketing world is one that keeps changing every day – and new opportunities for story-telling are always emerging.

So make sure you engage in continuing education – and school yourself on everything out there that can help you tell your tale in the best way possible.

About Lindsay

Lindsay Dicks helps her clients tell their stories in the online world. Being brought up around a family of marketers, but a product of Generation Y, Lindsay naturally gravitated to the new world of on-line marketing. Lindsay began freelance writing in 2000 and soon after launched her own PR firm that thrived by offering an in-your-face "Guaranteed PR" that was one of the first of its type in the nation.

Lindsay's new media career is centered on her philosophy that "people buy people." Her goal is to help her clients build a relationship with their prospects and customers. Once that relationship is built and they learn to trust them as the expert in their field, then they will do business with them. Lindsay also built a proprietary process that utilizes social media marketing, content marketing and search engine optimization to create online "buzz" for her clients that helps them to convey their business and personal story. Lindsay's clientele span the entire business map and range from doctors and small business owners to Inc 500 CEOs.

Lindsay is a graduate of the University of Florida. She is the CEO of CelebritySites™, an online marketing company specializing in social media and online personal branding. Lindsay is recognized as one of the top online marketing experts in the world and has co-authored more than 25 best-selling books alongside authors such as Brian Tracy, Jack Canfield (creator of the "Chicken Soup for the Soul" series), Dan Kennedy, Robert Allen, Dr. Ivan Misner (founder of BNI), Jay Conrad Levinson (author of the "Guerilla Marketing" series), Leigh Steinberg and many others, including the breakthrough hit *Celebrity Branding You!*

She was also selected as one of America's PremierExperts™ and has been quoted in *Newsweek*, *The Wall Street Journal*, *USA Today*, and *Inc.* magazine as well as featured on NBC, ABC, and CBS television affiliates speaking on social media, search engine optimization and making more money online. Lindsay was also recently brought on FOX 35 News as their Online Marketing Expert.

Lindsay, a national speaker, has shared the stage with some of the top speakers in the world, such as Brian Tracy, Lee Milteer, Ron LeGrand, Arielle Ford, David Bullock, Brian Horn, Peter Shankman and many others. Lindsay was also a Producer on the Emmy-winning film *Jacob's Turn*.

You can connect with Lindsay at:
Lindsay@CelebritySites.com
www.twitter.com/LindsayMDicks
www.facebook.com/LindsayDicks

CHAPTER 29

WE AREN'T ALL MEXICANS — ENTREPRENEURSHIP IN A MULTICULTURAL WORLD

BY JULIO ZELAYA

"Hello, my name is Julio Zelaya and I'm from Guatemala," I said with a smile. With a confused look on his face, Mr. 'A' quickly responded: "Oh yes, Mexico...I know."

Many people assume that Mexico is the same as all of Central and South America, but there are many differences. Now, I truly admire Mexico. We have many good friends and clients from this beautiful and successful country. We share much in common such as roots, history and work initiatives. Yet, in spite of the close distance, we also have a number of differences, which gets me thinking that we should appreciate such a diverse society especially in the area of business. We live in a large and small world at the same time, borders are continually dissolving, and in the case of Latin America we can safely say that it encompasses so much more than just the Mexican culture commonly known to Americans. Hence in order to extend the impact of any entrepreneurial undertaking, it's vital we answer the following question: How to better understand the Hispanic culture for the marketplace?

MEETING MR. A:

The meeting was planned for Tuesday at 11am. My flight was scheduled to leave Monday from Guatemala to Houston. It was going to be my first trip to Texas! I envisioned a vast desert with tumbleweeds rolling in the wind. I pictured Mr. 'A' in leather cowboy boots, a typical cowboy hat, chewing on something and greeting me with a warm, all too well known phrase, "Howdy stranger!"

Following a three hour flight, our plane finally landed. I went through immigration where an agent by the name of Lopez received me with a stern look on his face. "What's the purpose of your visit," he asked me in English? To which I replied in Spanish, "I'm here on business". "Here we speak English sir," he retorted in a reprimanding tone. To my surprise, agent Lopez didn't speak any Spanish. After the formalities, he stamped my passport and void of a single bit of hospitality he ended with, "Welcome to the United States." I thought, "Wow, talk about welcomes and first impressions for a Latin American. It's probably due to a rough cowboy upbringing."

I promptly arrived at Mr. 'A's office Tuesday at 10:45 a.m. and boy, was I surprised! His attire was just like mine, business suit and tie. I quickly scanned him, trying to find his cowboy boots, but all I saw was a pair of formal dress loafers which were way too normal to satisfy my western imagery. We greeted each other stretching my hand out saying, "Hello I'm Julio Zelaya and I'm from Guatemala." With a confused look on his face he quickly replied, "Oh yes, Mexico....I know." I immediately got the impression that he was just as disappointed as I was by our 'normal' appearance, and I couldn't help but let a small smile slip out.

"I know it's early but why don't we get a bite to eat. I know just the perfect place, they serve the best Chimichangas; the best Tex-Mex food in town," he uttered so enthusiastically that I didn't dare tell him that I was looking forward to some local Texan cuisine.

When we arrived at the "Chimichanga place", we were seated in picturesque, wooden chairs the likes of "Hacienda Cortez." A server quickly approached us with the name Juan Martinez on his name tag. We could immediately see his genuine effort to speak in English, though his accent was heavily pronounced. The perplexed look in my companion's face was obvious and without the slightest intent in trying to understand him, gave me a stare that said, "You know his language, talk to him." I quickly answered Juan in Spanish, which clearly gave him a sign of relief. He took our order and disappeared into the kitchen. "How is it possible that he can't speak any English?" Mr. 'A' pondered out loud.

MR. 'A' GOES TO GUATEMALA

A few months went by from my first trip to Houston and it was Mr. 'A's turn to visit my home country.

We traveled together from Houston to Guatemala City. Upon flying over our city and seeing our tall buildings and the extension of our metropolis, home to over five million people, he said, "I see you've got buildings here, not as much jungle as I thought!"

Approaching the immigration lobby, the agent quickly saw that he was from the USA, so he tried to address him in English. "Weelllccoommme, how was flight?" he painstakingly asked in a strong accent. "Very well, thanks for asking," replied my companion. In a surprising tone Mr. 'A' commented, "I can see that English is quite common in your country." To which I replied, "Not really, but we always strive to make foreigners feel right at home here."

"We have a number of possible restaurants," I continued. "I want you to enjoy the best of Guatemalan cuisine." "Excellent!" he agreed.

Upon arriving at a well-known typical restaurant, everyone quickly identified him as a foreigner and started greeting him. Right from the young lad helping us park our car to the waiters in the restaurant; they all said, "Hello sir, welcome." Oddly enough, the waiter in the Guatemalan restaurant was also named Juan.

No doubt that the events which transpired with my friend Mr. 'A' can effectively be used as an example of ten things we should seek to avoid when dealing with people from other cultures.

YET, WHY:

- do we tend to harbor a simplistic and generalized idea of a place or nationality before ever experiencing it? I had a completely erroneous idea about Texas, as Mr. 'A' had about Guatemala.

- is it common for Hispanics to try to "devalue" their roots, a phenomenon which sociologists have come to coin "covering"?

- is it when an Hispanic resides in the USA, they try to speak in English, however when an American visits a Latin American country or interacts with someone who speaks in Spanish, he doesn't make an effort to learn their language, which is normally Spanish?

- is it common for Spanish-speaking countries to use English as a status symbol in society?

- is it so customary for Latin American countries to receive foreigners so kindly and politely?

- is it that when a Spanish-speaking person visits the USA, they are normally offered Latin American foods, but when an American visits a Spanish-speaking country, they are commonly offered native cuisine?

The answers to these intriguing questions are found in the perception we have of the world and its cultural diversity. Latin Americans view English as a language vital to be successful, perhaps due in part to a remnant of the American Dream. However when we actually do the numbers, we come to terms with the fact that the *most used* language in the world is Mandarin with 935 million people, followed by Spanish with 387 million speakers, and English comes in third with 365 million people.

Enter SuccessOnomics, a book on how to engage in better and more effective business dealings. This is the motive behind sharing about my culture, to open new doors of entrepreneurship. The United States has a vast internal Hispanic market, not to mention the one beyond the borders of Canada and Mexico! We must come to the understanding that the possibilities are endless.

THE HISPANIC MARKET IN NUMBERS

According to Nielsen's[1] studies:

- The Latin population with over 52 million inhabitants is the largest minority in the United States of America, ever increasing towards ethnic plurality.

- Latin Americans are a vital component for success in business and not just a casual, marginal niche.

- Rapid growth of the Latin population is estimated at 162% by the year 2050, versus 42% for the general population.

- Latin Americans exert a different pattern of consumption and they do not have the same buying habits as the market in general.

- Hispanics have accrued much buying power equivalent to $1.5 trillion for 2015.

- Since Hispanics are the largest immigrant group, they present a significant cultural sustainability, not soon to dwindle in the US cultural melting pot.

- 51% of Latin Americans prefer ads and commercials in their own language rather than in English.

- Hiring Spanish-speaking talents to broadcast content causes a 30% greater impact in the Hispanic community.

COMMON ELEMENTS FOUND IN HISPANIC-AMERICA

Seven of them are decisive factors: family values, easy-going lifestyle, live and let-live attitude, respect for age, direct community involvement, separation of classes and national pride. Let's explore each of these to help expand our mindset and possibilities.

- **Family values**

    – As Latin Americans we tend to greatly emphasize family

---

1. Nielsen (2012) *Hispanic-American Report on Consumption*

values. Daily life revolves around the family, not the individual.

– Almost all activities, including shopping, focus around the family, not the individual.

– Children aren't considered "small adults," but they're expected to embrace and respect their parents' good judgment.

Consider: "Are you taking into account the family in your business decisions? How does your product or service contribute towards family life?"

• **Easy going lifestyle**

– Generally speaking Latinos take life at a slow pace.

– Business is done one-on-one through personal relationships. As Latinos we want to know you and we expect a shared interest in you knowing us as well.

Now ask yourself, do I really take an interest in getting to know the person before doing business with them?

• **Live and let-live attitude:**

– On the one hand Latin Americans have had the tendency of tolerating totalitarian and dictatorial figures of authority, but on the other Latinos prefer to live like there is no tomorrow. Though there is an increasing drift towards planning and saving, generally speaking there is open-mindedness, yet still with a strong inclination towards spending.

– Hispanics dislike when someone outside their family circle intervenes in areas such as drug use, sex, personal security and the likes. They tend to be much more reserved and discrete in their personal affairs.

Question: Do you have a respectful attitude towards individual, personal decisions?

- Respect for age:

  - It's commonly accepted to respect the elder as wiser, more experienced and worthy to be listened to.

  - The majority of families are patriarchal, in other words they are led by the eldest of the males.

  Analyze: Does your service or product respect and take into account the position elders hold in the family?

- Community involvement:

  - Religious practices are much more up close and relevant ties extend beyond the immediate family.

  - Hispanics tend to group, share, communicate and support each other at a personal level.

  Analyze: Is your product or service itemized at Hispanic groups?

- Separation of classes:

  - There are vast differences in power. It's normal for ranks to be determined by various positions of authority.

  Thought: In your business dealings with Hispanics, do you honestly have a respect for their positions?

- National pride:

  - The norm is to defend your country's honor at all costs.

  - In spite of there being various grades of nationalism, there's also a certain inherent pride with the country you come from, especially in 1st generation Hispanics.

- Key question: Do you take the time to be well informed and prepared in your customer's country of origin prior to doing business with an Hispanic?

Taking these premises into account should serve as a good starting point, since they basically summarize what much research has come to know as "commonalities" of the Hispanic culture.

COMMON PARADIGM MYTHS OF HISPANIC-AMERICANS AND THEIR REALITIES:

Though we have much in common, Hispanic-Americans also have notable differences, even among fellow countrymen. There are five common paradigms which are really myths:

- **All Hispanics speak Spanish.** According to a US census, approximately 25% of Hispanics do not speak their language at home. Additionally, there's more than three-times the amount of Hispanics now speaking indigenous dialects.

- **All Hispanics are immigrants.** There are a number of Hispanic families from various generations whose grandchildren were born and raised in the USA.

- **All Latinos view themselves as the same.** The Great Falls Tribune noted: "53% of Latinos identified as white in 2010, an increase from the 49% of Latinos who identified as Caucasian in 2000. Roughly 2.5% of Latinos identified as black on the 2010 census form."

- **All illegal immigrants originate from one same country or region.** According to the Pew Hispanic Research Center: "As of 2010, Mexicans comprised 58% of undocumented immigrants living in the U.S. Unauthorized migrants from elsewhere in Latin America made up 23% of the unauthorized population followed by those from Asia (11%), Europe and Canada (4%) and Africa (3%)."

- **All immigrants are uneducated.** There's a increasing trend towards education in Hispanic-America and each day we see more Hispanics with higher levels of schooling and specializations (JD, PhD, MD) functioning in high levels of society as well as valuable start-ups. One example of this is Luis Vohn Ahn from Guatemala, creator of Duo Lingo, one of Apple's most highly featured apps in 2013.

In my ample experience I have found the following principle to carry much weight:

Many barriers are broken when a true genuine interest in knowing the person precedes the product or service they are representing.

I cannot even begin to describe the rich, cultural heritage of each Hispanic country and individual. Discovering the person prior to inquiring about their ethnic background, provides a much more gratifying experience in life focused on individual human beings, each with their own unique and powerful world.

"We all should know that diversity makes for a rich tapestry, and we must understand that all the threads of the tapestry are equal in value no matter what their color."
~ Maya Angelou, African-American Poet

Just as we can say that Latinos are identifiable by a particular skin tone and our bodies have certain "features and forms," avoiding these labels will help us take the time to explore that rich cultural mosaic which the United States was built upon, making it a world power with so much potential.

The challenge then is how to do better business by cherishing the wealth diversity has to offer?

"People say that you and I don't make good company as water and oil, how ironic! Were we the same, how boring, for there would be nothing to speak about the next day"
~ Ricardo Arjona, Guatemalan Grammy Winning Singer and Song Writer

I believe in a world free of barriers, dwelled upon by people with great dreams and the force to make them a reality. Individuals set on overcoming not just cultural diversities, but every other hindrance which might set us back from the purpose we are destined to fulfill in life. Therefore I wish to close this part, inviting you to ponder transcending cultures and nationalities by speaking to our very human nature:

What are you doing to make your dreams come true?

About Julio

Julio Zelaya believes in a world filled with great and noble dreams and the people who'll reach them.

Founder and President of The Learning Group – a leading Latin American corporation focused on development and implementation of corporate universities, executive education and specialized Entrepreneurship programs.

Julio Zelaya holds a Post Doctoral Degree in Management and Marketing from Tulane University, a PhD in Psychology from Universidad Mariano Gálvez, an MBA from INCAE Business School and has various certificates in entrepreneurship and management from institutions such as MIT, Harvard, Babson, Cornell University and ASTD. Professor of several MBA and PhD courses in Latin America.

Julio is a bilingual, international speaker (Spanish/English) whose charismatic and inspiring style has led him to share the stage as a keynote speaker with some of the best in the world, the likes of Dave Ulrich and Sir Ken Robinson. He's been involved in the training and formation of over 250,000 people in the continental US as well as other countries in Latin America and the Caribbean, sharing how to live with purpose and entrepreneurship as a lifestyle. He was a conference speaker at TEDx Guatemala City sharing on "The Gift of Dreaming."

Author of twelve books, *"La Travesía del Emprendimiento"* (The Entrepreneurship Voyage), and "Sólo por ser usted" (Just because it's you), both written in Spanish, his articles are commonly published in prestigious magazines of Central America such as *Business and Strategy*. He co-authored the book *Transform* in English with Brian Tracy (available in October 2014). He's currently working on his next book on how to live a life full of purpose (available in English and Spanish in November 2014).

Among his clients we find: Novartis, Kellogg's, Abbott, Wal-Mart, Exxon Mobil, PepsiCo, Philip Morris, Henkel, World Bank, Chevron, World Vision, Save the Children, USAID, Merck, and others.

He has taught at conferences in Penn State University, Tulane University as well as in a number of entrepreneurial summits. He was selected as one of America's PremierExperts™ and has been featured on NBC, ABC, FOX and CBS television affiliates speaking on entrepreneurship and leading a life with purpose.

You can connect with Julio at:

julio@juliozelaya.com   www.juliozelaya.com
FB: Julio Zelaya   Twitter: zelaya_julio
www.thelearningroup.com

CHAPTER 30

CALCULATED RISK – THE KEY TO SUCCESS

BY JOSH FELBER

I'm not exactly sure where my sense of entrepreneurship came from, but I distinctly remember when the idea began to germinate within me. At the age of 14, I read two books that impacted my young mind and continue to influence me to this day: *Think and Grow Rich* by Napoleon Hill and *Unlimited Power* by Tony Robbins. I wasn't even a decade and a half into my life, but my course was set. I knew the direction I needed to go and I was determined to start my own business.

My new found interest in entrepreneurship and my awareness of the growing computer industry led me to investigate how I could buy computer products for less than the current outlandish prices. My research revealed that if I had a vendor's license, I could buy wholesale and sell at retail. So, at the age of 14, I obtained the appropriate licensure and was the first company in my geographic area to become a Commodore Amiga dealer. I sold their computers and accessories at computer shows as well as at user groups and continued that business throughout my high school years.

After graduation I went to college for a short time before getting bored and discontinued the traditional educational path. I then started working for a company in the Merchant Services industry. I did really well with them and, while still a teenager, moved to Louisiana to open six offices for the company. Shortly thereafter, I moved to Dallas and partnered with an individual who also had extensive experience in the world of Merchant Services. He was in his mid-fifties and I was only 19 at the time. We started our own company in that vertical and within 5 years we became the second largest Merchant Services company in the country with about 500 employees in various offices across the United States. At the right time, we sold our portfolio to a bank and walked away with a sizeable profit.

At the age of 25, I moved back to my geographical roots in Ohio with a large sum of cash on hand from the sale of the business and started a sports performance car company. That company was ahead of the "Fast & Furious" explosion and sales were mediocre. We decided to close the business after a short period of time when one of the partners moved.

I then invested in a satellite dish installation business and within the first 45 days set up an extensive marketing plan and brought in several telemarketing people. We sold about 500 satellite systems within the next 45 days and continued to increase to an average of 600 to 700 systems per month. We quickly became one of the largest dealers in the United States. However, the lagging economy after the horrific events of 9/11 caused that market to slow considerably and with the continued enormous weekly advertising investment with minimal sales, I decided to shut down the operation and focus my energy and money elsewhere.

Through several business associates, I was introduced to a nutraceutical company and a revolutionary weight-loss product called "Slim Mints." I jumped at the opportunity and became a partner as well as the Vice President of Sales. In about a year and a half we were in 40,000 retail stores across the country and in numerous other countries. After great success, when the appropriate offer came along, we sold that company to a larger nutraceutical company.

Following the sale of the nutraceutical company, I partnered with one of my long time friends and business associates to start a company in the green technology industry. Simultaneously, we also started another company in the products industry and began buying patents. We then took the patented products to the big infomercial companies to get them on television. These businesses didn't hold my interest for a very long period of time before I decided to change gears and pursue something for which I had a passion.

I have always been a big runner, and around 2003 I discovered CrossFit. I started using the methods of CrossFit and it was something I really loved doing. In fact, it had become a passion, which I decided to turn into my next business venture. In January of 2010, I began to do my due diligence related to opening a work out facility and by October of that year I opened the doors. I was definitely on the right track as was evidenced by the first year of business growth. Each year the operation has experienced a substantial increase in gross revenue and in 2012, I moved into a 7,000 square foot facility and also opened a second location with a partner. This tremendous success has attracted the interest of potential partners and investors to open additional locations with the third site to open in the latter part of 2014.

One of the unique features that sets apart my facility from others is an onsite chiropractic and rehab center within the gym facility provided for the benefit of the gym clientele. This was a value-added component to one of the facilities in 2013 and has proven to be very popular and successful. Going forward, this will be the model for additional locations that will be opened.

Another area of customer need identified was the availability of quality nutritional products. After considerable research and product development, I will also be launching a functional nutritional company to design, make and sell my own supplement lines.

Through the opening of the various gym locations, I have also had the opportunity to begin to acquire the commercial buildings in which those facilities are located. This has led me to move forward with plans to begin to expand my investing into commercial real estate in order to bring more diversification to my holdings.

I have shared my business history with you, not to try to impress anyone, but to make the point that with each of these very different business ventures, there was a certain amount of "calculated risk" I had to take when making a decision to invest my time and money. Most people are so used to being "risk adverse," they may look at what I have done in life and consider me to be an extreme risk taker. However, I'm not a "risk" taker. But, I am a "calculated risk" taker.

Taking calculated risk has been so much part of my life since I was just 14 years old that it doesn't feel "risky." Over the years and through multiple business experiences, I have learned much and have evolved into a "risk analyst" of sorts. Interestingly, I never went into a business proposition, after doing my due diligence, thinking it was too risky and that I was going to fail. I always evaluate all the factors to determine if I feel a particular business opportunity can be successful. I confidently know my skill set and what I can and cannot do. If I have confidence that I can put the right people in the right places and all the other aspects of the business are viable, I am confident I can enable the business to succeed. Now, not every business I had was a huge success. Sometimes I lost money. But, you learn to protect your downside as much as possible.

My experience has taught me "4 key elements to investing in a business opportunity" and "5 essential principles to calculated risk." Allow me to share those with you.

4 KEY ELEMENTS TO INVESTING IN A BUSINESS OPPORTUNITY

1. **Invest in income-producing assets.** If it doesn't have real potential to produce income, don't even consider it.

2. **Save your money to reinvest in future income opportunities**. When you begin making income on your business venture, don't spend it all on superficial luxuries. Reinvest in your business and other income-producing opportunities.

3. **Working to earn more money isn't greedy.** Zig Ziglar said it well, "Money isn't everything, but it ranks right up there with oxygen."

4. **Have fun and make money.** I strongly believe that you have to have fun while you're making money. If one of these two components is missing, you will be miserable and it may be an indication you are in the wrong business.

5 ESSENTIAL PRINCIPLES TO CALCULATED RISK

1. Taking Calculated Risk is the New Way to Avoid Risk

When it comes to risk, most people are raised with the words "be careful" echoing in their minds. They are told, "Go to college and get a secure job." There are thousands of people today that will tell you that plan is not working so well for them as they struggle to pay off their $50,000 student loan debt over the first 15 years of their working life. They are in debt for school, for a house, for a car and the list goes on. They are simply trading time for money so they can pay off their debt. And, just about the time they will be able to pay off some of those debts, they will go into debt for something new. Most people are always at the point of risk without realizing it. Anytime there is debt, there is risk.

On the other hand, if you put your money into a calculated risk such as an income producing asset or your own business, that type of risk may be able to pay you back 10 times what you would have had by not taking a calculated risk. For some people it may be as simple as getting involved in a multi-level marketing company because they love skincare or nutritional products and they want to share that with others. There are a lot of people that have done really well in multi-level companies and it usually takes only a minimal investment. It's a calculated risk with a very small upfront cost with great potential upside.

People have to move away from thinking that a good education will get you a good job that will get you a good life. It's just not that way anymore. By starting to take calculated risk, you can actually see things change in your life.

2. Do Your Due Diligence

The term "Due Diligence" in the context of purchasing or starting a business refers to a process of systematically researching and verifying the details of every aspect of the business to determine the validity and viability of the entity. The goal in due diligence is to ensure that all stakeholders associated with the transaction have all the information they need to accurately assess the risk. Taking your time to do this process thoroughly and accurately will potentially save you from many headaches, financial loss and will enable you to determine if the business can be profitable into the foreseeable future. This course of action will reveal where any risk may exist enabling you to determine if the risk is too great or if there are ways to reduce your risk exposure.

3. Use Other People's Money (OPM)

One way to mitigate risk is to use other people's money. Sometimes you can find a partner that will put up 100% of the funds. Or, multiple partners may share in the financing of the business. There are many ways to structure a deal so you aren't 100% at risk. You may have non-monetary value you bring to the business partnership. For example, you may provide the day-to-day operational oversight for the business or you may be a marketing expert. Every role in a business has value and can possibly be translated into an ownership role in lieu of putting actual dollars on the table.

I always put certain pieces in place to alleviate the financial downside for me. I can bring a great deal of business expertise to the table. If someone wants to partner with me, they may be a financial partner only and may not want to have anything to do with the day-to-day operation of the business. They just are there to reap the financial rewards. Whether it's my money or someone else's money on the line, in my mind failure is not an option. I will put my entire effort into making the business as successful as possible.

4. Adjust What Needs to be Adjusted
It is very common for a startup business to lose money in the first few years. However, whenever there is a revenue loss, you must carefully scrutinize why the loss took place. Was there anything you could have done to minimize the loss? After vigilant examination, make the necessary adjustments to mitigate those same losses in the future. Sometimes business people just assume they will lose money in the first 3 to 5 years and they consider some monetary loss simply a natural part of doing business. That shouldn't be the case. Don't just accept a financial loss. Diligently seek to understand the loss and, if it is preventable, put into place any necessary changes so those losses are not repeated.

5. Know When to Get Out
When I was involved with the satellite business, there was an economic downturn that made a significant impact on our sales. I saw what was taking place and determined it was in my best interest not to continue that business. The business may have been able to survive the economic downturn and pick up again on the other side. However, I wasn't willing to wait it out. Instead, I chose to close the business and put my efforts into another business that would be able to generate immediate income.

Also, if you're not having fun and you're not making money; that may be a clue that it's time to get out and cut your losses. If one of those pieces is there, you may be able to find a way to get the other piece. But, if both pieces are missing, you are putting your personal well-being at risk. There is no sense in being in a business you don't enjoy and that isn't making money.

YOU CAN DO IT!

Andre Malraux said, "Often the difference between a successful person and a failure is not that one has better abilities or ideas, but the courage that one has to bet on one's ideas, to take a calculated risk – and to act." I would encourage you to "be dangerous," don't follow the norm of "be careful." I don't mean literally light yourself on fire – not that kind of dangerous. But, I do mean challenge yourself. Take a calculated risk. Go after that goal. Find something you're passionate about, something that you love, something you can have fun doing and make money at the same time. Have fun and make money – that's what I always come back to. You can do it!

About Josh

Josh Felber is focused on challenging himself and those around him to consistent excellence. Blessed with the heart of an athlete, mind of a leader and an entrepreneurial spirit, he is not only effective in his approach to business, but also extremely gifted in motivating people to achieve their own goals. His intense drive and dedication to succeed has laid the foundation for his innovative approach to leadership.

Josh is the President and CEO of JF Ventures, LLC, Functional Fitness Labs, LLC (CrossFit Akron), F2 Nutrition, LLC and Primal Chiropractic, LLC, all based in Akron, Ohio. Since beginning his first business as a computer dealer at the age of 14, the seed of entrepreneurship was planted and long-term success was destined to follow. While still in his teens, Josh started Merchant Financial Services, which became one of the largest entities in that industry. He led the company to generate annual transactions of over $5 Billion.

Other businesses in Josh's career have included ventures in satellite dish installation, nutraceuticals and green energy solutions. In each of these opportunities he led the companies to be national leaders within their business vertical. As a Partner and Vice President of Lifemax, a nutraceutical company, he helped build the company from the ground floor and under his sales leadership, the company reached millions in sales within 4 years and their products were on the shelves of 40,000 retail outlets in 30 different countries.

His most recent endeavor includes the opening and operation of multiple functional fitness facilities, currently located in the North East Ohio area. As an avid health and wellness advocate, Josh has been a long time runner and CrossFit proponent. He has received numerous awards for various competitions including multiple marathons and half-marathons. He has now taken his passion for health and wellness to a new level through the creation of Functional Fitness Labs, LLC (CrossFit Akron) in 2010. Each year of business has demonstrated significant growth.

Josh has also incorporated a chiropractic and rehab center with the gym facility for the benefit of his clientele. This model has proven to be very successful and will be used in future locations. Additionally, he will be launching a functional nutritional company to design, make and sell his own supplement lines.

Josh has been recognized multiple times in the National Who's Who of Entrepreneurs, was a National Winner of the *ATT* and *USA Today* Investment Challenge, and has been featured on radio and television in the greater Akron area. He is an EXPY Award recipient for Media and Communications and recently appeared as a guest on America's Premier Experts® presentation of Health and Wellness Today, a television program seen on various ABC, CBS, NBC and Fox affiliates throughout the country. Josh holds numerous certificates in CrossFit, Sports Performance, and Nutrition, and is an Eagle Scout as well.

Josh and his wife Trina, an entrepreneur as well, reside in Akron, Ohio with their daughter, Mia, and twin sons, Cash and Roman. Additional information about Josh Felber and his companies can be found at: www.joshfelber.com.

CHAPTER 31

PLAN NOW RETIRE NOW

BY MICHAEL FOGUTH

In walked James and Linda late one evening, following an hour ride in from Detroit, where they both work. James and Linda both began working right out of high school, and have been saving their entire lives for what was about to happen in the next hour. You see they never really planned for retirement, and therefore, never thought about what they needed to retire. Because they both never planned to retire, they never thought about what they needed to do to retire. Like most retirees today, they were always taught to invest (save in a 401k), defer (taxes), and delay (taking anything out of your retirement account). So, what's the problem with that? The problem with that is you have no idea what the magical number means to you without a plan.

What most people see or hear is that you have to have some big number saved up in order to retire, and that may be true, but what is most important is how that number will impact your retirement lifestyle. What we have to remember is that we are all different. We all want to do different things and spend different amounts of money on different things. Everyone has a different ideal retirement, so why do we all try to fit our retirement into someone else's plan? Do you want to travel the world, buy another house, move to a different state, downsize, buy a boat, sell your boat, fix up your house or sell your house? The list can go on and on. The point is, you MUST have your very own plan!

Having your own plan is very simple. What you want to do is start with every dollar you have saved for retirement and place them into one of three categories. The first one let's label as "RED" – this is where you will list every dollar that holds risk. Examples are Stocks, Mutual Funds, Bonds, Variable Annuities, and many other types of accounts. Think of RED money as money that goes up and down based on what Wall Street is doing.

The second group of retirement dollars we want to label "BLUE" – this is where we will place all the funds that can go up and down in value but are not directly tied to Wall Street. Examples are GOLD, SILVER, GAS, HIGH GRADE RARE COINS, REAL ESTATE, CLASSIC CARS, GUNS, COLLECTABLES, and everything else we own for which we see increases and decreases in value. These investments will go up and down in value, but are not directly tied to the fortunes of Wall Street.

The last group of funds are labeled "GREEN" – these are accounts that are principal-protected. They cannot lose value no matter what happens in the economy. Examples of GREEN money are Checking, Savings, CD's, Fixed Annuities, Fixed Indexed Annuities, and any other account where you can invest your money, and no matter what happens in the economy, you cannot lose one penny of what you put into these accounts.

Now that you have your assets broken down into three categories we can take the total number of all three accounts, red + blue + green = total amount of retirement savings. Divide the number that you have in each account into the total to get your percentage of what you have in each category. Example: $750,000 in RED, $40,000 in BLUE and $75,000 in GREEN looks like 86% in RED, 5% in BLUE and 9% in GREEN. To keep things simple, use round numbers for this, later on we will break these down to see exactly how they all fit in.

The second part of the plan is the most important, income planning. Remember it's not how much you earn, it's how much you keep. Our goal in this phase is to understand how to properly take income during our retirement years. Retirement income is a lot like climbing a mountain; making it to the top of the mountain is optional, making it to the bottom is mandatory. When you retire is optional, but staying retired is mandatory and no one wants to have to degrade their lifestyle in retirement because they ran out of money, or go back to work against their will and chase a paycheck during retirement. Figuring out your number comes down to a simple equation. Think of this like a three-legged stool—leg one is Social Security, leg two is a pension or some other kind of defined benefit plan, and the third leg is the lifestyle leg. It is becoming more and more routine to see retirees only have one or two legs on their stool. The more legs you have in your plan, the more stable it will be, and remember the name of the retirement game is *safe*, *secure* and *enjoyable*.

Now that we know what we need to secure our retirement income, let's look at what we need to figure this out. Let's now take all guaranteed sources of income and add them up: Social Security + Pension + Lifestyle = What we know we can spend per year. One of the most important parts of our plan is inflation. Every plan MUST call for an increase in the cost of living; we like to use a round number of 3% every year. Some folks like to use smaller or larger numbers, but 3% is a good number to use based on the last 30 years. Let's look at why planning for inflation is important: in 1984, a gallon of gas cost 84 cents; in 1994, it cost 2 dollars, and in 2014, it cost 4 dollars. For James and Linda, they had $33,458 in social security income, $31,239 in pensions and that was it for guaranteed income. They had saved for retirement, but what they did not know was how much money they could pull out of their investments every year without running out of money.

James and Linda always thought they needed the magical number of $1,000,000 to retire. In fact, James and Linda really only need $20,303. That's per year, plus, remember we have to plan for a 3% rise every year, so that $20,303 number will go up. To help ensure a safe and secure guaranteed retirement for James and Linda, we must calculate how to invest their money in order to payout the income they require. It is a lot easier to solve for $20,303 a year than it is for $1,000,000 of total investable assets.

Solving for your guaranteed retirement income is the most important thing to do when you are ready to retire. It is as easy as *plan now, retire now*. Having the proper financial investment vehicles available for you to use when resolving these issues is the hard part. You have to make sure that you don't have too much of your money tied to any one area. Too much RED money will leave you vulnerable to the fortunes of Wall Street, and you may end up losing money in the market the same year you wanted to take a vacation, or redo the kitchen. Too much BLUE money may also leave you in a place where you are uncertain about returns or even liquidity. Buying a rental home to create another source of income sounds like a good idea at the time, but ask any part-time landlord, it's not always what you want. Too much GREEN money may leave you with not enough interest earned or too much money tied up for too long. Having a custom blend of all three will allow you to enjoy your retirement no matter the current economic times. Think of yourself never having to change the way you want to live your life for the next 30 years. No alarm clock going off, no worries about buying a new car, updating the house when you want, and so on and so forth. The ideal retirement is only one plan away.

At the end of James and Linda's first strategy session, we have the foundation to build the custom plan for them. You see, as much as you want to look at retirement as how much money you have saved, it really should be about what you want to do the next 30 plus years. In that first meeting with James and Linda, we talked about the places they wanted to go, the things they wanted to do, the stuff they planned on buying—everything you can think of that you want to do when no one can tell you what to do. For them, life was about traveling to Florida every year from December to March (in Florida they call them Snow Birds). They also wanted to buy a convertible within the next three years. They planned on traveling to Europe once again. We even talked about the curve balls we are thrown in life. James is a few years older than Linda, and wanted to make sure if something happened to him, that Linda would not have to worry about how she was going to live. The unexpected things that happen in our life are sometimes the biggest events in our lives. A good plan will always have a "what if" tied into it.

Same day of the week, same time one week later, in walks James and Linda. We sit down at the table and I ask them, "Well, do you have any questions?" James says to me, "When can we retire?" I say, "Well, when do you want to retire?" They both look at each other and say "NOW". What I did not know was that it took them two hours to get home from work today, and they both had it with the daily commute. "Well!" I said, "Let's talk about how we can get you both to feeling safe, secure and ready for the climb down the retirement mountain." We reviewed the page breaking down their assets into three easy-to-see categories. They currently had 90% of their assets tied to RED money, 0% in BLUE and 10% in GREEN. From there we went into the income breakdown, and their true magic number was $72,000 a year, and a 5% rate of return.

Once they knew what they needed, we had to discuss how to get there.

I always ask everyone the same question: "If you needed a 5% rate of return, knowing what you know about Red, Blue and Green money, where do you think is the best place to get a 5% rate of return." James and Linda both said the same thing. "I don't know. That's why we are here." We laughed for a minute and I said, "Okay, let's break this down." I turned to the dry erase board in the conference room and we started reviewing all their options. Fast forward a few minutes and we now had our answer. Creating a custom plan that is tailored for you and only you, allows for direct simple-to-see-and-understand solutions. Retirement planning can be as complex as you and your advisor want it to be.

When you think back over the 30 plus years you have worked to get to this point, take the time to secure the next 30 plus years. Understanding what you want to do and how you want to do is not that hard—if you have a PLAN.

If you would like to develop your own customized plan as James and Linda did, please visit www.foguthfinancial.com

About Michael

Michael Foguth guides his clients through the retirement planning process with custom-tailored plans designed to withstand whatever the road ahead may hold. Raised in Mid-Michigan by his parents Michael and Marie, he was taught that faith and family are the foundation to a successful journey through life. Family is of the utmost importance to Michael; his Father being one of 13 and his Mother one of 6 emulated the importance of strong family bonds. Michael and his wife Brooke support this belief with the four children they have together. Family is what drives Michael to continue his passion in the retirement planning arena. Having seen firsthand what improper preparation and market volatility can do to one's retirement, he makes it a point to educate others on what they can do to ensure history does not repeat itself.

Michael's passion led him to specialize in working with retirees and those nearing retirement who desire to protect their hard-earned money and ensure that it is there when they need it. Michael and his team at Foguth Financial Group pride themselves on the long lasting relationships they have developed with their clients and their families. Not only has he guided his own clients, but he has trained financial advisors across the country on exactly how to properly plan a successful retirement for their clients. Michael's clientele turn to him when they are faced with tough decisions that come up during their pre- and post-retirement journeys.

Michael is a graduate of Central Michigan University. He has been nominated for "Elite 40 under 40" by L. Brooks Patterson in 2014. He has been quoted in *Newsweek, The Wall Street Journal, USA Today, Yahoo Finance* and *Forbes* as well as featured on NBC, ABC, CBS, CNBC, MSNBC, FOX and FOX Business. Educating today's retirees plays a key role in the planning that Michael does; he is an educator for the Richness of Life Institute through Central Michigan University and Cleary College.

Michael has become one of the national premier experts when it comes to retirement planning in today's economic times. When he is not at work, you can find him coaching his children in whatever activity they are playing. The Foguths are very active within the community. They participate with local and national organizations such as; LOVE INC., A.L.S. of Michigan, Make-A-Wish Foundation, Relay for Life, Rally for the Cure and Michael also sits on the advisory board for DoorKeepers. Michael and his family are also members of Northridge Church of Plymouth.

You can connect with Michael at:
Michael@foguthfinancial.com

CHAPTER 32

THE 7 GOLDEN RULES OF RETIREMENT PLANNING

BY RICHARD EHRLICH, ChFC

Imagine you and your spouse taking off on a road trip. The car is packed, the seatbelts are on, and you are about to pull out of that driveway. Anyone who has been on a road trip knows that the next few hours, or the next few days, can go one of two ways.

Option A) You end up in the middle of nowhere with a flat tire, lost, late, out of gas, out of patience, and ready to rip your hair out.

Option B) You navigate toward your destination peacefully, enjoying the open road and the exciting prospect of the freedom that lies ahead.

Now, those two scenarios are obviously the extremes at each end of the spectrum, but unfortunately both are entirely realistic and possible, so what determines whether your road trip ends one way or the other? How can you protect yourself from "Option A" and the stressful experience it brings?

The difference between the two lies within the tools and resources that you have to help you along the way. Just as with any journey or adventure, there is a checklist of things you need in order to have a successful journey, making it to your destination happy and on time.

Before you take off on your road trip you need to ensure you have:

- ✓ A definitive destination: Where do you want to go?
- ✓ A Map/ Plan: How will you get there? Vehicle? Speed? Timing of pit-stops?
- ✓ An ETA: Realistically, when do you want/need to get there?
- ✓ A Travel Guide: Who will help guide you in the right direction and keep you on track?

Having each of these things can be the difference between a peaceful, enjoyable and successful journey, or ending up stranded, lost, and tearing each other's hair out.

At this point you might be a little confused... what does travel advice have to do with economic planning? The truth is that you are on the most important road trip of your life: the journey of your retirement.

This adventure that you've embarked on can be either the most peaceful and enjoyable experience, or the most stressful and discouraging challenge of your life. What determines whether this journey goes one way or the other? How can you protect yourself from the dangers along this road trip?

Just like a road trip, your retirement follows certain rules. Here are my 7 Golden Rules for a happy retirement. Follow them and your dream may be closer than you think.

RICHARD'S 7 GOLDEN RULES FOR RETIREMENT PLANNING

Rule #1 - Have a Definitive Destination

This is rule number one in any journey. You can't take off down the road until you know where you are going. Do you have well-defined retirement goals? How much money do you realistically need to retire?

It's easy to pick a nice round figure that sounds like it would be enough, but determining the REAL amount may be more complicated than you think and a lot more complicated than some online calculator will have you believe. It's important to determine these figures with a professional, and ensure that you aren't traveling off into an abyss with faulty information.

So what should you factor into your savings equation?

- **Lifestyle** – where do you want to live? Do you expect your living expenses to go up or down? Do you have travel and vacations planned and budgeted?

- **Tax Rules/Brackets** – Have you factored Uncle Sam into your budget? Will your retirement income place you in a new tax bracket? What are the taxation policies on your investment vehicles?

- **Debt** – Is your mortgage paid off? Do you have any outstanding loans to pay down? Have you already cleared all the "red" off your personal ledger?

- **Family Responsibilities** – Do you have specific goals like being able to pay for college for your two kids? Will you likely be supporting your parents as they age?

- **Healthcare** – Have you determined the estimated cost of healthcare for you and your spouse? Do you plan to utilize long-term care insurance? Have you budgeted for the likely continued rise in all these costs?

Determining your destination and goals, in a realistic, calculated manner, will ensure that you start your retirement journey in the right direction.

Rule #2 - Have an Updated Map/ Plan
This nuts and bolts portion will define the success or failure of your road trip. You know where you are, you know where you are going, but what is the best way for you to get there? Here are a few keys to a successful plan:

- **Details** – General directions are good enough. Make sure you have the turn-by-turn details outlined.

- **Up To Date** – the best route yesterday is likely not the same today. Make sure you take into account changes, alterations, or opportunities in the current landscape.

- **Personalized** – The path is different for everyone and having a personalized roadmap is essential for a successful plan.

Rule #3 - Pick the Right Vehicle

The investment vehicles you choose should match with your current financial standing and ultimate goals of your portfolio.

Do you opt for the smaller hybrid that will save you money, but might not have the most comfortable and secure ride? Do you take the SUV that might be a bit more expensive but has room for more luggage and is safer on the road? Something in between? Whichever vehicle you choose, make sure of a few things:

- You understand how to drive it – you know the details of how the investment vehicle will help you move forward.

- You've had it checked out - it has a history of performance that gives you confidence in its ability to help you reach your goals.

- It's fully loaded with the right features – are you optimizing it within your plan as far as maximum contributions, timing of withdrawals, and tax efficiencies.

Rule #4 - Don't Succumb to the Need for Speed

How fast do you feel comfortable pushing your investments? There is a delicate balance between risk and reward with any retirement plan. Driving fast, and taking on high risk, could help you make up time on the road, but this also leads to a higher likelihood that something could go awry.

Whether it's another market downturn, a lack of diversification, or an unexpected life event, having a higher volatility investment strategy than is necessary could cost you both time and money. Make sure that your plan has a speed and a risk that you are comfortable with, and provides you the peace of mind in knowing that you will reach your destination safe and sound.

Rule #5 - Plan for Pit-Stops

It's never a good idea to simply look at the map at the start and then tuck it away for the rest of the drive. It's important that throughout the journey you are stopping to evaluate where you are. Circumstances change. Maybe your destination has moved. Maybe you encountered set back and you have to make up time. Maybe you've decided it's time to slow down and take a less risky route.

Make sure you plan for periodic pit-stops to assess your initial strategy, refuel or get a quick tune up on your investments, and correct your course if you find yourself a little off track.

Rule #6 – Determine Your ETA

There are new reports coming out every day with different numbers and ages and estimations, but there is one underlying trend: people are living longer and the age of retirement is going up. We've all heard that 70 (or 80… or 85) is the new 60. Healthcare costs are going up, taxes are going up, the "real age" for social security is going up, and with all of that to contend with, the number of people able to retire and stay retired at the age they expected is going down.

The important thing to remember is that your ETA for retirement is unique to you, your goals, and your strategy. If your neighbor is retiring at 65, this doesn't mean you should follow suit. If your brother finds himself back in the workforce at 70, it doesn't mean that has to be your reality. Every retiree's road trip starts and ends in a unique place, and everyone has a unique path they are traveling in between.

How should you estimate your time of arrival? *Take a close look at your destination.* How much do you realistically need saved to enjoy your retirement? *And then take a close look at your route.* If you follow your current strategy, and don't veer from the course, how many years will your assets last? Are you taking the safe secure roads, or are you taking a shortcut that could lead to some unexpected delays and potential downfalls?

Keep in mind this is your ESTIMATED time of arrival! Make sure you give yourself some flexibility, some time to stop and enjoy the drive, take an unexpected turn, buy that new home, or be able to recover from any unanticipated setbacks. After all, this journey is your life, and if you plan it right, you shouldn't have to rush through it or end up stranded 10 miles from your destination with a flat tire and an empty tank of gas!

Rule #7 - Hire an Experienced Travel Guide

Chances are you will only be making this road trip once, and you are likely traveling through unfamiliar territory. This is where having a guide who knows the terrain, understands your journey, and is an expert in navigating this treacherous path is invaluable to your success and peace of mind.

The big question: how can you ensure that you select the right person to join you on this trip? Here's a few essentials:

> **Experience** – Your guide should have experience with each facet of your travel plans. They should be familiar with the local areas, understand the inner workings of all the vehicles available, know how to fix, tune up, or adjust to any unexpected events, and have a clear vision of your destination. Look for someone who specializes in comprehensive wealth management, investing, financial and retirement planning, and insurance strategies that will all contribute to your success. There is a reason you have a guide: this person needs to have the knowledge and experience to show you the way.

> **Philosophy** – Everyone has different ideas of what makes a good road trip, and many of these aspects were discussed in your mapping and planning stage. What level of risk are you comfortable with? What kind of vehicle best suits you and your goals? What is your preferred ETA? It's critical that you and your guide are on the same page with how to travel this road. Maybe you prefer safe, secure investments, but your advisor chooses to take a more dangerous route. Or you would like to take a pit stop to pay for your children's college, but your advisor didn't plan or understand that. Make sure that your guide believes in, and plans for, the route that fits you and your journey.

> **Trust** – This is the most important trip of your life, so make sure you are taking navigation pointers from someone that you trust. Before you hand over the wheel you need to be confident that your advisor understands you and your journey, and has your best interests in mind with every turn they take. If you don't feel comfortable and secure with your guide, you will likely find yourself lost and confused later on in life.

Throughout this checklist there have been a lot of questions asked about your retirement and your financial situation. Many of those questions you might not have an answer for, or maybe you have an answer, but you aren't sure if it's right. That's where having a guide, to help you determine these answers, to ensure that your answers are correct, and to identify any questions you may have forgotten to ask altogether, is one of the biggest keys to a successful retirement voyage.

Your retirement journey should be an enjoyable one. You should have the security and peace of mind to experience every mile and see every sight. Don't let the anxiety of an incomplete financial plan add stress to your life. Start off in the right direction for your future and follow your path to retirement success.

For up-to-date financial advice, read Richard's weekly financial column at: RichardsWeekly.com

Have questions? Email Richard at:
Richard@SecureWealthPlanningGroup.com

About Richard

Financial retirement professional Richard Ehrlich, ChFC, started his career in NY in 1994 and has been helping clients secure their wealth for almost two decades.

Richard Ehrlich is not your typical financial advisor, having gotten his start on Wall St. with the prestigious firm Drexel Burnham Lambert, and working directly under Wall Street genius Michael Milken, Richard did the unthinkable and moved out of the corporate sector and set up shop in Boca Raton, Florida.

As Richard says, "Life is more than a paycheck. After seeing my father lose his entire life savings to the market and poor financial decisions, I realized that something had to be done."

In 1994, Richard moved out of Wall St. and set up shop helping local retirees and soon-to-be retirees avoid the same mistakes his father made. The founding principal behind the Secure Wealth Planning Group is that a sound financial plan is more than just the ability to pay your bills, it's about planning for the future, planning for the luxuries, the unexpected and the inevitable.

Since then, Richard made the move to Boca Raton and has been assisting individuals, retirees, professionals and business owners, physicians and surgeons, and professional athletes and entertainers with financial preparation.

Richard continues to keep up-to-speed with the most advanced planning strategies available—to provide his clients with products and services that impact them and their families for decades to come.

In his free time, Richard enjoys spending time with his wife and two sons, Eliyah and Shlomo, swimming and reading.

Questions? Richard Ehrlich is a licensed fiduciary. Call 561-340-2667 or email Richard at: Re@SecureWPG.com

Like Richard on Facebook > http://facebook.com/SecureWPG

Follow him on Twitter > https://twitter.com/SecureWealthPG

Or Connect with him on LinkedIn at > http://www.linkedin.com/in/richehrlich

Investment advice is offered by Horter Investment Management, LLC, a Registered Investment Adviser. Insurance and annuity products are sold separately through The Secure Wealth Planning Group, Inc. Securities transactions for Horter Investment Management clients are placed through Pershing Advisor Solutions, Trust Company of America, Jefferson National Monument Advisor, Fidelity, Security Benefit Life, and Wells Fargo Bank, N.A. Horter Investment Management, LLC does not guarantee or endorse any annuity or life insurance product or their performance. Insurance and annuity products are not sold through Horter Investment Management, LLC. Products are subject to the terms and conditions of the contractual language of the life and annuity companies. Past performance is no guarantee of future results and investors could lose money.

The content of this book, Successonomics/Nick Nanton with Celebrity Press Publishing, does not reflect the views of Richard S. Ehrlich, ChFC or Horter Investment Management, LLC. Investors are encouraged to meet with their advisor, tax professional and/or attorney to discuss their plan and/or recommendations of change.

CHAPTER 33

AVOIDING THE PITFALLS AND TAKING ACTION FOR A SUCCESSFUL RETIREMENT

BY BOB HALL

After earning my business degree from Arizona State University, I immediately entered the financial services industry and joined a very large firm. In the mid-'90s after being in the business for a relatively short period of time, I was really struggling as most representatives do within their first few years. At a training meeting I attended I happened to meet one of the leading producers in the country who was also part of the firm for which I was working. He was kind enough to lay out for me his formula for success. He said, "There are two groups of financial advisors. There are the ones that work in a target market where there are 70% of the competitors and only 30% of the money and they work evenings and weekends to fight for their share of that business. The other group is working where there is only 30% of the competition and 70% of the money in the United States and they work 9 to 5, Monday through Friday." Then he asked, "What group do you want to be in?" I replied, "Of course, I want to be in the second group." He continued, "Then you need to stop seeing people under the age of 60."

That is when I started focusing my emphasis on talking to retirees and understanding their unique needs related to retirement planning. I have always had a very healthy respect for seniors, but the time I have been able to spend with them has given me an even greater appreciation for them. The World War II generation in particular, is responsible for the prosperity we enjoy today because of the hard work and sacrifice they made for all of us. I have a deep respect for those people and thoroughly enjoying talking with them.

The new retiring generation, known as the Baby Boomers, has also worked hard and has been known as the "saving" generation. The disciplined savings practice of this segment of our population has influenced the stock market more than any other generation. Now, there are an estimated 10,000 Baby Boomers that are retiring every day in our country. That means there are thousands of people daily that should be meeting with a qualified financial advisor to determine their strategy for the next thirty-plus years of their life.

To better serve my clients, I left the large financial services firm in 2000 to become an Independent Investment Advisor. That was a pretty dangerous time to start a business given the condition of the market. Alan Greenspan called the late 1990's "the period of irrational exuberance." That period had come to an end right about the time I started my business. However, I didn't feel I could properly serve my clients if I was working for a large corporation. For the benefit of my clients, I started my own company so I could offer them more objective advice. My clients like that because I don't have to be locked into proprietary products for one company. I don't work for any one company now, I work for my clients. As an independent financial advisor I am much better positioned to help them with their pre-retirement and retirement planning needs.

There are four basic rules by which I am guided: Show up on time, do what you say you're going to do, say please and thank you (treat people with respect), and make yourself available. That's how I live my life and how I treat my clients.

THE BIG PICTURE

A country can't go from a national debt of $9 Trillion in 2008 to $17 Trillion in 2014 and expect that our economy will continue unscathed. If you really analyze what the market has done over the past 115 years or so, the bull market cycles are followed by bear market cycles that average twice as long. This pattern has repeated itself for over 100 years. The bull market of the 1980's and 1990's lasted 17 years. The bear market started in 2000 and hit bottom in 2008, then the market came roaring back. However, if history repeats itself, that 17-year bull market of the 80's and 90's should result in a 30-year negative market. The only thing that caused a very sour market to come roaring back since 2008 is that that it has been infused with a lot of artificial sweetener. However, this artificial sweetener dump cannot continue indefinitely.

What really caused the market rally of the 80's and 90's? There was a paper published by the Federal Reserve Bank of San Francisco that talked about how stock prices have been closely tied to demographics over the past half-century. They also suggested that this is a negative forecast for equity net values moving forward. If you look at the stock boom of the 80's and 90's, it is directly correlated to the Baby Boomers who were saving money for retirement. Corporate America realized they couldn't continue to fund pensions for all the Baby Boomers, so instead, they began to offer 401(k)'s.

The idea was that if all these baby boomers started pouring money into 401(k)'s, the stock market would benefit based simply on the sheer volume. That approach works great when a large segment of the population is putting money into the market. But, now those baby boomers are starting to retire. The first one turned 65 last year and there are 10,000 baby boomers leaving the workforce every single day in America. And, that number will only be getting bigger over the next 10 years. The Baby Boomers that infused the market via their 401(k) are now starting to pull money out of the market to use it. What does that mean for the future of the stock market? Well, it's very difficult to predict the future of the market because there are so many influential government controls in place that could impact it.

Don't count on the generation to follow the Baby Boomers, Generation X, to bolster the stock market. Gen X is known as the "spending generation." If they make $1.00, they spend $1.50. That begs the question, who is going to replenish all the Baby Boomer money currently beginning to exit the market? Some analysts suggest there are many foreign investors that are looking for places to invest their money and may choose the U.S. market. This may offset some of the coming deficit, but it will only have a limited impact. Needless to say, today's financial world is a quagmire and you need a qualified specialist to help guide you through these unsettling times.

PRACTICAL CONCERNS FOR RETIREES

The frightening thing is that when most retirees go to see their typical Wall Street broker, they are directed to make their portfolio more conservative because they are too heavy in equities. They shift them from equities over to fixed income. In a typical Wall Street brokerage account or mutual fund portfolio, what does fixed income actually translate to? In plain English, bond funds. What happens to bonds when interest rates rise? Bonds drop in value. Can interest rates possibly go any lower than they are now? The logical conclusion is that interest rates are destined to rise.

Whenever interest rates rise, bond funds will be the next bubble to pop. However, I don't anticipate the government allowing interest rates to rise quickly. I think it will be a soft landing because the economy is so fragile right now. But, even a slight movement in interest rates can result in a drastic drop in the value of bond prices.

Another concern for retirees related to the current low interest rates, is the resulting pain for CD investors who are counting on interest rates in their CD's to produce income. When you factor in tax and inflation to today's CD rates, you are actually losing your purchasing power every year.

3 IMPORTANT CONSIDERATIONS WHEN INVESTING

There are three considerations you must always make when investing:

1. Growth Potential

2. Safety

3. Liquidity

Unfortunately, you can't have all three. If you find someone who tells you that you can have all three, run from them as fast as you can.

To get growth and liquidity, you will have to sacrifice safety. This means you could lose money – possibly a substantial amount of money.

To get growth and safety, you will have to sacrifice some liquidity. Otherwise, how could a company guarantee that you're not going to lose money?

To get safety and liquidity, you will have to sacrifice growth. You will actually have to settle for little or no interest.

Developing the appropriate and personalized investing strategy for you comes down to prioritizing those three things. What is your number one priority? What is the number two and three priority? Once you come to that conclusion, then we can look at your overall assets and determine how much money can be used for growth, how much for safety and how much for liquidity. Then you can begin to compartmentalize that money to establish different pools of money from which to draw.

A RETIREE'S GREATEST FEAR AND HOW TO OVERCOME IT

The number one fear for American retirees is running out of money. How do you alleviate that fear? I have found there are only three things that can cause a retired person to run out of money:

1. Overspending income. If there is more going out than coming in each month, eventually you're going to run out.

2. A stock market correction. If you're taking unnecessary risk in the market, when the market drops substantially that can cause you to run out of money. Usually the first and second points go hand in hand. If a person can't conservatively stay within their means and stay within a budget, they often will try to take wild risks in the market to get the returns they feel they need. It then becomes a double-edged sword.

3. Long Term Illness. A long-term illness can very quickly deplete a portfolio. However there are ways to protect yourself from this danger and to cover many of your expenses should this happen.

If you're not overspending your income, if you don't have too much exposure to the market and if you have a plan to pay for long-term care in case you ever get sick, then your retirement becomes bullet proof.

AVOID REVERSE DOLLAR COST AVERAGING

Reverse Dollar Cost Averaging is when you are drawing consistent income from a portfolio. A retiree will typically need that consistent income whether the market is up or down. So, if you have to draw that money out when the market falls, that means you will have to sell more shares to get the amount you were expecting and that can quickly deplete your portfolio. When you need consistent income from a variable portfolio, that can be a recipe for disaster. If you are in that situation, you should spend some time with a knowledgeable financial advisor to explore an alternative plan.

DON'T PROCRASTINATE ABOUT YOUR RETIREMENT PLAN

Don't let procrastination cause you to put things off, saying, "Someday I'll do it." People are full of "Someday I'll..." However, if they never make it to "Someday Isle," then they can find themselves in a lot of trouble. Procrastination is probably the biggest challenge that anyone faces. It's so easy to put things on the back burner.

Change requires action. I had a client about 10 years ago who came into my office. She said, "I need to change the beneficiary on my account." I responded sympathetically, "I'm sorry to hear about your husband." She said, "Nothing has happened to him. We are just getting a divorce." Now this is a client that had been married nearly 50 years. I quizzed her as to why she was getting a divorce. She said, "My husband has always been abusive to me." I asked, "Well, why have you stayed with him this long? If he was abusive you should have left 50 years ago." She replied, "The reason I remained in that situation was because the fear of changing was greater than the pain of staying in a bad situation and taking it." I think there are a lot of people that do that exact thing regarding their retirement planning. They know they're in a bad situation, but rather than taking action and fixing it, they decide to stay there and take it. Your future depends on you taking action.

WORK WITH AN INDEPENDENT FINANCIAL ADVISOR

One thing I strongly encourage retirees to do is to find an independent financial advisor that specializes in the retirement market because that's the only way to get true objective advice. Stay away from a financial advisor that tries to be the "Jack of all trades." If you have a financial advisor that is also an accountant, that is kind of like going to a doctor because you have a heart condition and having the doctor tell you he can also do a root canal if you need one. Work with someone who is a specialist. If they are specializing in multiple services such as investment advising and tax preparation, then they are likely mediocre at both.

WORK WITH A RETIREMENT SPECIALIST

It's very important that retirees work with a retirement specialist because, even the best financial advisor that will guide you through your accumulation years, is probably not the best financial advisor to get you from retirement to the rest of your life. They have completely different focuses. One is geared toward accumulation and the other is geared toward preservation and distribution. As a retirement specialist, I do not ignore accumulation because you need to hedge against inflation. But, at the same time, if you are heading into retirement and you are investing like you are a 40 year old, you are in dangerous territory. There are very specific strategies and considerations that must be evaluated and a retirement specialist will be the best person to help you.

Find a retirement specialist that is younger than you. You want someone that is young enough to still be there with you throughout your entire retirement. Sometimes people get a financial advisor who is about ready to retire. In 10 or 20 years when you need his help, he's not going to answer your call because he will be retired and not in the business any longer.

Find an advisor that makes them self readily available. If you need help, you should be able to call your advisor Monday through Friday and maybe even Saturday. These days, usually when most people need help with something, they are instructed to call the 1-800-WHOCARES number only to get a computer to try to resolve their issue. I would much rather work with someone that I can see face to face to resolve an issue or answer a question. You should expect that same service from your financial advisor.

About Bob

Bob Hall and Absolute Financial have been working with individuals and businesses in the San Diego area for many years. Bob has extensive personal and professional experience. Bob is licensed to represent a variety of investment and insurance products.

Bob and his team are dedicated to developing lasting relationships with all of their clients. They believe in helping them assess their financial goals and participate in the management of their finances.

One of the benefits of working with Bob is his ability to provide clear, easily understood explanations of financial products and services. The personalized program that he can provide is a roadmap to working toward a more secure financial future.

Learn more about Bob Hall and Absolute Financial at: www.AbsoluteFinancial.net

CHAPTER 34

DID THE PROGRESSIVE MOVEMENT REMOVE THE "INVISIBLE HAND" FROM THE U.S. ECONOMY?

BY RICK POSTON, ChFC, CLU, CASL

The Invisible Hand, is a metaphor used by Adam Smith, the economist, which describes the *self-regulating* behavior of the economic marketplace. The term self-regulating refers to the fact that there are opposing forces present in the economic marketplace that create a state of equilibrium. You can find an example of this relationship if you look at the relationship between supply, demand and prices. As each of these variables react to market conditions, there are opposing variables with negative correlation that react to counter the movement and keep the marketplace in a balanced state of equilibrium. Self-regulating markets tend to operate under the premise that for every action there is an equal and opposite re-action. This law of physics describes a completely different set of actions and re-actions, but it accurately describes the activity within the self-regulating marketplace.

I like to compare the Invisible Hand to the 12th Man in football. The Invisible Hand doesn't actually exist in economic markets any more than there is an actual 12th Man in football – but because of the efficiency of the opposing forces in the marketplace, it would appear that someone or something was altering the behavior of the marketplace or the football game.

The next hand that I feel deserves mention is the manipulating hand of the Progressive movement or politically liberal regime, which has strategically committed to flooding society with welfare and entitlement programs for the American public to keep their political party in power. Can the Invisible Hand, quietly influencing market forces toward equilibrium, overcome the intoxicating power of over 80 different entitlement programs—specifically, food stamps, healthcare, cell phones, money and housing? The simple answer is a resounding NO.

The liberal agenda is manipulating economic behavior with their vast entitlement programs the same way the Federal Reserve is manipulating the stock market to keep prices artificially high—by printing $85 Billion per month and buying securities and treasuries in open market transactions—while 26% or almost $4 Trillion dollars of our currency in circulation today has been printed under the guise of "Quantitative Easing." Quantitative Easing is another term for currency manipulation – the same immoral behavior that we have chastised China for doing.

The U.S. is supposed to be the most powerful nation in the world and set the example for the rest of the world to follow. Due to its stable reputation, the U.S. dollar was adopted by the International Monetary Fund as the global currency. Because of the out-of-control Quantitative Easing experiment, several countries along with the International Monetary Fund have questioned if the dollar should remain the global currency, or if it is now necessary to create a new neutral currency that can be safeguarded against abusive manipulation. Needless to say, if the U.S. dollar is removed by the IMF as the global currency, it will create a day of reckoning in this country when we see the tremendous devaluation the dollar could experience. Imagine for a moment how we will survive a potential 30-50% drop in the purchasing power of our money.

We also must take responsibility for our own financial well-being, so that we are not vulnerable to the lure of government handouts. Poverty is a weakness that liberal government preys on to control voting blocks. Liberal politicians assume that everyone who is dependent on their entitlements for assistance will be a secure vote in the next election. The more people the Liberals can intoxicate with their entitlements, the more votes they secure to enable them to remain in political power. As a society, we must instill the value of honor in resisting government handouts and being proud to take care of ourselves and experience true freedom. Freedom does not exist if you are dependent on Big Government to feed you, give you a cell phone or provide a roof over your head.

The opportunity to create personal wealth has always been the American Dream. The pursuit of the American Dream has motivated people to take risk and embrace entrepreneurship in true free markets. Our personal financial stability brings with it the power to withstand rogue politicians that try to defeat the free enterprise system. The free enterprise system has been the foundation of this country's success and elevated the U.S. to become the envy of the world.

For the people who watch from afar, America has been termed the "land of opportunity." The current administration, for the last 5 years, has had policies fail one after the other, because the policies are designed on reducing inequality and wealth redistribution rather than increasing economic growth. Now we have become a debt-ridden country with a decreasing credit score that has far too many of our citizens living in poverty and on welfare. The infectious entitlements have created a growing segment of society that has developed an entitlement mentality. They actually believe that society owes them the entitlements that they are given. I recently saw the statistic that over 46.2 million people or 1 in every 7 Americans live in poverty. For the last 20 years, we have averaged 35 million people living in poverty – this sudden 31% jump has occurred in just the last 2 years (2012-2013).

The current administration continues to tell us that the economy is improving, but the actual numbers reveal to us a different story. We have spent the last 13 years in recessionary conditions, hoping and praying that the economy will turn the corner and we will begin to see growth again. Economic recovery begins with job creation. People have to earn money at a good job to be able to spend it. It is the consumer spending money that fuels the growth of businesses.

Today we have over 50 million people on food stamps. 53% of Americans do not have any investment savings. The administration tells us that the narrow U-3 definition of unemployment is about 7.0%, but we all know that number doesn't accurately represent the real unemployment this nation is experiencing. There are 6 official definitions of unemployment.

When you take a look at the U-6 broader definition of unemployment at 14.4%, you get a more accurate reflection of the difficulties people are facing and the negative impact the Affordable Care Act has had on businesses' hiring practices.

We have more Americans on an abused welfare system of food stamps and government subsidies than we have ever had in this country's history- even more than during the Great Depression. People have lost their houses to foreclosure in record numbers and cities are declaring bankruptcy. We are having to print money just to pay the interest on our national debt as it approaches $20 trillion dollars.

Obamacare was sold to the American people as "The Affordable Care Act"—but in actuality there is nothing affordable about it. Obamacare stands to increase the cost of health insurance for the middle class in this country by 30-50% while taking over $550 million dollars away from an already weakened Medicare program. Obamacare will change the American way of life as we know it.

We are seeing a groundswell of people that feel compelled to homeschool their children because public schools have spun out of control – they have become the training ground for a liberal agenda. We have taken God out of schools and the Supreme Court has taken God out of the Pledge of Allegiance. We are quickly becoming a Godless society that is losing hope and faith.

Under the current administration, the American people have been exposed to scandal after scandal – like the IRS profiling conservative organizations. Then we experienced the NSA scandal with unconstitutional violations of privacy by wiretapping and storing cell phone conversations and texts. Just days after being assured that Al-Qaida had been defeated and presented no threat of an organized attack, we had the attack on the embassy in Benghazi – with no military response to try to defend the U.S. consulate, as terrorists murdered four American diplomats. Rather than admit to the American people that we had endured another act of terrorism, the American people were told the terrorist attack was the reaction to a YouTube video.

Don't forget Fast and Furious, where a Presidential executive privilege was issued to Eric Holder, Attorney General, when he was found in contempt of Congress for refusing to cooperate with Congress by turning over documents about their plan to give automatic weapons to Mexican drug cartels in the border towns – cartels who used those very guns to murder a U.S. Border Patrol officer.

We have identified that the U.S. has the largest reserves of oil and gas in the world, but the current Administration insists on stonewalling the Keystone XL pipeline – the artery needed to transport the oil and gas from the drill sites to the refineries. Instead, our President has given over $100 billion dollars, money that we had to borrow and add to the national debt, to "green energy" companies to spend on research and development. We have since found out that over 80% of these companies who received this government money were donors to the Administration's re-election campaign. Most of these companies, like Solyndra, have filed for bankruptcy and closed their doors.

The scandal that upsets me the most are the attempts to violate our 2nd Amendment rights as they try to remove guns from the American people. The liberals are so possessed by their desire to outlaw gun ownership that use of an Executive Order to accomplish his goal has been considered.

One scandal after another with dead bodies to account for and the American people are being told that they are "phony scandals."

The fact is clear that the current Administration has completely disregarded parts of the U.S. Constitution. Specifically, Article 2, section 3, which states that the President "shall take care that the laws of the land be faithfully executed." This is a duty, not a discretionary power. A couple of weeks ago, the employer mandate of the Affordable Care Act was suspended. In June of 2012, deportation proceedings against some 800,000 illegal immigrants were stopped after Congress refused to approve The Dream Act legislation, which would have allowed these illegals to stay.

Obviously, our forefathers knew of the challenges facing a growing nation and that is why they took the time to write out for us The Constitution and The Bill of Rights. It is ironic to see how laws that were established over 200 years ago could be so timely and applicable today. Our forefathers even imagined that over time the values of society could change and so they designed systems for new or revised laws to be written to accurately reflect the needs of the day; they literally left us operating manuals on how to run the country. It is a shame they are being ignored to pursue personal and party agendas. The entire design of our Government was based on Biblical law and the way the Bible says dispute resolution should occur.

You see, this country was founded by men seeking religious freedom and they knew that if we followed the teachings of the Bible, we could not fail as a great nation. I believe that the reason we are having the problems in our government and our economy is all due to one issue – we have elected people to run this country who do not embrace Christianity and our Christian heritage. If we put God first in our lives and live to serve Him, I believe the United States can remain the super-power it once was. On the other hand, if we continue down the path that we are on, we will continue to become even more divided – until we tear ourselves apart at the seams. Must we really hit bottom before we realize that as individuals and as a country we have strayed too far from the God-fearing nation we were designed to be?

We need an Invisible Hand now more than ever to counteract the negative forces in our economy and our government. I pray we get the Invisible Hand of God and that he will have the mercy to guide us back to the path of righteousness.

Richard Poston, ChFC, CLU, CASL
Empowered Wealth Financial Services
Copyright pending

About Rick

Rick Poston is a 19-year financial veteran who has helped hundreds of small business owners take their companies to the next level – by helping them grow their personal savings and retirement accounts.

Establishing himself with American Express Financial Advisors for seven-and-a-half years before launching his own company, Poston Financial Services, the Shreveport-born, Dallas-based adviser, has worked with a diverse client base of private practice professionals and many small business owners.

Rick has been chosen by *Bloomberg's Businessweek*.com and *Forbes Magazine* as one of the Top 20 "Game Changing" financial advisors in the country. Rick stays in touch with his fans each week by hosting an educational hour on Talkradio with the *Empowered Wealth* radio show every Saturday morning at 10 a.m. on 660 AM, The Answer, and on 100.7 FM, The Word.

Beyond his media presence, Rick continues to work directly with clients in his full-service boutique practice. Rick currently maintains three professional designations: Chartered Financial Consultant (ChFC), Chartered Life Underwriter (CLU) and Chartered Advisor for Senior Living (CASL).

For additional information or to schedule an appointment with Rick, please call 469-361-4020 or go to: www.rickposton.com.

CHAPTER 35

SHEILA MAC TALKS SMACK ABOUT SUCCESS

BY SHEILA MAC

Dear Friends,

I believe you are reading this resource because you are an elite group of achievers, *Lifelong Learners and Wisdom Earners.* There is no accident that you have found this book or that it has somehow found you. I ask that you read it from cover to cover, for one of the authors will whisper to you directly touching your heart and soul. This *will* change your life *if* you take action immediately. In this action resides the key to your own true success in business as well as in life. For this knowledge will not only afford you fiscal fitness, it will offer you the precious gift of time.

I believe that one of the best ways to learn is though the hearing of stories. So in the hopes of helping you on your personal path to success I wanted to share with you my story of growth, turbulence and all of the secrets to achieving success that I have learned along the way.

I started my journey in Glendale, California. I spent my first two years of life raised by a mother with severe disabilities and a father with an elementary school education who spoke only Spanish. The trials of parents' lives filed our home with much frustration and anger. Shortly after my second birthday my parents divorced and I was taken in by my grandparents. We moved into a lovely home in the foothills of Southern California. From the outside our home was a beautiful scene, lush nature and small animals surrounded us. But unfortunately for me there were no children nearby for me to play with and my grandparents were not interested in filling that role.

I made friends with the animals and nature around me all the while tied to a tree in back so that I would not stray or need supervision. I remember sometimes hearing the echoes of children laughing through the hills around me knowing that I could not be a part of their games. Alone I was living in this new place called home. It was here that I quickly learned to speak English because ever utterance in Spanish was met with a hard slap across my face. I learned to find contentment in the silence, finding comfort in the solitude. These were the years that taught me just how powerful my imagination could be. I had to use my mind to create adventure and escape from the monotonous cycle of cooking, cleaning, and yelling that filled my days.

Create happiness in your environment. Happiness leads to success in life. Although this period of time in my life was not particularly happy it taught me to be the master of my own emotions—a lesson that has carried me through the most difficult of my days. Soon enough I began school. I only had one outfit for the school week and each family member was only permitted one bath per week as well. As we all know children can be cruel and my lack of nice things did not win me any popularity contests among my classmates.

Embrace all of your emotions, through being teased and ignored I received the gift of true compassion, learning to look deeply into another's heart. I promised myself to always have unconditional love for others. I found escape in a very special book that I acquired among my grandparents collections: Think and Grow Rich by Napoleon Hill. I must have read this book a hundred times through. Folding its corners and underlining every passage that spoke to me. I read and reread every page hoping that it would give me the knowledge and peace I desired.

Study, learning from the Masters in any craft will save you years of time bringing you closer to living the life of your dreams. In his book, Napoleon Hill said, "Tell the world what you intend to do, but first model it." *When you hear something that truly speaks to you apply the concept within 24 hours.* At nine years old I finally decided to step out of my comfort zone and the world of solitude that I had become accustomed to. I began writing advertisements for local businesses and speaking up in my classes at school, winning the respect of my peers. With my new found confidence and desire for more, I left that place I called home in search of a different life.

Choice has magic. No matter where you find yourself in life, you always have the power to chose your next step. We are all presented with so many opportunities every day—what sets the successful apart is being a strong enough person to choose a different path. These paths may not be easy and more often than not, they take guts to walk down, but it is in walking towards the best choices in your life with conviction that leads to the most success. I bounced around from friends homes, Foster Care, and spending time with the homeless. Along my travels I met a young boy who was waiting on a bus bench with me. We got to talking and sharing our stories with one another and he told me that he had been contemplating ending his life. For the first time in the middle of my own youthful adventures, I was called to service.

Go forth in service. If you are seeking employment or knowledge in any business model, you first need to ask yourself one thing, "How can I serve?" Most of the income I earned early on came from my initial work in service. This young man showed me a strength in myself that I had not known before. He taught me that getting out of self-pity and living in service was the key to my own success and happiness. By 13, I was living in a stable foster care group home and when I heard that the old orphanage that I once lived at was converted into a museum, I marched straight up to their doors and offered my services as their new personal assistant. Hired immediately, I began expanding my knowledge, learning how to run a museum, plan events, entertain guests and design buildings. The hours of stimulating work would be over too quickly and I would soon find myself back in the group home counting down the hours until I got to return to the museum. It was then that I realized the choice was mine, what world did I want to play in?

Stay out of conflict with yourself and in alignment with your hearts desire. Although my two worlds conflicted, I knew that in my heart I wanted more than a life in a group home. Working at the museum showed me what else was out there and gave me the confidence to follow my hearts desire. At 15, my heart wanted to be famous. Off to a talent agency I went, and as luck would have it, I was offered a commercial the very same day. My parents refused to sign the documents allowing me to work so I chose to emancipate myself in order to chase my dream. The next few years were full of many dreams and my following the smallest of opportunities to reach them. I studied and tried my hand at any and everything from real estate to interior designing. My quest for knowledge and desire to follow my heart wherever it may take me filled these years with beautiful gifts of adventure, mystery and success.

At 23, I made my first investment in property by opening a few gift stores. I also used these stores to create a unique hands-on training program for at-risk youth to begin their careers. This gave me a channel to serve these young adults in the foster care system while helping my community. I married young, had three beautiful children while fostering three more, and enjoyed my time as a wife and a mother. Throughout my family time, I never stopped learning, my desire to grow and better myself in the business world was always there and I did my best to nurture both passions. What you do in business will always have a direct effect on all other aspects in your life. When one separates business from the rest of living, conflict is assured. Being in conflict is what causes one to become immobilized. When in conflict ask yourself, "When would making the choice to do the things which my heart desires to do, feel right?" Know that those things occur when you are in complete alignment with your truth. Each time you find you are living in congruency with your authentic soul, magic will happen. Instead of spending time on things that are not in alignment with your truth, use your energy towards something that moves you towards the life your heart desires. My heart desired to live every day in service. Service to my family, service to my friends, service to my community— while still finding time to care for myself.

I have been blessed to find a career that allows me to fill all of these desires and feel so much gratitude for the act of coaching in my life. I have re-embraced all of my secrets to success while on my newest journey in coaching. Shortly after learning about coaching, I acted. I sought information and found the best people to guide my journey. I spoke my truth. I allowed my life both personally and professionally to guide my training and my eventual coaching. I stayed out of conflict with myself and followed my hearts desire—allowing my heart to lead the way and trusting in my deep desire to serve. I chose to follow my passion. I made the business and family choices necessary to dedicate myself to learning and applying the Tony Robbins coaching techniques, as well as doing the required self-work. I created happiness in my environment.

Although it has not been difficult to find the joy in training, I have taken it one step further by making the most out of all of my encounters. Whether it be with mentors, clients, or other coaches, I make it a point to find something I can learn from every exchange. I have studied and studied and studied some more—attending every seminar, class and workshop I can to further my knowledge. And finally I have lived in service. The last one combines all of my secrets to success, because for me, if I live every day in service I also live every day in congruency with my hearts desire. My journey has always been a bit of a dance. Within this sacred dance I am constantly challenged, inspired and excited... ever-moving and changing towards the person I want to be.

My dance towards success taught me and continues to be driven by these key "secrets":

1. When you learn something that truly speaks to you, apply that new concept within 24 hours.

2. Speaking your truth and knowing what it is, is your key to success.

3. Stay out of conflict with yourself and in alignment with the knowing of your heart's desire.

4. Choice has magic, no matter where you find yourself you have that power to choose!

5. Create happiness in your environment, wherever you find yourself.

6. Study with and from the masters.

7. Go forth in service.

Dear Friends,

Success is an Expression of the "Authentic Soul."

Remember:

"We are ONE and THE DANCE OF THE SOUL is SACRED, it all begins when BEAUTIFUL AUTHENTIC ME and BEAUTIFUL AUTHENTIC YOU live in COMMUNITY and IN FREEDOM!"

As always, I wish you Life, Love, Laughter and Light.

Sheila Mac

Connect with me at: www.SheilaMac.com
www.SheilaMacTalksSmack.com
www.linkedin.com/pub/sheila-mac/11/b4/796/
https://twitter.com/SheilaMacSmack

About Sheila

As a Southern California native, Sheila Mac is no stranger to sunlight. However, her innate ability to find a glimmer of light in even the darkest of situations sets her apart from the rest. As a Personal Coach and Strategic Interventionist, it is Sheila's desire to teach all of her clients how to find that light as well. Sheila focuses on the ever-present opportunities before all of us. She teaches her clients not only how to seize said opportunities, but more importantly how to recognize them. Sheila shows her clients that there is always a chance to better yourself whether that be personally or professionally. Sheila Mac's unwavering perseverance and continual dedication to being a life-long learner has lead her to become the successful Entrepreneur she is today.

Sheila Mac's passion is helping people learn the skills they need to live their authentic lives. She is an expert on moving forward – Sheila has spent her entire life growing an impressive spiritual and fiscal living from nothing. Her unique story allows her to connect with any client, regardless of background, in order to help them reach their full potential both personally and professionally.

Born in Glendale, CA, Sheila was bounced between family, Foster Care and an orphanage before emancipating herself at the age of 15. Although to some being dealt this hand of cards may have been the makings of a difficult life, Sheila simply saw all of the possibilities in front of her. Her entrepreneurial spirit and ability to seize opportunities was first shown at the ripe age of 15 when she emancipated herself from her foster parents in order to begin working and building a better future for herself. By 23 Sheila had saved enough money to purchase the first of her successful gift stores teaching her about the profitability of running a business and property investment management. Sheila hired top interior designers for her store, then asked them to personally train her in the field as well. The focus was to learn how our environments can shape our family and business successes. Sheila knows being a wisdom learner never ends.

A product of the foster care system herself, Sheila Mac understands the importance of giving back to the community. She worked with the Job Training Partnership Act—creating a program to train young adults from foster care as well as low income homes in all aspects of retail management. Creating an open source hands-on training program helping students to begin their careers was one of the ways Sheila lead others on the road to success.

Continuing her desire to give back and motivate others, Sheila received a degree in Business Management from Woodbury University, then studied through the Tony Robbins and Cloe Madanes Coach Training Program, as well as Mastery University and Platinum Partnership Courses. This training along with her certification from The Ojai Foundation in "The Way of Council and Council in Schools" gave her the tools to be able to take her natural abilities and effectively help others turn their lives around and find their true light.

Wishing you a legacy of:
Love, Laughter & Light!
Sheila Mac

**Connect with me at:
www.SheilaMac.com
www.SheilaMactalkssmack.com
https://www.facebook.com/sheila.mac.777
savm@sbcglobal.net

CHAPTER 36

A FORCE AS POWERFUL AS COMPOUNDING INTEREST

BY JAMES RYAN

Hello. My name is James Ryan and in a moment I will reveal cutting-edge power principles to you that I am excited about, because they allow you to capitalize on what I believe is the biggest growth opportunity since the Internet. What's more, this power principle will keep on giving each year to create exponential growth just like the powerful force of compound interest.

Yes. I can imagine quite a few readers with a raised eyebrow and a skeptic's smirk as you read this. I would be skeptical too had I not been lucky enough to gain over five years of firsthand experiences with these power principles. And now, studies have been released by leading universities like MIT and Harvard that confirm that organizations who adopt this power principle become 20% more profitable than their nearest competitors.

That's right, 20% better margins. Who wouldn't want that type of growth? And, I believe this statistic is actually looking in the 'rear view mirror' and will be even better over the next few years. What's more, we are early on in the trend because only 2% of Fortune 500 organizations have adapted to date and the rush to be a fast follower is just beginning.

But, let me warn you, achieving these gains and more requires a paradigm shift. If you are in a static industry that has great margins and only weak competitive threats in your arena, then this power principle may not be for you. On the other hand, if you are an executive looking for innovation and growth and you are in dynamic market environment with increasing cost pressures, shifting customer demands or new threats in your arena, then these power principles may be a godsend.

I discovered these principles after years of seeing the exact same systemic root challenge as I consulted across a wide range of Nations, US domestic firms, multinational Fortune 500s, the telecommunications sector, the financial sector, the defense sector and Start-Ups. I don't mention this to impress you, but to impress upon you that the root challenge impacts just about every organization on the planet today – it is ubiquitous and solving this systemic root challenge creates opportunity for firms of all sizes and a wide range of geopolitical locations.

The systemic root challenge is that there is a wall, perhaps bigger than the Great Wall of China, between business executives and IT guys. As you consider why this remains to be the case, I am reminded of the saying: *What man does not understand, he fears; and what he fears, he tends to destroy.* Ask an IT guy about a business matter and the response you receive will often be, 'Oh, that isn't something I am paid to think about.' Likewise, ask a business guy about an IT matter, and you get 'Isn't that an IT thing?'

It isn't like this is an entirely new challenge. Many of us have heard 'we must align the business and IT strategy' or 'we need more IT governance', or 'we need Enterprise Architecture.' It is, however, a challenge that most organizations have yet to fully solve. If earning 20% better margins is worthwhile, it's time to solve this challenge because that's just the beginning of the opportunity. Let me state the first success principle as a short sentence, and then we will expand upon it in the following sections:

Digital Leaders build *Highly Digital Businesses* through *Digital Transformations* that deliver break-through performance

WHAT IS A HIGHLY DIGITAL BUSINESS?

Go ahead and try to imagine a company that does not use IT today. Really. Go ahead and take a few seconds.

It's hard, right? And if you are like me, you probably had quite a few companies pop into your mind that DO use IT. We are in the digital age after all, and just about any viable business today is a digital business.

So, if most businesses are digital today, what's does being 'highly digital' mean? To put that into perspective, consider the difference between Amazon.com and Borders. You can imagine that the IT staff at Borders reported 99.9% uptime from their IT investments and sizeable annual budget right up until Borders declared bankruptcy. The thing is, Amazon.com didn't have better IT than Borders, Amazon used IT better than Borders. This difference is subtle yet essential. From this example we can characterize a 'Highly Digital' Business:

A 'Highly Digital' Business Places More Attention to the Use of IT to Create Advantages and Value.

James Redfield once said, "Where attention goes, energy flows." 'Highly Digital' business had a moment where they 'flipped the switch' and decided to place more attention on the strategic use of IT and their digital transformations followed.

WHAT IS A DIGITAL TRANSFORMATION?

First, let's do a quick pattern spotting exercise to put a frame around digital transformation.

What comes next?

1st Industrial Revolution -> Industrial Age -> 2nd Industrial Revolution

1st Digital Revolution -> Digital Age -> _____

Yes, the 2nd Digital Revolution comes next and 'Highly Digital' businesses understand this. In the first digital revolution, we 'dipped our toe' into information technology. Most of our activity has focused on automating mundane processes and re-engineering processes. But now we are 'jumping in' with both feet and the spoils will go to those who achieve *digital transformation* – fundamentally shifting the way business works by allowing the strategic use of technology to radically improve business performance.

History does tend to repeat itself and factory electrification gives us a great example of how business 'dips its toe' first and then 'jumps in'. You see, electric motor technology was innovated and business began 'dipping its toe' by swapping electric motors as exact replacements for steam engines. Electrified factories realized productivity gains as a result but it wasn't until 30 years later when factories 'jumped in' and discovered that huge productivity gains were available by redesigning factory layouts to follow the natural flow of work. This was a fundamental change in the way factories worked – a transformation which was only possible by using electrification, and only envisioned after the strategic evaluation of electrification technology in the broader context of factory design.

Factories that became 'highly electrified' saw productivity on assembly lines double and more. In the 2nd digital revolution, similar gains are available for companies that become 'highly digital' by fundamentally changing the way business works through digital transformations.

WHAT IS A DIGITAL LEADER?

Digital leaders are like other leaders in their ability to influence, cast vision, coach, and chart a course. The difference is in adding digital competence.

John Maxwell once wisely said:

"Competence goes beyond words. It's the leader's ability to say it, plan it, and do it in such a way that others know that you know how - and know that they want to follow you."

Digital leaders are competent in thinking strategically about both business and technology. As result they are able to see more opportunities borne by technology, see them sooner, anticipate the trends, and then influence the full extent of the organization to innovative and create competitive advantages.

Does this mean that every CEO must have digital competence to build a 'highly digital' business? No! We all have our strengths and businesses do not pay for mediocre. Successful CEOs will either be digital leaders or will include digital leaders in their inner circle. In both cases, CEOs will require the full extent of the company's leadership team do the same. Not all leaders must have digital competence, but all 'Highly Digital' business must have and create space for digital leaders.

HOW TO BECOME A 'HIGHLY DIGITAL' BUSINESS

As an executive coach I am often asked by my clients for the silver bullet to capitalize on the 2nd digital revolution. My answer—a fleet of digital leaders. Most executives know that people are their most important asset and digital leaders are the new assets needed to unlock performance gains in this 2nd digital revolution. Grow the talent, hunt for it, or rent it. But, be forewarned. The awareness of the 2nd digital revolution has grown and fast followers are now moving to capitalize on the opportunity too. It's no surprise that in 2014 executive search firms are reporting spiking demand for digital leaders.

In the remainder of this section allow me to describe four (4) areas that I believe are the most fertile ground for incorporating digital leaders into the enterprise:

Boards: How many members of your board of directors / board of advisors are digital leaders with both business and technology competence? Board's provide advice to CEOs and ask difficult questions of senior management. Doing so effectively in this digital age requires multiple digital leaders on the board. I often find leaders envy the IT of organizations like Amazon.com, Google, and Cisco. Not surprisingly those companies each have multiple digital leaders on their board.

Strategic Planning: To what extent do you include digital leaders in the strategic planning processes? The most successful companies in the 2nd digital revolution will innovate new business models, strategies, and organization structures that were not possible without information technology. When digital leaders are included in strategic planning processes they bring forth their digital perspective, identify emerging technologies, and consider the digital trends. Who else believes that Garmin's previous CEO, Min Kao, wished he had more digital leaders to warn him about mobile phone providers in the arena?

Cyber Security: It's time to rethink cyber security. When we think about cyber security, let's think about competitors not computers. At the moment that we realize that cyber criminals and organized hackers are competing with us, the penny drops on what to do about it. Go ahead and think for a few seconds about how businesses handle any competitive threat…that is how digital leaders approach cyber security. Digital leaders in cyber security will help the organization select strategies to compete against the hackers and criminals and implement them to stay one step ahead of the dynamic and evolving competition.

<u>Organizational Change:</u> Change is one of few certainties and most organizations do it poorly when IT is involved. In 2012, Gartner reported to its CFO customers that IT projects deliver target benefits less than 60% of the time. If you are like me, then you also believe that investing tens and even hundreds of millions dollars in IT projects where the probability of achieving target outcomes is only slightly better than flipping a coin isn't a great strategy to stick with. To add insult to injury, the 2nd digital revolution will amplify the repercussions – as IT will be involved in more and more changes. Fortunately, Digital leaders use more holistic change methods that keep both business and technology in view, cut through complexity, and deliver outcomes much faster and more reliably as a result.

A FORCE AS POWERFUL AS COMPOUNDING INTEREST

Albert Einstein is said to have called the power of compound interest "the most powerful force in the universe." Whether he actually said it or not might be questionable, but the mathematics behind compound interest certainly favors making a deposit early. The sooner the investment is made, the larger the balance grows each year.

Just like compounding interest, the earlier an organization develops its leaders, the more growth it can achieve. John Maxwell summarizes this concept in *The Law of the Lid,* which essentially says that no organization since the dawn of time has ever risen above it's 'leadership lid' – the artificial cap on an organization's potential created solely by a shortage in leadership skills. To raise the lid, develop the leaders.

For this 2nd digital revolution, the more an organization grows its fleet of digital leaders, the more growth the organization will achieve. The foot race to develop digital leaders has begun.

SUMMARY OF POWER PRINCIPLES

- *Highly Digital Businesses earn 20% better margins – and that is looking in the rear view mirror*

- *Highly Digital Businesses place more attention on the strategic use of IT*

- *Digital Leaders build Highly Digital Businesses through Digital Transformations*

- *Not all leaders must have digital competence, but all 'Highly Digital' businesses must have and create space for digital leaders*

- *Growing your fleet of digital leaders is the silver bullet for achieving compounding growth year over year*

About James

His mom was on her way to become a nun - until she met his dad. James Ryan likes to say that he learned to study important books from his Mom and to achieve the unthinkable from his Dad. ☺

By combining strong research skills with practical leadership skills, James often finds himself in super smart teams who are driven to achieve – even when the trail has not yet been blazed. By way of example, he has had the privilege of enjoying exciting work with gifted teams where he was:

- Pioneering with a Fortune 500 Defense Industrial Base firm to earn D.o.D. trust when cyber security became a front-office issue to meet shifting customer demand

- Leading the development of a revenue-generating two-factor credentialing product for a Fortune 500 financial services firm

- Defining an Identity and Access Management Strategy with NASA and HP to allow the Federal Government to achieve target mission objectives as stated in executive orders

- Transforming a Cyber Security Program in 1.5 years to allow Federal Agencies to rise from an F to an A grade in their congressionally-reported FISMA score card

As the middle child between two sisters, he was naturally a peacemaker and diplomat. Well, he might question 'naturally', but he once read that we can master anything after 10,000 hours of deliberate practice, so he does have the reps!

James has a collaborative leadership style and natural curiosity to see the opportunity, multiple perspectives, find the YES, 'make things work', and anticipate needs. He leads, follows, coaches, teaches, and pitches in – whatever it takes to achieve positive outcomes.

To share his message and cyber security expertise, he is also a public speaker and author. He has appeared on the History Channel and he has shared the stage with luminaries such as the Honorable Howard Schmidt and Patrick Reidy. His articles have been published in a broad range of publications including business journals, contracts magazine, and security management magazines.

James graduated *Summa Cum Laude* from Virginia Tech as an Electrical and Computer Engineer in 1997 and later earned his Masters. He joined Lockheed Martin in 1997 as a member of its prestigious Engineering Leadership Development Program (ELDP) and joined the .COM craze in 1998 to build high-tech telecommunications companies and managed service providers. In 2001, he founded Litmus Logic (http://www. litmuslogic.com) to deliver strategic cyber security services. In 2012, he partnered with Gopal Khanna, Minnesota's first CIO, to build the first cyber security summit, and he continues to serve on summit's board of advisors. In 2014, he founded the Digital Leadership Review (www.dlreview.org), an online magazine to give a podium to digital leaders, and partnered with John Maxwell to teach advanced leadership skills.

In his downtime, James plays competitive table tennis and volunteers to coach children in the USA and Ethiopia. You can connect with him online at: james@litmuslogic.com or: james@dlreview.org.

CHAPTER 37

THE IRS WEAPON'S 3 SILVER BULLETS FOR KILLING AN IRS PROBLEM (FOREVER)

BY TRAVIS WATKINS, ESQ.

When you have an IRS problem, it's easy to get scared, depressed, and down on yourself. Who wouldn't?

There was once a man who managed, through years of hard work, to provide for his family and even acquired some lease properties later in life. When the tax man came knocking at his door in the early 1970's, asking for detailed financial records on the properties, his mind began to race. "Had I done something wrong?" he must have thought. "Will they discover some accounting error and separate me from my hard-earned money and property?" he undoubtedly said to himself.

Before he could answer those questions, before the audit began, it became clear *to him* that he was worth more to his family dead, than alive. He withdrew all the money in his bank account and returned home and took his life. That's an extreme case, at a time in America when sensibilities may have been more fragile, but for the most part, the IRS hasn't changed that much. That is also the true story of my grandfather, Ed.

See, the IRS doesn't know what human frailties and dispositions people have when collecting taxes, and mostly it's irrelevant to them. That is the primary reason that I have chosen to devote my professional career

331

to helping taxpayers with IRS problems, and I have helped many over my 15 years of practice. I firmly believe that Americans are generally earnest and good people who want to make a living, pay taxes even, with the least amount of government interference possible.

Boiled down into three simple concepts or bullets, here is what my experience in dealing with the most brutal collection agency on the planet (the IRS) for the last 15 years has shown to be the most effective strategies for beating tax problems.

1. AVOID BEING TOO HARD ON YOURSELF AND PROCRASTINATING

There are an estimated 500,000 people in the U.S. and abroad with some type of an IRS problem. Heck, some of that number (1,100 or so) are IRS employees with a tax problem! Now, are you ready for this? The IRS doesn't care why you got into tax trouble. So, you shouldn't either.

Let that sink in for a moment. The problems that are so personal to you and may have even led to your tax problem are of no consequence to the overall purpose of the IRS to close the ever-growing tax gap (which is government-speak for the difference between the amount of taxes owed and taxes actually collected).

With a plethora of taxes in America, there has to be a plethora of rules, regulations, exceptions, and special interests supporting them. Translation, it has to be complex, and it is. It is so complex that not even the IRS knows exactly how to apply it. The IRS' own watchdog, the Treasury Inspector General, issued a 2013 report that gave the IRS a 70% grade when it came to IRS seizures (the highest form of governmental taking--homes and other property). That amounts to a "D+" in applying its own rules and regulations!

So, is there really any reason to keep blaming yourself and being lulled into inaction? No. All that matters now is that you man-up, dust yourself off and fix the problem.

Now, the IRS is not speedy on anything other than bank and wage levies (or garnishments). Maybe your problem has somehow slipped through the cracks? Maybe it has, maybe it hasn't. But, don't be so sure.

IRS agents coincidentally share the same motto as the Royal Canadian Mounted Police. When it comes to justice, "we always get our man!" IRS agents don't think of themselves as unreasonable, unfair, unconscionable or un-American. Quite the contrary, they see their job as their patriotic duty.

Whether you run or not, most people can't escape that heavy feeling that someday this is all going to catch up with them. The #1 demographic that people with a tax problem share is insomnia, almost without exception. And that, my friend, is no way to live.

I know what you may be thinking at this point. I'm not trying to game the system or be unrealistic. I simply don't have the money to pay now, and the IRS won't cut me any breaks if I have no money, right? WRONG! The best time to settle with the IRS is not when things are at their financial best. It's the opposite. The less disposable income you have (that's gross income less allowable expenses), the less it looks like the IRS will collect the debt within its limitations period, which is 10 years.

So, here's how to start attacking your problem today:

   a. Start filing and paying THIS year. It's the law anyway, and the IRS won't cut you any deals if you are not in filing compliance when you make a request for relief.

   b. Get your withholdings straight with your employer if you are a wage earner, so you don't owe taxes at the end of the year.

   c. Start making some payments to your old IRS debt (newest periods first).

   d. Obtain your master tax file from the IRS and diagnose the nature and extent of your problem. It may not be as bad as you think. On the other hand, it may have to get worse before it gets better. However, I promise you that the first step back to a more peaceful night's sleep is to determine what years are unfiled, if any; what years are filed but unpaid; and the first day that the IRS will stop coming after you for a given tax year, i.e. the statute of limitations or CSED (literally, the Collection Statute Expiration Date).

2. GET REALISTIC ABOUT TAX RELIEF

It is possible for a taxpayer to have huge savings. Mostly, those big savings come from the IRS' Offer-in-Compromise Program. IRS reports show the average accepted offer is 14 cents on every tax dollar owed. Since the IRS' "Fresh Start" initiative in 2012, getting an offer approved is much easier and more cost effective than it used to be. However, *acceptance is still not the norm.* In fact, <u>about 2 of every 3 offers get rejected the first time.</u>

Here's how it works:

First, the IRS considers the equity you have in assets (like your home for instance) that could be seized. Pay close attention to this one.

Next, the IRS considers the amount of your disposable income. Disposable income is your paycheck, minus allowable expenses (like housing, food, transportation, health insurance, state and federal taxes, etc.). In its most simplistic form, the IRS then takes your disposable income times 12 and that's your offer amount.

For example, let's say you have no assets and your income is $4,000 per month and your expenses are $3,000 per month. The offer calculation would look like this: 0 assets. Then take 4,000, less $3,000 for a total of $1,000 in disposable income. Take that $1,000 times 12.

    $4,000 income
  -<u>$3,000</u> allowable expenses
   $1,000 disposable income X 12 = $12,000

Your offer would be $12,000.

It doesn't matter if you owe $100,000 or $1 million in this scenario. You only pay $12,000!

You must put down 20% of your offered amount ($2,400) to make the offer request and you have a full 5 months from its acceptance to pay the remaining 80% of your offer (or $9,600). Processing of the offer takes 6 to 9 months. Meanwhile, collection stops while the IRS considers your request, so long as a wage levy is not in place when you make your request. In that case, a stay of collection is at the discretion of the IRS.

Looks pretty good so far, what's the catch? First, remember that the IRS considers the amount of equity in the assets it could theoretically seize. In other words, if you have equity in your home (i.e., the value of the home on the open market, less the amount you owe on the home) or a retirement account, a 401(k), for instance, the floor of your offer is the equity in those assets. This is true, even if you could not liquidate these assets by sale. This knocks out quite a few offer candidates right off the bat. Taxpayers who receive huge tax savings usually have little to no assets.

Second, IRS offer examiners like to play a little game with the law. They make a lot of hay about one provision in the IRS regulations. It says that an offer is not available *"IF IT IS BELIEVED"* the taxpayer can pay off the debt in the time the government has to collect it. And guess what? The government always BELIEVES it can collect the debt in time. Incidentally, the "if it is believed" standard prevents many taxpayers from even getting a simple payment plan with the IRS.

3. TO TIP THE SCALES IN YOUR FAVOR, HIRE A LOCAL, LICENSED LAWYER TO EXPLAIN YOUR OPTIONS AND GET YOU THE BEST RELIEF AVAILABLE

There are a lot of debt relief outfits out there claiming they can fix your tax problem for cheap. Unfortunately, many of the national tax- help chains are mostly salesmen (or worse, thieves), not problem solvers. Here is why you need a local, licensed lawyer instead:

(a). *A tax problem is a legal problem.* If you aren't prepared to keep up with the daily changes to the already voluminous and confusing laws that govern the agency (they literally change daily), don't expect the IRS agent assigned to your case to tell you what your options are. If you can't pay, there are different types of payment plans, currently not collectible status, penalty abatements (forgiveness) and the offer-in-compromise program, mentioned above. If your spouse caused the problem, there is innocent/injured spouse relief. In some instances, bankruptcy will kill old taxes. In others, simply filing an amendment or an original tax return (if you haven't filed and the IRS has created a substitute return for you) may do the trick. Because a tax problem is a legal problem, your communications with a qualified local tax lawyer are privileged. You don't have to share those communications with the IRS upon demand. This is a power that a CPA, bookkeeper or non-lawyer representative from out of state DOESN'T HAVE!

(b). *Revenue officers (IRS tax collectors) are, themselves, local.* When IRS computers don't have enough information on you to spit out a lien or a bank or wage garnishment, you are likely going to deal with one of these IRS bulldogs in your area. If you have an IRS Form 2848 Power of Attorney on file with the IRS, these officers can't talk to you. You can legally call the police on them if they refuse to leave your premises. I don't recommend that, initially, but the point is, a lawyer is best suited to create a buffer when the stakes are this high. Simply put, let a local lawyer talk to the IRS exclusively, face-to-face with the Revenue Officer, on your behalf, so you don't have to.

(c). *Lawyers have appeal and the power of the lawsuit.* Alas, the most important reason of all. Remember how I told you that few offers in compromise are initially granted? Luckily, virtually any IRS decision can be appealed ad nauseam with IRS appeals. But, you have to know when to timely wield those appeals or to drop them and try a different route. Also, the rubber really meets the road for IRS relief when you can effectively keep the IRS honest with a U.S. Tax Court action or other Federal lawsuit. Some IRS actions carry these rights and some don't. Exercising these rights in court is another one of those things a local, licensed lawyer is best suited to do for you.

So, find yourself a qualified, local, tax lawyer who charges on a flat fee basis.

HERE ARE FIVE WAYS HOW:

(i). *Look for flat-fee lawyers who practice before the IRS every day.* IRS relief can be a time consuming process, and if your lawyer charges by the hour, you can quickly run up a new problem for yourself – a lawyer's fee problem. An experienced tax lawyer can effectively estimate how much time it will take to get you across the finish line with your problem.

If your lawyer can't do this and wants to send you a monthly bill for services, run!

(ii). *Watch the solver-to-salesmen ratio.* Many tax relief firms are stacked primarily with salesmen, not tax problem solvers (ratios often as high as 8:1). Tax problems are highly emotional problems, which means they are very lucrative cases for relief outfits. To cut corners, many firms use seemingly knowledgeable sales personnel to get you in the front door. Then, your tax problem takes a back seat in line for a solver to work on your case. Unfortunately, some cases in that firm model never get worked at all. So, how do you find out what a firm's solver-to-salesman ratio is? Just ask! Personally, I love to field questions like this. Why? My solvers (associate lawyers) and I are the only sales representatives. In other words, our salesmen are our solvers.

(iii). *Research your tax lawyer on consumer-rating sites.* Now-defunct tax giant, JK Harris, had an "F-" rating with the Better Business Bureau (BBB.org). Bad, right? Now, consider this. Harris never applied to be BBB accredited, but BBB has integrity. For that reason, BBB is still the gold standard for consumer/commercial help outfits. Don't settle for less than anything less than an "A+" or an "A" rating with BBB. By the way, Harris and another tax juggernaut, TaxMasters, both folded as insolvent, in a storm of class action judgments and state attorney-general actions. These outfits were greedy, no doubt. However, there was a bigger problem here. They advertised in every U.S. state and territory. They boasted about having offices in each one. They didn't. They had central bases of operations in one office, and rented regional conference rooms by the hour.

(iv). *Research your tax lawyer on peer-review sites.* Martindale-Hubbell (Martindale.com) has been the premier rating site for lawyers for decades. Judges, former clients and other practicing lawyers rate the lawyer at issue. AV-rated is preeminent/superb. It is the highest designation, and the voting is rather strenuous. Other lawyers and judges don't hand out this designation willy-nilly. BV-rated is distinguished, while the "Rated"-rating simply means that the lawyer has not achieved the two distinctions mentioned above. You need an AV-rated tax lawyer to navigate the laws with experience dealing with the IRS daily, so you don't have to.

(v). *Settle for nothing less than an American Society of Tax Problem Solvers (ASTPS) CERTIFIED lawyer.* ASTPS is a national, non-profit organization of professionals who specialize in representing taxpayers before the IRS. ASTPS trains "rescue squads" for troubled taxpayers. ASTPS is the only authoritative organization that certifies lawyers as experts/specialists as IRS problem solvers. In other words, your brother-in-law lawyer who is a general practitioner (or even a tax planning lawyer, for that matter) is just not suited for this highly specialized niche. The ASTPS certification process is rigorous. It requires continuing education with the organization and passage of a test similar in difficulty to the bar.

About Travis

Travis Watkins, Esq., CTRS is Your IRS Weapon™. He is the principal and senior attorney at The Law Offices of Travis W. Watkins, P.C., with offices throughout Oklahoma, Arkansas and Texas. His firm is unique, as it devotes 100% of its practice to fixing IRS problems for select clients and keeping those problems fixed forever.

Travis has represented hundreds of companies and individuals before the Internal Revenue Service, since 1999. He received his law degree from Oklahoma City University in 1999. He attended Oxford University and received his B.A. in Arts and Letters from William Jewell College in 1995. He is admitted to practice before the Internal Revenue Service, and the United States Supreme Court.

Travis is a Christ follower and his faith walks on "all fours" through a life of helping others. He is the son of a foreign missionary. He grew up spending summers in Haiti, Kenya, Rwanda and Europe assisting his earthly and heavenly fathers in the fight against hunger for impoverished children. He brings those experiences and his grandfather's untimely death, preceding a tax audit in the 1970's, to every fight against the IRS.

Travis is a peer-review "AV-Rated" Preeminent lawyer by Martindale-Hubbell. He is a CTRS (Certified Tax Resolution Specialist) by the American Society of IRS Problem Solvers, a national, non-profit organization of tax professionals who trains 'rescue squads' for troubled taxpayers.

Travis is also the creator of the Tax Help Legal Network™ (THLN), a consortium of local, licensed, lawyers in a growing number of locales throughout the U.S. THLN embodies Travis' strongest belief about tax resolution: the hope and future of America's troubled taxpayers lies locally in the experience, courage and accessibility of lawyers trained to do battle with the IRS for fair treatment under the law.

Travis lives in Oklahoma City with his wife and two children. He is an active member of LifeChurch.tv. He is an avid football and basketball fan. He is also the host of a public service, regionally-syndicated radio show, *Your IRS Weapon*™, on Sunday afternoons. The show is a tax news, tips, strategies and answer format, set to the tunes of your favorite rock and country classics.

Travis can be reached 24 hours a day at 1-800-721-7054 or log on to: www.taxhelpOK.com for more information on the firm and what it can do for you.

CHAPTER 38

WHY BUY AN ONLINE BUSINESS VERSUS AN OFFLINE BUSINESS?

BY ISMAEL WRIXEN

"If everyone is thinking alike, then no one is thinking."
~ Benjamin Franklin

THE DECISION

The decision to buy a business is a major one, usually with significant personal and financial commitments attached. There are a vast array of business models to invest in and it is estimated that with so much choice, the average buyer ends up searching for 18 months before giving up entirely. The advent and rise of the Internet has only complicated matters further by introducing a host of unique e-businesses (e.g. SaaS, lead generation) as well as a range of hybrid models (click-and-mortar, e-tailers). If you're in the market to purchase a business, even from an offline or non-technical background, it's worth considering the many benefits of acquiring an online business versus an offline business.

TAPPING INTO GROWTH

The explosion in growth of Internet users and usage in the last decade is remarkable. It is estimated there were 2.7bn Internet users globally in 2013 (39% of global population), up more than 6x from 10 years ago. The demographic has switched significantly as well. In 1996, 66%

of Internet users were from the US and now that figure is just 13% -- with Asia and Europe accounting for nearly 70% of all Internet users (Source: ComScore).

The introduction and proliferation of smartphones and tablets has been a major driver of both Internet adoption and average usage time. Multi-device ownership is increasingly becoming commonplace in developed markets with 1 in 4 smartphone owners in the US and EU5 also owning a tablet (Source: ComScore). Early signs from these markets indicate that multi-device ownership has not served to cannibalise desktop browsing but instead complement it with overall usage time rising.

But what does all of this really mean for online businesses, and for you, if you're looking to acquire one? Well, it points to a number of things. Firstly, the number of consumers online is growing significantly each year and as the Internet becomes an increasingly popular purchasing channel, eCommerce businesses will continue to experience explosive growth. In fact, according to eMarketer's latest forecasts, worldwide business-to-consumer (B2C) eCommerce sales will increase by 20.1% this year (2014) to reach $1.5 trillion, up a staggering $400bn from 2012. That growth is coming primarily from the rapidly expanding online and mobile user bases in emerging markets, increases in mCommerce (mobile commerce) as well as advancing shipping and payment options for online customers.

Interestingly, the latest research indicates online consumers are more valuable than offline ones. McKinsey research suggests online consumers are, on average, older and more affluent than their offline counterparts. In a recent comprehensive study of European consumers, the consultancy firm found that 38% of online buyers had household income greater than c.$54,000 versus just 25% for offline channel buyers.

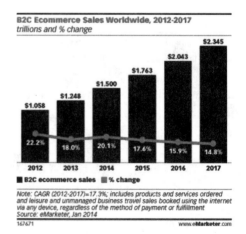

B2C Ecommerce Sales Worldwide, 2012-2017
trillions and % change

$1.058 — 22.2%
$1.248 — 18.0%
$1.500 — 20.1%
$1.763 — 17.6%
$2.043 — 15.9%
$2.345 — 14.8%

2012 2013 2014 2015 2016 2017

■ B2C ecommerce sales ■ % change

Note: CAGR (2012-2017)=17.3%; includes products and services ordered and leisure and unmanaged business travel sales booked using the internet via any device, regardless of the method of payment or fulfillment
Source: eMarketer, Jan 2014
167671 www.eMarketer.com

Secondly, the attractiveness of the Internet as an advertising medium for major brands continues to increase with the rise in Internet adoption and value of the eCommerce market. Digital advertising revenue is now worth $37bn in the US alone, second only to TV, and rising at 15% per annum (5x faster than any other medium). Don't think that it is just search engines benefiting from increases in advertising spend: $7.7bn was spent on banner advertisements alone in the US in 2012 (Source: ComScore). Website owners with authoritative content in the right niches, and of course the right traffic, can command a good price for onscreen real estate.

YOU CAN MAKE MUCH BETTER MARGINS

An often cited benefit of the online business model are the potential cost savings. There are typically much lower start-up costs to creating and running a website. Without physical assets there is often no large outlay, and instead the focus is on creating relevant content and outreach. With so many e-business models and unique monetisation methods, accurate studies on the differences in cost structures between online and offline businesses are somewhat sparse. One good comparison is an analysis of profit margins between retailers, e-tailers (click-and-brick operations) and pure eCommerce stores. Matt Carroll at FailHarder has written extensively on the economics of each. His analysis of the average profit margin achieved in the apparel niche (he models the sale of shoes) shows retailers on average achieve 51% gross margins whilst eCommerce achieve 65% through charging for shipping. Note, gross margin does not then take into account the savings in operating expenditure for the online model (rent, utilities, employees) which can take the **typical net margins of eCommerce stores to c.30% versus c.10% for offline equivalents.**

Aside from eCommerce, there are a number of e-business models that offer extremely attractive profit margins to business owners. Using data from the sale of over 150 online businesses in the last four years at FE

International, we have compiled the following net margin comparison table for the most common online business models:

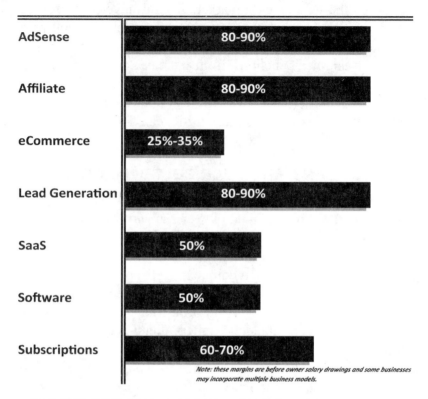

AdSense	80-90%
Affiliate	80-90%
eCommerce	25%-35%
Lead Generation	80-90%
SaaS	50%
Software	50%
Subscriptions	60-70%

Note: these margins are before owner salary drawings and some businesses may incorporate multiple business models.

ONLINE PROVIDES MORE MARKETING INSIGHTS

"The aim of marketing is to know and understand the customer so well the product or service fits him and sells itself."
~ Peter Drucker

Good marketing is at the heart of many successful businesses and the online space is no different. What is interesting about Internet marketing is that whilst it requires a slightly different skillset to traditional businesses (Search Engine Optimisation, Conversion Rate Optimisation) it offers a number of major benefits versus marketing in the offline world. The tools and strategies for marketing to consumers online provide much more data to the marketer in terms of customer engagement, relationship building and fine-tuning the conversion funnel. There are at least four major benefits to marketing online:

#1 – You can make changes on the fly – marketing online allows you to instantly split test new landing pages, site layouts, order forms, email sequences and newsletters, all within the click of a button.

#2 – You can track real-time results – with Internet traffic you often have enough of a customer sample to observe the impacts of your changes in just a few days or a week, allowing you to tweak, analyse and decide on what works best within a comparatively short time period and with low operational impact on the business. Using Google Analytics you can create goals to observe changes in precise detail.

#3 – You can target specific demographics in your advertising – the rise in social media as a platform for marketing has enabled Internet business owners to target specific demographics and customer profiles (e.g. age, gender, ethnicity and location). Paid-traffic campaigns can be run on specific locations to expand awareness in particular areas (local and national) as well as drive the right traffic to your business.

#4 – You can use a wide variety of methods for marketing online – including email, audio, video, blog, social media and newsletters – marketing strategies online are increasingly adopting a multimedia approach to initiate and develop relationships with consumers. E-mail marketing continues to be a powerful tool to help raise brand awareness, build relationships and bring in sales.

ONLINE GIVES YOU MORE FREEDOM

One of the major draws of the online business model is of course, the ability to operate it from home, and in fact, from just about anywhere in the world. With more people looking to supplement income from their main jobs, the attraction of an online business as a means of passive income is only increasing. Latest figures show 1 in 6 people in the UK alone are operating an online business from home as a way to do this. Without employees and infrastructure to manage, the owner time commitment on a well-established online business can be very low.

Using the same transaction data from FE International, we have compiled an estimate of the average weekly owner time commitments for the most common online business models:

Average Weekly Owner Time Commitments

MORE LIQUID AND LOWER RISK THAN YOU MIGHT THINK

Any prudent investor should be mindful about the liquidity profile of their investments and buying an online business is no exception. The good news is that a website is typically a much more liquid asset than an offline business. Given online businesses are geography-independent and are quite often easier to operate, there is both a lot of buyer demand for them and shorter due diligence periods during the transaction itself. At FE International, depending on the size and complexity of the asset, we typically see websites sell from 24 hours of listing to 3 months, with the average being somewhere in the middle. Many offline businesses can take 12 or more months to sell with 3 of those months set aside for due diligence alone.

BUSINESSES THAT HELP THE ENVIRONMENT

Whilst probably not a deciding factor in your decision to make an online versus offline business acquisition, being environmentally conscious is becoming increasingly important in this day and age. An online business offers significant carbon footprint savings with fewer employees, remote working (thereby no transportation costs) and no requirement for utilities like water and heating. Information is processed electronically and stored online too which helps to save on materials. eCommerce provides significant benefits to traditional retailers. Approximately 65% of total emissions generated by the traditional retail model stemmed from customer transport, according to research by Carnegie Mellon University. Consequently, online retailers use 30% less energy than traditional retail operations. Equally, unnecessary uses of manufactured materials can be avoided entirely with online retail. Granted, the Internet presents another source of power consumption, but research conducted by the ACI found that eCommerce will still achieve a net reduction of 1bn tons of greenhouse gas emissions per annum, constituting 11% of U.S. annual oil imports.

EASE OF SCALABILITY

Taking all of the points raised so far into consideration, there is one other very compelling reason to get into online businesses: scalability. Operating an online business can require little in the way of upfront costs and the low time requirement can often mean it is very easy to own and run several businesses simultaneously. If we look again at the traditional offline retail example, how easy would it be to acquire or open another store? It may take years to raise the funds and find the right location with enough footfall and you might end up signing a lengthy lease to secure the premises. Operating online is somewhat simpler in this respect; you can take a model in one niche and apply it to another with relative ease if you have the relevant experience and knowledge. There is no physical presence involved and you do not necessarily need to duplicate yourself, or other members of your staff, to run more than one online business. You can synergise your skills and resources, significantly increase your ROI and get you one step closer to financial independence.

HOW TO GET STARTED

Choosing and vetting a suitable investment opportunity is certainly the first step and one of the most difficult when acquiring any business. Data from FE International suggests that at any given time, in the sub-$5 million range, there are less than 200 online businesses that are revenue-generating, professionally vetted and being offered by an established broker that specifically deals in the sale of online businesses.

Regardless of whether you're relatively new to online business acquisitions or a seasoned investor, you should use a broker for information, guidance or advice where needed. Whilst they are vested in the sale of the business, a good broker will provide invaluable advice to the buyer on all areas of the transaction process.

Once you have partnered with a broker and found a suitable acquisition target, here are just a few things to look for when assessing an online business:

A reputable broker will be on hand to educate and support a buyer through these expansive topics, highlight due diligence areas of interest, provide relevant business referrals and nurture a good relationship with the seller.

Following the successful completion of due diligence, always involve your attorney, but be mindful that their knowledge may be limited only to the contractual elements of acquiring an online business.

THE KEY IS FINDING SOMETHING RIGHT FOR YOU

"This is a fantastic time to be entering the business world, because business is going to change more in the next 10 years than it has in the last 50."
~ Bill Gates

It is important when approaching any business acquisition to find something that fits your background, skill set and acquisition goals. With major growth potential, improved margins and often a reduced time commitment, an online business can be a very attractive alternative to a traditional offline venture. That's not to say there aren't other considerations, but it could well be the case that with a little bit of research and sound professional advice, an online business will help you reach your financial goals much faster than a traditional offline investment.

About Ismael

Ismael is co-owner of FE International (FEI), along with his long-standing business partner, Thomas Smale. Ismael's background is in M&A investment banking, and he has executed high profile deals across several sectors, namely Technology. Ismael is fluent in several languages and graduated from the University of Bath, England, with first class honours in Business, gaining the Accenture prize for excellence in the process.

FE International (formerly Flipping Enterprises) was founded in 2010 to provide brokerage services for mid-market online businesses. The company has become the pre-eminent advisor within the industry and enjoys a well-earned reputation for integrity, creativity and delivering results. In 2013 alone, the firm successfully executed an industry-leading 71 transactions.

The team is comprised of professionals from investment banking, strategy consulting as well as online entrepreneurs, all of which have extensive transaction execution expertise. FEI's brokers complement this formal experience with unique and innovative approaches to deal marketing and structuring.

Originally established in London, the company expanded internationally to San Diego in mid-2013 to bring its dedicated brokers closer to the US client base.

Offering direct access to an established network of pre-qualified international investors, FEI is perfectly placed to drive demand to your business and maximize value for your company.

To learn more about FE International:
www.FEInternational.com

To reach Ismael Wrixen directly:
Ismael@FEInternational.com

General Enquiries:
info@FEInternational.com

CHAPTER 39

P.E.A.C.E.

BY TAMARA WORD-MAGALOTTI

A friend called me today lamenting her recent break up with a long-term partner, her financial woes, and her exhaustion from working unlimited hours at her new job. She chronicled her struggles of the previous year and expressed that she was apparently unloveable, that she had gained weight from the financial stress and that her new job, although a good one, was making her look old due to her complete exhaustion.

Taking a deep breath, I began to console her in the way a friend does for someone they have known most of their life, then, I stopped myself. She needed comfort, yes, but my friend also needed a different perspective. She needed abundance.

Not long ago, I was in my friend's shoes. You have probably been there too. All seems lost and you feel like you need to claw your way out of a deep, dark hole. The clawing seems to be getting you nowhere but deeper into the abyss. Then you realize it, you have hit rock bottom and the only place you can go now is up. What my friend could not see was the abundance already present in her life.

I said to her, "Starting tonight, I want you to list five things for which you are grateful."

She replied, "What have I got to be grateful for?"

I replied, "For today, you can be thankful for the roof over your head, your fuzzy pajamas, a hot cup of tea, the remote to the television and your friends." Everything else she needed would come in time, but today, she needed to keep track of the little things.

Abundance is not money, houses or fancy cars. Abundance is a mindset. Abundance is the difference between thinking that you don't have anything left to give and knowing that you have so much you can give it away. Abundance thinking enables you to plan long-term because you know that your short-term needs will be met.

How much more powerful would you be everyday if you could devote more energy to your customers or to developing that new business idea you have? Have you considered the amount of time you waste each week agonizing over things?

Choose to be happy right now, in this moment. You have everything you need to be happy. You might not have the house, job, body or circumstances you desire, but you can still be happy now. You must be happy NOW, because life is never perfect.

Abundance thinking creates PEACE in all elements of your life, including your business. Instead of worrying how you will pay bills or make payroll, you will plan and dream bigger, knowing that if you can conceive it, you can make it happen. We can use the acronym PEACE to demonstrate the five steps to bringing about abundance in your life both personally and professionally.

(I) PROJECT GRATITUDE.

Gratitude is thankfulness for the people, things and experiences already in your life. Gratitude clarifies the channels of your mind and illuminates your sense of purpose. When you begin to recognize the value of everything around you, you can better see the areas on which you do not have to spend your valuable time and money.

Keep a gratitude journal to remind yourself of all the things for which you are grateful. Before you do anything else in the morning—maybe before your feet touch the floor--list five things in your gratitude journal for which you are grateful. Every evening before you go to bed, list another five things for which you are grateful.

You can start small with simple pleasures like my friend who listed her fuzzy pajamas. After a while, you will feel gratitude for things you once took for granted. In the beginning, my gratitude journal reflected my thankfulness for excellent hair stylists and the cooperation of my hair at a big event. It slowly transitioned to gratitude for the safety of people in mudslides half a world away and to things much bigger than the life I took for granted.

Gratitude prepares your mind to receive and acknowledge the abundance in your life by reminding you of the control you have over your own thoughts.

(II) EMPOWER YOUR THINKING.

Change your thinking from the negative to the positive. Phrases like "Why would anyone want to do business with me? I am too old, too fat or not smart enough…" create negative thought-patterns that cause your attitude to take a nosedive. We often do not realize how our self-talk is affecting our lives until it's too late. We begin to emit negativity into the world around us, creating a pattern of bad juju. Instead of berating ourselves when something goes wrong or when negative thoughts enter our heads, we need to change how we speak to ourselves.

If you normally tell yourself, "He broke up with me because I didn't spend enough time with him and I worked too much." Consider telling yourself, "He required more time than I have to give because I have chosen to work hard on my career at this point."

If your company loses a large contract, instead of telling yourself, "we failed to provide adequate service to that customer," tell yourself, "We learned from ABC Corporation that we need to be more in tune with our customer's needs and to respond more quickly."

The next time that situation arises you will feel more empowered to manage the situation differently. Managing the situation, rather than letting it manage you, reduces the stress in your life. After 21 days of speaking positively to yourself, you will have created a new habit of empowered thinking.

You can progress to a *90-day mental diet* during which you think positively and allow only positive, healthy thoughts into your mental diet. If a negative thought creeps in, write down the thought and figure out how to (a) improve the thought, (b) cancel the thought, or (c) get rid of those thoughts altogether.

In the same way that dieting makes you notice the large amounts of junk food that used to make up your meals and snacks, a mental diet causes you to notice other people's negative thinking. You may suddenly find that your friends and colleagues are "junk food" in your life that do not provide healthy, positive thinking. Beware. Your friends and colleagues can have a negative impact on your life. If so, maybe it's time to let them go.

(III) ALLEVIATE STRESS.

Sometimes you just have to let it go. How many times have you given hours of thought to things that you later realized were inconsequential, unavoidable or unchangeable? Stress occurs when we give undue attention to things over which we have no control.

Gossip is one of those things that saps our energy and creates stress. When we gossip, we give up valuable time during which we could have effected change in our own lives in exchange for talking about something or someone over which we possess no control. We do not get that time back, therefore, our own projects, family or responsibilities suffer as a result. The ensuing guilt and stress create a viscious cycle.

Everyone deals with stress differently; however, I believe that following your passion can help you alleviate your stress. Things about which you are passionate dissolve stress in ways nothing else can. If you have work-related stress, is it possible that the discord comes from working in the wrong industry? Building the business about which you have always dreamed changes your focus from "Ugh, another day at the office" to "Yes! Another day to build my dream."

If changing jobs or removing the stress from your life is not feasible, change the way you manage your stress. Massages, spas, mediation, prayer, healthy eating, intense exercise like Crossfit or distance running, kick boxing, hot yoga, or joining a sports league can all help you better manage your stress.

Have you ever felt stressed over your personal or business finances? Most people probably have felt stress over money issues a time or two. Yet, the majority of people spend less time planning their finances than they do planning their next vacation. Creating a financial plan will help alleviate stress.

(IV) CREATE A FINANCIAL PLAN.

Money is neither good nor bad. Money is not the root of all evil. But excessive love of money or misuse of it could be evil. Money cannot buy happiness, as evidenced by the number of rich, Hollywood stars one could name who died when they spent their money on drug overdoses, or dangerous adventures.

Money is a tool we use. Using money to fund a cancer center is good. Using money for 50 bags of crack cocaine is bad and potentially deadly. How we manage our money is key. Creating a financial plan allows a person to track their financial pathway and have a plan for every situation.

A financial plan frees up energy you might otherwise have sacrificed to the stress of making ends meet. You will no longer lay awake at night worrying about "what if" scenarios because every financial emergency has a plan. No longer fretting over paying employees or about what will happen if your car needs repairs free you to live bigger, live more abundantly and live debt-free. Freedom comes from the discipline.

I recommend creating a financial plan that is a zero-based budget system. A zero-based budget is a unique plan than plans *every* dollar on paper before *any* money is spent. You categorize everything, right down to investments and personal hygiene products like your toothpaste. You know where every dollar is going from every avenue of income you have. You do not end up with anxiety when you don't have money to pay bills.

I have had clients in the past who came for loans that just don't have the income to qualify, so we put them on credit repair and teach them zero-based budgeting to help them to track every dollar so that they can save money every month. Surprisingly, many business people do not track their finances in their business any more accurately than they do at home. I am happy for readers to contact me directly for more information about zero-based budgeting. In addition to dissolving stress, a financial plan removes the emotions from money management, which in turn, eliminates emotional spending.

(V) EMOTIONAL SPENDING IN CHECK.

Women often call it "retail therapy" but emotional spending can wreak havoc on finances when needs and wants become a gray area. Part of your financial plan should include a "for me" account into which you place money each time you resist an impulse purchase.

For men the purchases might be sports cars or new golf clubs, but the intent is to still fill a void with things. You have to fill that void with self-love and self-respect.

Instead of buying that sweater you keep eyeing in the department store window each morning on the way to the train, deposit the $75 you would have paid for the sweater into your "for me" account. Instead of the instant gratification of the sweater when you have had a bad day and lost a client at work, you delay the gratification and curb the tendency toward impulse purchases. If, after time, you decide you need the sweater, you can always purchase it. If you delay the purchase each time you would have made an impulse buy, you will eventually have amassed an account with a larger sum of money that you can use for self-improvement, donate to charity, spend on a mission trip or invest for retirement.

Henry David Thoreau said, "What is called genius is the abundance of life and health." Be a genius. Recognize and appreciate the abundance you already have in your life. Create PEACE in your life so that you have more energy to expend on positive and important life experiences: building stronger client relationships, spending quality time with your family, saving money for a rainy day and appreciating the world in which you already live.

About Tamara

As a business banker, the philosophy that Tamara Word-Magalotti always maintains is to continuously treat your clients like precious golden nuggets, and you will reap the rewards one thousand fold. Growing up with a family of missionaries presented Tamara with the unique opportunity to find her niche in the business world. Deeply influenced by her family's faith, Tamara wanted to find a position that would truly help others in a profound way. As Tamara always says, "Business Banking gives others the unparalleled opportunity to reach their financial potential in a very positive way."

Tamara is the Founder and Owner of Tamara Magalotti & Associates, LLC, a consulting firm that helps businesses and individuals reach all of their financial objectives through their unique product offerings, as well as their specialized attention to each and every client. Tamara is also CEO of TriCity Business Management, LLC., a firm specializing in telecommunications, energy, and essential services for both residential and business clients. Her goal is to help small businesses provide customers with a professional touch. TriCity Business Management, LLC., meets the ever-changing needs of small businesses by offering a complete line of essential services, including phone service, natural gas and electricity, and simple and affordable credit card processing. Services are tailored for a company's individual needs and are designed to grow right along with the business.

Tamara attended San Francisco State University until she found her passion in the Fashion Industry working and traveling worldwide with such giants as Chanel, Dior, Versace, Calvin Klein, Donna Karan and many others. She was also selected as one of America's PremierExperts®.

Tamara is also very passionate about giving back to the community as well, with 5% of all company profits going to St. Jude Children's Research Hospital.

You can connect with Tamara at:
Tamara.Magalotti@gmail.com
www.facebook.com/TamaraWMagalotti

CHAPTER 40

CONFIDENCE IS THE BACKBONE OF SUCCESS

BY NOEL TIPON

Growing up, I was a shy kid. I rarely raised my hand. I never went out of my way to get noticed. I didn't volunteer. I was not the child you would predict would become a successful international criminal defense lawyer able to comfortably argue before judges and juries. While confidence didn't come naturally to me, I truly believe it became the backbone of my success.

Today, I am the Managing Partner at Bilecki & Tipon, the premier law firm representing servicemembers in the Pacific Rim. Operating out of our headquarters in Honolulu, Hawaii, we provide legal services for servicemembers who are facing the most serious criminal charges or are struggling with personal matters in family court.

I built my confidence—the result of hard work, long hours, experience, and mastering my craft—which culminated in my obtaining the highest level of competence in my field. You, too, can reach this pinnacle. No matter how great your natural talent, you can build confidence.

Seven years ago, my career took a drastic turn. I was a Major on active duty in the United States Marine Corps stationed at the Marine Corps Base, Hawaii. My time in Hawaii as a Marine was coming to an end. As with all active-duty military assignments, you rarely stay anywhere for too long, and three years in paradise was about all the Marine Corps was going to let me do. My nearly ten-year career included Marine Corps

Officer Candidates School (OCS), The Basic School (TBS) in Quantico, Virginia, the Marine Corps Air Ground Combat Center in 29 Palms, California, the Washington Navy Yard, and a deployment to Fallujah, Iraq from 2004 to 2005.

I was given orders to relocate to the East Coast. This time was a crossroads in my life in many ways. As a Marine and criminal defense lawyer, I was doing well. I was winning cases and earning promotions. I could easily accept my orders and move on. But this option represented the least challenge for me. I saw the next phase as an easy jump into another secure job with guaranteed income and benefits for my young family. But I knew I would never have the kind of financial success or professional freedom deep inside I knew I needed, if I stayed in the Marine Corps. In 2007, America was still fighting wars in Iraq and Afghanistan. Leaving the Corps in the middle of two wars didn't seem like the honorable thing to do; it felt like abandoning my brothers in arms. I wanted to continue to support and honor servicemembers, yet I needed to start down the path to achieving my personal goals through self-employment.

"Throw off the bowlines, sail away from the safe harbor, catch the trade winds in your sails. Explore. Dream. Discover."
~ Mark Twain

Taking the leap from the military world into the abyss of the private sector isn't about ability. The courtroom came easy to me. I had the ability to win over and convince juries. My success in the courtroom was a blueprint for success in my business. Work hard. Be prepared. Know the facts. Master my craft. Have confidence in my ability to win.

Through hard work and dedication over the past seven years, I reached near the top of the court martial lawyer niche market in my private practice. I was trying cases in military, state, and federal courts. I had hired an associate and an office staff. My practice was financially stable and thriving in a relatively short period of time. But I realized that if I wanted to continue to succeed, I needed to shake things up and take a few risks. I was reminded of the African proverb that teaches, "If you want to go fast, go alone. If you want to go far, go together." So the evolution of my law practice was to combine firms with another heavy hitting and talented court martial lawyer in Hawaii, Tim Bilecki.

Together we would go farther than either one of us would go alone.

People who become the best typically have ambition; they tend to not be content with the success they have and have a deep desire for continuous improvement and more success. Successful people don't allow mediocrity. Don't become complacent. Don't settle for what is given.

When the opportunity presents itself to go up against the big boys, you have to take that opportunity. If the opportunity doesn't happen on its own, then you find ways to make your own opportunities. Even after sixteen years of practice, I continue to seek out mentors and experts in both the law and in business in order to improve in the courtroom and in the office.

Being confident, and in translation, being successful, is not easy. Some people make it look easy, but it is hard. Only through hard work can one achieve the intangibles of confidence and success. Tom Brady's legendary come-from-behind Sunday afternoon wins should look easy to you and me. What the football fan doesn't see is the hard work: the two-a-days, the late nights and early mornings studying film, and the time in the gym. Why does someone with natural skills do all of these other things? …Because he is driven to be the best.

Does hard work really trump natural talent? If I had worked my tail off practicing my layup on my backyard basketball court every day from the day I turned eight years old, I would have a good pickup game. Would I be better than LeBron James? Not a chance. There are some things that the lack of natural talent cannot overcome. By the same token, I would be a very good lawyer with natural talent to win in the courtroom. But I wanted to be the lawyer.

Confidence is not a push-button implementation. To build my confidence, I had to put in the hard work and long hours. I had to do things over and over again. I had to do things well. Realize that mistakes will be made but you learn from them. Successful people don't make the same mistake twice.

Early on, I had to make a tough decision about which type of business I was going to be: low-margin, high volume or high margin, low volume. I specifically chose the latter; to take on a smaller number of the most serious and more intricate cases over a large number of clients with minor offenses. Once I did, I had to stay true and everything I did, from marketing to choosing clients to charging fees had to drive my business in that direction. I had to have the confidence to be able to adhere to this strategy and not bend. As my law partner Tim Bilecki says, I had to "be Morton's and not McDonald's."

3-Time Emmy® Award Winning Director & Producer, and Celebrity Branding expert Nick Nanton says, "Price is only an issue when value is a mystery." Don't make the value of the service you provide a mystery to people seeking your service. Starting out, I was often asked, "What do I get for the money I will be paying you?" That question is generally asked by people who don't do their research or are looking for the cheapest lawyer. These are the characteristics of the client you don't want. Learn to identify these clients within a few minutes on the phone.

Winning over clients isn't simply about a witty sales pitch and a catchy jingle. That might work for soda beverages or running shoes, but it will never work in the services industry where, as JW Dicks, best-selling author, entrepreneur and business advisor to top Celebrity Experts preaches, "People buy people." And to that, I add, "People want to buy winners." Without being the best at what you do, you will never secure clients you want, those who pay premium prices for premium service. There are potential clients that want the best deal. But you want to represent clients who want the best.

In the legal industry, I believe there are two reasons why law firms reach the top. First, managing partners understand the value of what the firm does and charge accordingly. But more importantly, clients realize the value of what the firm will do and pay accordingly.

KEYS TO BUILDING CONFIDENCE

There are several key things anyone can do to build confidence. First, accept challenges. The message behind John F. Kennedy's speech in 1961 about the space race was that as Americans we will not be content with doing the easy things, but the goals achieved in doing that—which is hard—are the things that make Americans successful.

Never be afraid to fail. Almost every great entrepreneur suffers failure. Henry Ford, generally considered the inventor of the modern age, suffered failure and even bankruptcy, before his company succeeded. Steve Jobs was fired from Apple, the company that he founded, before he made it arguably the most influential computer company and one of the most recognized brands in the world. If you are afraid to fail then you are unlikely to take that one step that could separate you from great success. In a profession where coming in second place means my client goes to jail, I understand the consequences of failure. But I never let the fear of failure push me into taking a deal or prevent me from giving my clients the representation they deserve.

Take calculated risks. Taking risks is not a new idea. Everyone acknowledges it is important to take risks. Some may think that getting out of the Marine Corps to start my own law practice was a crazy risk. I would argue that it was a calculated risk that I was ultimately willing to take. How do you take a calculated risk? Look for models of what you want to be and accomplish, do your homework, execute your plan, and don't look back.

"Don't let perfect be the enemy of good." The saying is derived from the writing of Voltaire. There is also a saying in the military that a bad plan is better than no plan at all. The message I take from both is that decisive action, even if imperfect, is paramount. All too often we fail to get the job done because of perceived imperfection. It helps to know when building confidence that perfect is rarely attainable.

Associate and compete with the best and the brightest. You're never going to get better in life if you only associate or compete with mediocrity. You have to challenge yourself. If you don't, complacency sets in. And bad things happen when we become complacent. Even the most confident people succumb to complacency. They become enamored by the success they have achieved. Because of this, they will fail to grow or change with the times. Staying in the Marine Corps for me would be settling for the successes that I achieved, but for a life that was not my own. Successful people do not settle for what is given to them.

Never stop learning. The hunger for knowledge can fuel the success needed to sustain confidence.

Don't take things too seriously. The consequences of failure in the courtroom are serious matters. But that doesn't mean that you have to take your Sunday afternoon softball game just as seriously. Part of being confident is the knowledge that not everything is about winning, especially outside of the office. Also take the time to reap the rewards of your hard work when you can. And when a gnarly south swell rolls into Waikiki, ride it.

For every rule in this world or in this book, there are probably a dozen or more reasons to break it. It would be easier if I could just lay out a 10-step plan for achieving supreme confidence, but it wouldn't be honest if I did. Anyone reading this book is starting from a different point in the confidence scale. And every business and every person has different goals and pathways for getting where they want to be. Don't be discouraged if you hit a snag or two along the way. Remember what I said about not being afraid to fail: *If you come up short once, get up and start again.*

About Noel

Noel Tipon is an international criminal defense lawyer based in Honolulu, Hawaii who defends U.S. Military service members worldwide. Noel is the Managing Partner of Bilecki & Tipon, the Premier Law Firm Defending Servicemembers in the Pacific Rim. Noel is a co-host of The Tipon Report, a grass roots radio program reporting on and tackling contemporary legal issues in Hawaii.

In March 2014, Noel was featured in *Forbes Magazine* as one of America's Premier Experts providing Forecasts and Strategies for the New Year and Beyond. He is a National Academy Of Experts, Writers and Speakers EXPY Award winner. In May 2014, he appeared on the Biography Channel special, Times Square Today. The National Trial Lawyers Association recognized Noel as one of the Top 100 Trial Lawyers in the nation. The National Academy of Family Law Attorneys heralded Noel as one of the Top 10 family law attorneys in Hawaii.

Noel is a graduate of UCLA, and Golden Gate University School of Law. Noel is an experienced Hawaii criminal lawyer who specializes in military law, including court martial defense, family law, criminal law, and immigration law. Noel represents clients in military and civilian courts and is licensed to practice law in both Hawaii and California. As a proud veteran of the Armed Forces and former judge advocate for the United States Marine Corps (USMC), he has over sixteen years of experience representing Marines, Sailors, Soldiers and Airmen in military proceedings and civilian courts. He continues to support the men and women of the Armed Forces by representing servicemembers with military law issues.

Noel, a former Marine, began his military career in 1998 serving as a commissioned officer and military attorney in the United States Marine Corps. During his career, he worked as a criminal defense attorney at the Law Center at the Marine Corps Base in 29 Palms, CA, with the Navy-Marine Corps Appellate Defense Division in Washington, D.C., and the Law Center at Marine Corps Base Hawaii. He was deployed to Iraq from 2004 to 2005. While in Iraq, he served at the Headquarters for the 1st Marine Expeditionary Force and 11th MEU in the Al Anbar province, where he investigated claims against the United States and conducted humanitarian assistance missions. Following his deployment to Iraq, Noel was stationed at Marine Corps Base Hawaii, where he provided legal services and counsel to clients in Hawaii and Japan. He left the Marine Corps in December 2007 with the rank of Major. He continues to support the men and women of the Armed Forces by representing servicemembers with military and civilian issues.

CHAPTER 41

WHAT'S YOUR GAME PLAN?

BY RYAN COINER

As an entrepreneur and financial professional I have a great affinity and strong skill set to work with other business owners and entrepreneurs and have a great connection and chemistry with this market. These are business owners that have not been afraid to roll up their sleeves and build their businesses. Now, as successful business owners, they need a partner that will help them preserve and grow their assets. That's my "sweet spot," so to speak.

After growing up in Southern California, I played professional soccer in the United States and Germany. Then I moved to the Dallas/Fort Worth area in 2007 where my wife and I purchased an advertising franchise. We took out a loan to purchase the franchise, and launched the business out of our living room in a rental home in Fort Worth a month after we moved to the area. I got up every day and went door-to-door talking to business owners about their business and how I could help them in their marketing. For three years, we worked extremely hard at building the business by selling advertising and building relationships. We went through the life cycle of the business very quickly from start up to growth to stabilization to maturity and then selling it – all within three years. We became a million dollar shop and sold the business for fifteen times the purchase price.

Interestingly, once you start making a decent amount of money in business, financial folks have a way to find you and I was no exception. I started to be called on by various financial professionals. I listened to quite a few of them and asked a lot of questions. I basically told them all, "No," because the thing that was missing was that none of them understood me as a business owner and an entrepreneur.

That got my wheels turning. Why didn't these folks understand my world? I didn't want to just lock up all my money for retirement. I wanted to reinvest some of it back into my business and make it work for me. That experience actually caused me to take a look into the financial services industry to possibly fill this gaping hole that I perceived existed. I then talked to one of the financial professionals about my interest and he set me up with an interview with his company.

My motivation to help business owners actually goes back much further. My grandfather was a World War II veteran. He got off the Navy ship in Long Beach, California in the 1940's and went to work for a painting company while in his mid-20's. A year later he started his own commercial painting company and within 10 to 15 years had one of the largest commercial painting companies in Southern California. He eventually sold the company and walked into retirement at the age of 40.

My father, following his own entrepreneurial path, began working in commercial real estate when he had a young family. He was very successful and was making a six-figure income in the 1980's. One day, while driving through an intersection, he was t-boned by a woman in another vehicle traveling at about 60 mph when she ran a red light. That day changed my father's world and our family forever. You see, he was providing for his family and we were living very comfortably, but he had not put into place certain safeguards to protect himself and his family from unforeseen tragedy such as a very serious automobile accident. He spent eleven weeks in the hospital with over $1 million in medical expenses.

The woman who hit him, even though she was clearly at fault in the accident, didn't have a penny to her name, and there were no insurance or personal assets to go after as compensation for the tragedy she caused. My dad didn't have any risk management plan in place and had no way to provide for our family because he couldn't work for the next four years. As you can imagine, because of all the medical expenses, the family's expenditures escalated. All the earnings, the lifestyle, and more importantly, my parents' marriage relationship – began to be taxed severely. As a result of all the stress and the chaos my parents eventually separated.

As a result of my father not being able to bring home an income, these problems started to compound. As I have become more and more involved in planning for my clients, I am saddened by the fact that this unexpected tragedy did not have to become a complete financial tragedy as well. There are measures that could have been taken to ensure this event didn't wipe us out financially.

My grandparents stepped in to keep our family afloat financially by using their retirement dollars – which wasn't part of their plan. They helped my family keep our house, put food on the table and put my brother and me through school.

One of the great tragedies of this story is that when my grandmother passed away in 2013, she was living on government assistance. My grandparents went from humble beginnings to significant resources, then back to a meager existence because of extended family circumstances and their desire to help in a time of need. The real problem was that there was no proper financial planning done for my grandparents or my parents. This tragedy could have been mitigated if they had the proper plan and risk management resources in place. A solid financial plan could have reduced the impact on everyone affected.

This scenario of very real life circumstances has motivated me not to push financial products, but to help business owners protect and grow their assets. I want to help my clients prevent what happened to my parents and grandparents. This is not a job for me; it's a very personal passion.

The biggest challenge is to get today's business owner to slow down. I get that. I understand their drive and motivation because I've walked that same path. They are often wearing multiple "hats" and constantly have people calling them or needing them to make a decision about something. It is mentally and emotionally taxing to own a business that in many ways owns you. Most of the people I talk to have very serious goals for which they are striving. Sometimes these individuals are doing very well as far as income goes, but managing that income and leveraging it to their greatest advantage is not always one of their strengths. Evaluating one's financial future, establishing achievable financial goals and making the necessary adjustments requires time – which is often a fleeting commodity for today's entrepreneur.

It is important to understand that not all financial services professionals are equal. I have a unique perspective because I know, through experience, exactly what it's like to be a business owner. I know the challenges very well. Now, because I have access to most financial strategies available today, I am in a position to help any business owner that will take the time to plan their future. I also have a team of very experienced specialists and a robust network of highly trained professionals with which I work. So, once I understand what my client is trying to accomplish, I can gather the necessary experts from my team to help them accomplish their goals.

Allow me to use a football analogy to explain the general categories of what every business owner needs to consider when establishing a comprehensive financial plan:

Offense – The offensive strategies needed to win include the things that you are doing to build wealth. This is how you put points on the scoreboard, so to speak. It is important to have a financial professional to help you evaluate how you manage your income stream. Obviously, some money has to return to the business for continuation and growth, while there needs to be a plan to utilize other dollars to be able to enjoy the lifestyle you choose and to create an accumulation strategy.

Defense – Let's face it, things don't always go as planned. It doesn't matter how good your offense is, you have to also have a strong defense to win. If you take one step forward but consistently take two steps backward, you aren't going to win. You must have specific strategies in place to mitigate the risks that every business owner faces.

Special Teams – There are two components to the Special Teams analogy. The first is having the proper tax strategy in place. Most people are extremely tax "inefficient." They're worried about write-offs and paying the government as little as possible with no mind for how the tax system really works, and how they can make it work to their advantage within legal parameters.

Succession and Estate planning are the other Special Teams components. You will want to make sure your business and estate is properly situated so that your legacy is not defined by the planning you didn't update or ever do. A handshake agreement or outdated documents will usually cause quarrels or allow someone else to determine how your assets will be distributed. Unfortunately, it is all too common for people to leave little or nothing to those for whom they worked so hard to provide because they didn't engage in proper planning.

Now that we have established the important components of your financial plan, let me ask you this question. Who is your head coach that is orchestrating the offensive and defensive strategies as well as the special teams to make sure everyone is working in harmony? When I ask this question, the answer usually is, "Nobody." Some people will have a CPA, but he's limited in his involvement. Some have an insurance representative covering some of the defensive strategy needs, but not the offense. There may also be another person helping on the offensive side with some investments. But there usually is no "head coach" orchestrating the entire team to make sure everyone is doing their job in a cohesive manner.

My strategy is to come alongside of the business owner and help them create a comprehensive plan in all four areas – to be the "head coach," so to speak. I provide guidance and fulfillment in the "offensive," "defensive," and "special teams" strategies to ensure efficiency and harmony. It's not effective to have multiple people working on your financial strategy and not communicating with each other. Realistically, to do this effectively, you must have a head coach to give oversight to the entire process and to make sure each area is working in coordination with the other areas. The wrong plan or a fragmented plan could cost you hundreds of thousands or millions of dollars over your lifetime. You work much too hard and have taken too much risk to just squander that much money simply because of inefficient planning.

A lot of business owners have a preconceived notion about what financial services professionals do. When I ask people what they think I do, the general answer is something like, "You help people buy stocks, bonds and mutual funds." That is such a small sliver of what I do. Often business owners don't know what an asset it can be, to have someone with a finger on the pulse of all the potential financially-related strategies available for today's business owner and how they can coordinate those strategies for them. When a business owner has preconceived notions based on something they heard on the radio or television or read in a book, they sometimes think that's the only option. That's why I take time to listen to my clients and prospective clients. When they tell me what they are trying to accomplish, I can then offer specific solutions, many of which they may have never heard.

Based on my experience of working almost exclusively with business owners in my financial services practice, below are some suggestions for business owners to consider:

1. SLOW DOWN LONG ENOUGH TO PUT FINANCIAL STRATEGIES IN PLACE BEFORE IT'S TOO LATE.

The biggest downfall I see is that business owners often put off their planning – thinking they will start doing it next quarter, or next year... or sometime in the next five years because that will be a better time to do it. The reality is that there will never be a perfect time to stop long enough to create a viable financial plan and there will undoubtedly be other projects on the horizon. The best way to get to where you're trying to go is to start now and then make adjustments along the way. It doesn't have to be an "all-or-nothing" proposition. Financial planning isn't an "event," it's a "process." It's a living plan that will need to be adjusted at various times, and if you work with the right financial advisor, he or she will walk alongside you to help keep all the moving pieces going in the right direction.

2. FIND THE RIGHT PERSON WITH WHICH TO WORK.

Make sure your financial professional knows the mind of today's business owner, is very knowledgeable about effective financial strategies, and is someone with whom you can work. I don't try to make someone a client if we don't have good chemistry. If I find someone I like to work with and they like me, then it's a match that is workable and can develop into a long-term relationship.

3. WORK WITH A FINANCIAL PROFESSIONAL THAT ISN'T A PRODUCT PUSHER.

Make sure your financial professional is skilled in multiple aspects of the financial arena. Going back to the sports analogy, you don't want a coach that only has three plays in his handbook. You want somebody who can help guide you to victory by taking into consideration the financial climate and your personal financial goals. In my practice I gain a clear understanding of my client's needs and then recommend a specific strategy. I don't pitch products and my clients find that to be very refreshing. Also, because of the platform from which I work, I am aligned with some of the most reputable firms in the world – which gives my clients great peace of mind.

4. HIRE THE BEST.

If you want to win, you don't hire the first coach available. You hire somebody who is going to help you achieve victory in your financial affairs. In today's world of technology, you can work with a financial professional literally anywhere in the country and have a strong working relationship. I have clients from the West Coast to the East Coast and communicate with them on a regular basis.

5. WHAT'S YOUR GAME PLAN?

Making lots of money or simply working real hard does not necessarily mean you will hit your financial goals. The best thing you can do is slow down, develop a proper plan, and then implement it. The clarity this process will bring to what you are doing and why you are doing it, from my experience, is often worth another million bucks!

About Ryan

Ryan Coiner is a business leader, financial advisor, and mentor to financial professionals. Ryan is no stranger to success. His resume includes such accomplishments as graduating from the University of San Diego and being recognized as a two-time NCAA All American athlete. Ryan played professional soccer both domestically and abroad. After retiring from professional soccer, Ryan jumped head first into the business world. He built and sold a seven-figure business before starting his career in financial services. After selling his business, Ryan found his true business passion as a financial professional and rose to the top of the industry within his first year in the business. He is a part of the elite Blue Chip Council for a Fortune 100 financial company. Ryan has been recognized by the Wall Street Journal as a financial trendsetter, and received an EXPY award by the National Association of Experts, Writers, and Speakers.

Ryan works hard to have significant impact in the financial services profession. He splits his time between partnering, mentoring, and coaching other financial advisors and working with select clients on their individual financial plans. Currently Ryan serves as the General Manager and Managing Partner for one of the largest and most reputable financial firms in the industry. This position allows him to mentor financial advisors who want to take their businesses to the next level. Many financial advisors are good with numbers and planning but don't necessarily have the skills in growing a successful business and need help putting the nuts and bolts of business planning together. Ryan also works with select clients in his own financial practice, mainly entrepreneurs and business owners. Ryan finds they are great at what they do but often lack the vision, planning, and time to get their businesses and personal finances where they want them to be. Because Ryan thrives both in financial planning and business strategy, he is able to help both financial professionals and his select clients meet their goals.

Away from work Ryan enjoys a simple life spending time with his family, relaxing on the lake, taking walks with his wife, and golfing. Ryan also is involved in many community organizations and serves on the finance committee at his church. He has centered his career on the Bible verse Proverbs 10:9: "The man of integrity walks securely, but he who takes crooked paths will be found out." He tries to live this out daily in his business and with those he mentors.

CHAPTER 42

IS IT YOURS, OR IS IT TheIRS? — THE BEST-KEPT SECRETS TO KEEPING TAXES OUT OF YOUR RETIREMENT INCOME!

BY GARY MARRIAGE JR.
CEO - NATURE COAST FINANCIAL

One of the biggest challenges today facing many of the consumers and business owners I meet across our great country is keeping the excess taxes out of their retirement, and their businesses. This is in addition to protecting their assets from all the variables that can damage their life-savings—like market losses, rising healthcare costs, lawsuits, creditors and on and on… Now, I not here saying there is a 100% full proof way to guarantee you will never pay taxes, and I am not saying taxes are such a bad thing either. Taxes do help our country's infrastructure, and pay our Teachers, Firefighters and our protections. But there are unique planning opportunities that you can do to ensure the majority of your assets are free from excess taxation and at the same time be safe and protect you from future market losses.

HISTORY HAS A HISTORY OF REPEATING ITSELF:

As we all know, there are many unforeseen challenges we will face going into the future. One of these challenges we face as a country is how are we ever going to pay off all of our debts? Most, if not all, publications and analysts say we can't even afford to pay the interest, let alone pay the whole thing off! Because of this, I think most of us can agree taxes will be going up in the future. History has been known to repeat itself. If you look back at the 1970's some of the highest tax brackets were up to 70%, and we have also seen tax brackets as high as 90%. We have already started to see some of these new tax increases beginning in 2014. So, as you are planning for retirement, or planning on having funds set up for your future income, you may be able to start a foundation now that will protect you from the increased taxation that I feel is on the horizon.

WHAT'S YOUR IDEA OF THE PERFECT INVESTMENT?

We recently conducted a poll with our clients and asked, if you could have the perfect investment what would it be? How would it grow? The majority answered, "One that gives me tax-free income, doesn't lose money, and when I die my family gets it all tax-free." I'm sure most of you would agree with my clients. I can't think of anybody who wouldn't want to have an account like this. I'm here to tell you, it is available, and has been available for quite sometime…

THE LAST GREAT TAX SAVING PLAN?

Over the past several years, this plan has generated a lot of attention, and many Americans are now funding large amounts of money into them. It could be called the number one secret, or one of the last great tax savers for your retirement. The secret is: Index Universal Life (IUL) structured inside a Trust. As I said before, this product has been around for quite some time, but unfortunately has been underutilized and most people are completely unaware that it exists. I have personally met with many advisors throughout the country who never knew they had this great tool at their fingertips to offer their clients, nor how to structure them in a way to provide tax-free non-reportable income. For my clients, it has increased their future income and net worth tremendously, and at the same time protected them from the elements. Now some of you may say I don't need life insurance… life insurance is the last thing I need…or I already have enough life insurance. This may be true if you are looking at it like your grandfather's old life insurance contract or your current term policy. Most of the life policies currently owned by policyholders are purchased to be used as a death benefit, or income replacement for the surviving spouse, and 90% are used for this very purpose. But most have never seen an illustration or a plan where they can access their cash values and the interest earnings tax-free. Or how these can be used as another source for income planning needs in the future. What's great about this is if you don't use up all your cash value, the policy still could have a remaining death benefit that could go to your named beneficiaries tax-free. These funds can go your family, your church, or organization of your choice. I have illustrated several plans where clients have seen 300% to 500% increases in their overall nest egg.

There are a number of ways to fund these types of policies and accounts that you can use to help offset your future taxes and protect you from market losses. I want to also add that the index features for growth offered by some of these policies are outstanding. Most of them have the ability to capture a portion of market-like returns while also eliminating market losses. Most will have a "cap" which is the maximum that you can earn in that policy year, for example: 12% to 18%, but also offer a floor, or a guaranteed minimum rate of return, for example: 1% to 3%. This is just one of the many features that have attracted so many consumers to add these types of plans to their portfolio.

LET ME SHOW YOU HOW WORKING WITH A "TEAM OF ADVANCED ADVISORS" COULD CHANGE YOUR RETIREMENT OUTCOMES.

Our client, Mr. Larkin age 43, is a very successful business owner with a net worth of almost 9 million dollars. Having a great amount of income, Mr. Larkin felt he was limited to what other possible options that were available to him. He couldn't fund a Roth IRA because he makes too much income, and he was maxing out all of his current qualified plan contributions to get all of the tax deductions he knew of. He asked, "What could I be doing different to better my retirement, and what am I missing out on?" Some people would say he has done pretty well and should quit and move to the beach, he's made enough! However, it's that American drive that's in us, and our motivation to achieve more and do better. I was able to sit with his current accountant and introduce them to my team of professionals; by doing this we were able to come up with several different ways to improve Mr. Larkin's retirement outcomes that his current advisors were unaware of.

For one example, we created a specific Trust to protect his business from lawsuits and litigations. We then loaned $100,000 in annual premiums for fifteen years into his trust and had the trust use these funds to purchase an Indexed Life Insurance policy that would protect everything he has built. The life policy is the crucial part in protecting his business assets and liabilities, but also allows him to have a nice steady flow of tax-free income for the future. We illustrated how this trust and policy could allow growth of the cash values to be paid back to him through loan repayments and as <u>non-reportable tax free income</u>, which we plan on taking out when he wishes to retire at age 60.

Policy Trust Illustration:

- Annual Premiums of $100,000 for 15 years = $1,500,000.

- Starts taking income out at age 60 by way of loans each year = $374,590.

- We illustrated if he takes this income for 40 years and passes away at age 100. The illustration shows he could receive a total income of $15,358,190!

- His Death Benefit at age 100 could be $27,846,686.

As you can see these concepts can be a tremendous asset for many pre-retirees and retirees to grow and protect their business, retirement, and estates. Another great feature these plans offer is they don't have all of the restrictions that most IRA's and other qualified accounts have.

Such restrictions as:

1. Being able to take funds out before age 59½ without IRS penalties.

2. They can allow you to take income out non-reportable and tax-free, versus withdrawals from qualified accounts that are fully taxable at your current tax brackets.

After learning these concepts, some have now chosen to stop contributing to their IRA and or 401k accounts, because of the growing tax time bomb and looming tax increases on top of them. So by using some of these advanced planning concepts I have shown you what we have established for our clients, and how it has allowed them access to cash values as "loans" from their policies tax-free. What's also great to mention is if and when they pay back these loans, they're actually paying <u>themselves</u> back, and their policy cash values increase as well! Some have called this, "Private Banking Strategies" or "Family Banking Strategy."

Section 79

Another advanced concept we use for Business Owners is Section 79.

Our client example is Dr. Allen, who operates his successful practice as a C-Corporation. He is 41 and takes an annual salary of $200,000. He has 5 employees that have an average age of 35, and average compensation of $40,000 a year. Dr. Allen decides to offer a Section 79 plan of 10 times compensation to his employees. The corporate tax-deductible cost for the employees based on their selected coverage of $50,000 is $6,000. They selected the $50,000 to avoid any personal taxation on the benefit. The tax-deductible contribution for Dr. Allen's coverage is $100,000, which he pays for 5 years.

Dr. Allen is taxed on the value of the permanent benefits provided by the policy *(defined as the permanent direct cost by the IRS)*, which in this example is $65,000 per year as well as the Table I costs for benefits above $50,000, which is approximately $3,200. The net personal tax is $27,280 for 5 years for a total of $136,400. After funding this plan for a period of 5 years, Dr. Allen now has a personal policy that he can use for his future retirement income.

So what's his benefit to all this? At age 65, Dr. Allen can now receive over $65,000 of loans for 20 years. This amounts to over $1,300,000 of supplemental retirement income that is tax-free. His policy still has a death benefit in the case of premature death to protect his business, or provide a benefit to his named beneficiaries.

IRA AND 401K OWNERS

Uncle Sam wants you! That is, he wants you to spend your IRA in a manner that he finds appropriate. Millions of Americans have put away money into their IRA/401k's throughout their professional life, which the government encourages with tax-deferred growth throughout the working years, allowing employees to accumulate more money faster... but there's a catch.

The government's Required Minimum Distributions, RMDs – including 401(k)s, 403(b)s or 457 plans – "paint retirees and their employer-sponsored retirement plans into a corner." That's because by the time retirees reach the age of 70½, RMDs require individuals to make withdrawals, which are heavily taxed.

Let's process this further with the example of James and Betty:

Smooth sailing…at first: By age 65, this couple has saved $500,000 in their IRA, and because they have been taking no income from it, they're averaging a 6% return each year. They sail along smoothly, compounding the growth in the account and gain an additional $40,147 by age 70. But halfway through that year… The compounded tax liability has arrived. At 70½, James's IRA has an accumulated value of $669,113. Therefore, his RMD *(the amount he's required to withdraw)* is $24,420. James and Betty were not expecting the tax bill this has now created, which in their 25 percent tax bracket, is a staggering $6,105! More upsetting to the couple, however, is that this scenario will continue for the rest of their lives…

Down the road: Fast-forward to age 90 and the total withdrawals the couple have been forced to take reaches $908,005. The total taxes owed are a staggering $227,001—which goes straight to the IRS. Worse still, when James and Betty pass away, their children will pay taxes on the remaining money, and likely be at a much higher tax rate than their parents.

THE SOLUTION TO THE NIGHTMARE

Rather than wait for the inevitable RMD, James and Betty can convert to a Roth IRA. This entails taking their distributions early, at age 65, even though they are not required to do so. Each year for 10 years they withdraw $67,934, pay a tax bill of $16,983 from that sum and return the balance to the account. The net effect throughout the 10-year period is a total taxable distribution of $679,340 for a total tax bill of $169,835. The good news for James and Betty, is that they are now done paying taxes on this account, forever. They went from taxable distributions of $1.6 million to just $679,000, thus reducing the amount they owe on taxes by almost $1 million dollars! And the money that their beneficiaries receive will be now tax-free.

A WELL-EARNED VACATION BECAUSE OF A ROTH CONVERSION

We have also been able to create outcomes for some clients where we converted 30% of their current IRA to a Roth, and after paying the tax on the conversion, the total net result was higher account values than they started with.

Short example: $100,000 IRA, 30% converted to Roth IRA.

End result after paying taxes and rolling them into 2 new accounts =$103,690.

We told them to take the $3,690 gain and spend it on a nice vacation!

"These scenarios consider a number of variables, all of which are different for every client we work with. In my experience as a general rule, however, the sooner you begin the conversion process, the more you stand to gain."

RECAP: PLANNING CAN WORK FOR YOU

As you can see knowledge has worked quite well for not only for pre-retirees, retirees, and business owners, but it also works well for high net worth individuals, athletes, and celebrities. It is extremely critical to utilize an advanced team of knowledgeable and experienced advisors to help you set up these types of plans and have a true solid and safe financial future. I hope you have discovered the importance and seen value in having your retirement set up properly. The value of having non-reportable tax-free income of course is, it's not included, nor added with your current income on a tax return. It will not put you into the next higher tax bracket, it may now aid in lowering it.

So, if your plan is to bounce the last check on your way out, but unfortunately don't get the chance to do so… these funds can now go to your heirs… and not TheIRS.

About Gary

Gary Marriage Jr., is the President/CEO of Nature Coast Financial Advisors, Inc. an Independent Insurance and Financial Services Firm based in Crystal River, Florida. Gary and his team assist individuals and business owners develop stable retirement plans to ensure their savings will be there when they need it. Gary uses "The Team" approach, which he feels works best for his clients when building them a solid financial future. To accomplish this, Gary utilizes his own expertise, as well as several of the top local and national Attorneys and CPAs in the country. He feels that one person simply cannot have all education, knowledge, and experience to do it alone.

Gary educates groups and various organizations on the local and national levels. Along with educating the public through these speaking engagements, he also is a mentor to other professionals in areas where they can help their own clients better protect their retirement savings and lower their income/estate taxes. Gary also specializes in planning for high net worth individuals such as athletes, celebrities, and business owners. He designs plans that have drastically increased their estate size, but also reduces their net worth from future excess taxation, which helps keep more in their pockets. For business owners, Gary helps them retain their valued employees by setting up various retirement plans and protects the businesses with different types of trusts that have numerous amounts of benefits available to them – which most entrepreneurs are completely unaware of. Currently, Gary offers his services in 13 states throughout the country.

Gary is a member of the National Ethics Association and has received several industry awards. He has been a featured guest on local and national TV, radio, and numerous online and print publications such as *The Wall Street Journal,* Bloomberg, CBS, NBC, and Fox Business.

Gary is very involved within the area communities, charitable, and supporting organizations such as the YMCA, the American Cancer Society, the American Heart Assoc., Wounded Warriors, National Wildlife & Turkey Federation, Relay for Life, and many others.

Gary is a family man who values spending time with his wife Jennifer and their son Mason. He also enjoys being in the outdoors – Golfing, Fishing, Diving, and attending football games. Recently he was selected to play in the 2013 Annexus Pro-Am at the Waste Management Phoenix Open, which is the highest-attended golf tournament held in Scottsdale, AZ. He was grouped with PGA Pro Brendon de Jonge, finishing in 6th place!

CHAPTER 43

MITIGATING 6 COMMON RETIREMENT RISKS THROUGH FINANCIAL PLANNING

BY STEPHEN A. SCHWARTZ, CFP®

My interest in finance and investing goes back to my childhood and the influence of my Great Aunt. I was very close with her and she had a significant imprint on my upbringing and eventually my career choice. A child of the depression era, Aunt Bea did not come from a family of great financial means. She married as a young woman and her husband, an educated businessman, taught her how to invest in the stock market. The time period was the early 1950's and she began with small sums of her weekly salary and invested in blue chip stocks. Her husband unfortunately died a young man, leaving her with some savings and a small life insurance policy. She wisely invested those funds in her blue chip stock portfolio, which began the foundation for her long-term financial security. In some of my earliest memories, I recall her showing my brother and I how to read the stock tables published in the newspaper. She would explain in simple terms how companies like IBM, Bristol Meyers and Proctor & Gamble made money. She was a woman who worked throughout most of her life, managed to consistently save every year, and as I got older, it was clear that she never worried about money. She passed away about two years ago and it was astounding to see the wealth she was able to create after 50 years of investing and compounding interest. Her financial success and the time she took to offer me instruction and guidance left a significant mark on my life. It would be hard to review my career without acknowledging how impactful she was to me – on my path to becoming a Wealth Management Advisor.

For the past 15 years, I have had the privilege of working with many outstanding individuals, assisting them in developing their financial plans and helping them prepare for retirement. Working with high net worth and emerging high net worth individuals, I spent a great deal of time helping them create investment portfolios that match their specific goals and objectives. Considering the longevity of today's retirees, there is a great deal of specialized planning that must take place. The hallmark of this planning is helping retirees create a portfolio with a well-designed distribution strategy that can sustain them through retirement.

The work I do with my clients is very process-driven. I never instinctively suggest a product. Instead, I follow a process that is based on listening to people and understanding their financial needs and objectives first and foremost. I want to find out what they value most, where they came from, and how they feel about their financial situation. I also want to understand what their vision and goals are regarding financial planning. After I fully understand their current situation and objectives, we begin a discussion about planning and execution.

After talking with thousands of people and preparing an equal amount of financial plans, I have discovered certain risks that every person planning for retirement, or presently in retirement faces. Below I have outlined and explained the importance of these risks and how to successfully navigate these potential hazards. *Please note that while having a financial plan is key to financial health, all investments carry some level of risk including potential loss of principal, and no investment strategy can ensure a profit or protect completely against loss.*

1. LONGEVITY RISK

Every person that is about to retire, whether they have $1 million or $20 million in assets, are concerned about the same thing: Will I run out of money at some point during my retirement? After spending 30 years climbing the mountain of wealth accumulation, they are petrified to take the first step down the other side of that mountain. They know they have to make this money last for possibly three decades or more. Let's face it, thirty years is a long time to make a fixed amount of money last.

Awareness is the starting point. This involves having a financial "check up" or assessment of your financial condition. This can be accomplished by designing a retirement schedule which demonstrates the longevity of your financial assets. Based on this schedule we can determine if a funding gap exists, to what extent, and explore strategies to close the gap.

When you create a financial plan it provides you with an understanding of what sustainable annual income can be generated from a plan. That plan will be constructed based on a thorough analysis— including many different variables—and then compared to what your consumption expectations are. After composing a plan, one should integrate those components into an overall investment policy. With this type of approach, you're utilizing your financial plan to dictate investment policy instead of speculating on a specific asset category for your investments. By not exercising the integration of a financial and investment plan, one jeopardizes their financial health and can potentially lead to them outliving their money.

Many retirees have a misconception regarding their portfolio constructs when entering retirement. This misconception is bestowed upon them by mainstream media, and the message calls for a portfolio largely weighted in fixed income securities. This message is being conveyed due to the conservative nature and stability that fixed income securities provide. This general theme of investment advice is not comprehensive or all encompassing. When discussing a retirement plan with an individual it is often uncovered that retirees need investment returns that are greater than what is being offered from a portfolio concentrated in fixed income securities. When planning for retirement a significant requirement is one of strategic thinking, comprehensive planning, and the consideration for assets that could provide growth in order to sustain a multi-decade retirement.

A real life example that I have seen materialize is a particular family that began focusing on the creation of a retirement plan in their early 50's. Given their asset and income levels, their expectation regarding retirement was very insecure. After several meetings and the engineering of a comprehensive plan, they began to have more comfort in securing their retirement objectives.

As a by-product of our discussions, the underlying plan and objectives instilled a newfound appreciation for fiscal discipline. With this insight, they began to systematically save more money each year. This resulted in an earlier retirement than they expected. Looking back, they were quite surprised how they were able to substantially increase their wealth base and accelerate the timeline to commence their retirement. Reflecting on the work we did with this particular family, one of the most critical aspects was their willingness to engage and commit to a sound process of financial planning.

2. MARKET RISK

I find that most retirees are more focused on protecting their asset base rather than growing it. Instead of following conventional theory, I believe an objective financial plan should be based on your unique circumstances and be the guiding factor for an investment strategy.

While bonds can provide a predictable stream of income payments, these payments might not offset the rising costs associated with inflation, and just as stocks have certain risks, bonds also carry risk, including potential loss of principal and interest rate risk. A more optimal approach may call for owning bonds and stocks together in a portfolio. This asset class posture can provide both a predictable stream of income payments with relatively low risk while stocks can potentially provide growth to help fight off inflation. Over time, financial markets and economies move in cycles. Given the uncertainty of asset prices, a risk retirees need to be cognizant of is called, "sequence of return" risk. This is the risk of receiving lower or negative returns early in a period when withdrawals are made from the underlying investments. The order or the sequence of investment returns is a primary concern for those individuals who are retired and living off the income and capital of their investments. One strategy to mitigate this risk is to maintain a few years of cash equivalents accessible that are commensurate with your income needs. By committing to this discipline you are reducing the likelihood that you will need to liquidate your portfolio assets from a forced liquidation strategy in a declining market.

3. INFLATION RISK

Inflation is one, if not the biggest, risk a retiree faces. Inflation over time has the effect of eroding one's accumulated wealth. It's a difficult concept for individuals to grasp because they don't notice it in their day-to-day lives. One doesn't realize the impact of inflation because prices of particular goods and services typically do not increase a significant amount from month to month or year to year. Rather, they move gradually over time. The best example I can provide is the US postal stamp. In 1980, the cost of a US postal stamp was fifteen cents. In 2012, approximately thirty years later, that same stamp cost forty five cents.[1] Given these increasing costs, its important retirees understand the impact inflation can have on their nest egg. Let's assume a retired couple age 65 needs $100,000 prior to retirement to meet their income needs. Assuming a rate of inflation of 3%, this couple will need approximately $135,000 in the 10th year of retirement and almost $180,000 in the 20th year of retirement. In summary, inflation is a hidden expense that shows up over an extended period of time, and can jeopardize our financial security in retirement.

4. TAX RISK

Taxes are uncontrollable from an individual standpoint because they are imposed through government regulation. Tax risk can however be mitigated with proper planning. Investors can exercise some control by diversifying their investments from a tax point of view.

There are some strategic ways to diversify your assets as you plan for retirement. One way is to view your assets in three different structures. The first is a pre-tax bucket, the second is an after-tax bucket and the last is a tax-free bucket. To clarify, "pre-tax" is income considered or calculated before the deduction of taxes and "after-tax" is the amount of money that an individual or company has left over after all taxes have been deducted from taxable income. Each provides their own unique tax efficiencies, which are a result of their varying tax subjectivity. Accumulators who segregate their assets in this fashion are afforded choices at the time of distribution.

---

1 http://www.prc.gov/%28S%28g532al30p52gnjnrc2bfk33n%29%29/PRC-DOCS/aboutprc/offices/
  PAGR/stamphistory.pdf

Commonly known retirement accounts that would fall into the pre-tax bucket would include 401(k)s and Traditional IRAs (Individual Retirement Accounts), and can also be described as "tax-deferred." They allow you to postpone paying taxes on the amount you contribute and the earnings that are generated as long as they remain in the account.

A commonly-known retirement account that would fall into the after-tax bucket would include an Investment Portfolio which could be comprised of marketable securities or real estate holdings. These types of investments are made with dollars that have already been taxed. The growth on these assets (interest, dividends, and capital gains) may be taxed as ordinary income or as capital gains based on the type of investment, how long it was owned and a variety of other factors.

Commonly known retirement accounts that would fall into the tax-free bucket would include a ROTH 401(k) or ROTH IRA. Funding comes from after-tax contributions, and can create a source of tax-free income in the future if certain qualifications are met. Contributions are not tax-deductible in your saving years, but tax-free growth and tax-free withdrawals can help reduce your total taxable income when you reach retirement.

As an example, a retiree who has accumulated $1,000,000 in each structure should consider first the withdrawal of funds from their after-tax bucket. By following this, the tax-deferred and tax-free structures are able to experience growth for several more years. The tax-deferred structure such as an IRA is required to begin distributions for most individuals upon age 70 1/2. On the other hand, a tax-free account type such as a ROTH IRA does not require distributions for most individuals. Given this extended period of tax-free returns, one can increase their asset base, and again avoid taxation at time of distribution. A ROTH IRA can be an attractive estate planning tool given there are no minimum distributions required from this structure. Given there are no distributions required, an effective planning strategy can be naming a family member such as a non-spouse as the beneficiary. In that regard, one additional and lesser known benefit of maximizing a ROTH IRA is the ability to transfer unneeded assets to the next generation. By implementing such a strategy, one can promote asset accumulation, tax diversification and additional security for their beneficiaries.

Please note, there may be other factors that go into this type of strategy, every situation is unique, and everyone should consult with their tax professional on their individual circumstances.

5. LONG TERM CARE RISK

Long term care is clearly a risk based on "unknown" factors. It is impossible to know if you or your spouse will get sick to the point that you need some type of long term care. You also cannot predict what the financial consequences will be for that care. Nursing homes, assisted living facilities and in-home skilled care are very costly and continue going up every year. As a result, required care can create a lot of financial stress in retirement. It has been predicted that by the year 2040, long term care costs are set to double.[2]

Just 5 to 10 years ago, the majority of people were less receptive to having a conversation about long term care risk. Today, I find, the majority of people are receptive to engage in this conversation. The reason they are receptive is because of real life experiences that they have been exposed to or are currently dealing with. They see long term care issues happening in their families or in the families of friends and co-workers and the financial and emotional burden it can cause. The Baby Boomers are really the first generation to experience their parents living to very old ages, which often requires specialized care. They are seeing first-hand long term care risk as a reality.

6. LEGACY RISK

Philanthropy is often a changing dynamic over the course of a person's retirement. As people age and have more time to interact with family and grandchildren, they have an appreciation or desire to pass assets to their children and other heirs.

It is very important for retirees to review their financial plan regularly because situations, intentions and priorities will often change over time. Specifically, legacy goals may change as they develop an interest in bequeathing money to the next generation. Legacy planning is integrated with financial and retirement planning, and it's important to have conversations about the subject in order to see how it integrates into

---

2 http://www.cbsnews.com/news/boomer-out-of-pocket-health-care-costs-to-double-by-2040/

your plan. Furthermore, you should consider an investment portfolio that is aligned with your legacy objectives.

PLANNING IS YOUR MOST STRATEGIC TOOL

As noted previously, a common concern for retirees is financial longevity. Moreover, will the accumulated assets that one currently has provide enough income for the remainder of their life? When it comes to the risks noted above, many retirees are not fully aware of these risks and their exposure to them. Whether you are in retirement or in the pre-retirement phase of your life, make sure you connect with a qualified financial professional that can help mitigate these risks and develop a dynamic plan that will assure the greatest likelihood of the retirement you envision. In closing, it's important to revisit your plan regularly to make sure you are staying the course. Your future depends upon it!

About Stephen

Stephen A. Schwartz, CFP® helps high net worth clients achieve their goals and objectives related to accumulation, protection, and distribution of wealth by applying a special blend of knowledge and skill. He began his career in finance 15 years ago and has met with over three thousand clients since then. Stephen is a Wealth Management Advisor affiliated with Pioneer Financial based in New York City.

Stephen earned his Bachelor of Science in Economics while attending Quinnipiac University. His commitment to higher learning has allowed him to not only differentiate himself from his peers but significantly advance his competency, knowledge, and skill set. He holds the CERTIFIED FINANCIAL PLANNER™ professional certification and is a licensed Investment Adviser Representative, maintaining securities Series 6, 7, 63, 66 registrations and Life/Health Insurance licensing.

Stephen has achieved various professional accomplishments over the years, including qualifying for membership with the prestigious Million Dollar Round Table (MDRT), The Premier Association of Financial Professionals®. In 2003, he also received the *National Quality Award* from The National Association of Insurance and Financial Advisors (NAIFA). In 2013, he was honored with Northwestern Mutual's Forum Membership and *Top Office Leader* honors within his network office. Early in his career, he was acknowledged as among the leading new Financial Representatives within the Northwestern Mutual field force for his first four years and later received *Most Valuable Producer (MVP)* honors. He is a consistent *Forum* qualifier, which is an accolade achieved by the most elite financial representatives within the Northwestern Mutual distribution system. His recent accomplishments have been displayed online by *Reuters, The Wall Street Journal's Market Watch, The Street, Yahoo Finance,* and *Worth.*

Stephen was asked to be a featured speaker at The National Student Initiative Summit *Next Generation Finance,* a financial literacy event open to students and professionals. He is also constantly sought after to speak at company forums, sharing his experience on building and sustaining a comprehensive financial planning practice. Additionally, Stephen and his colleagues teamed up in 2013 with the Northwestern Mutual Foundation, dedicating his time and donating money to Alex's Lemonade Stand Foundation, a leading national nonprofit organization focused on fighting childhood cancer and helping families.

You can connect with Stephen at:
stephen.schwartz@nm.com
www.pioneerfinancial-ss.com
www.linkedin.com/in/pioneerfinancialsschwartz

CHAPTER 44

I AM THE CHEESE — THE BAITING OF DERIVATIVE STRATEGY

BY TOM A. PUENTES & J. ERIK KIMBROUGH

In the crime novel *I am the Cheese*, written by American writer Robert Cormier, Protagonist Adam is biking from his home in the fictional town of Monument, Massachusetts. During his journey he recounts memories of his previous life with his parents, his friend Amy Hertz, and the discovery that he is not who he seems. He sings many songs throughout the novel, the most notable of which is the childhood nursery rhyme, "The Farmer in the Dell." The song lists the residents of the farm who all choose partners to take with them as they leave with the farmer and his wife; yet in the last verse of the song, the cheese is left with no one. Adam believes that he is the cheese. He is alone in the world because his mother is dead and his father is missing. Also, there is a dual meaning to the title. The words "I am the cheese" may also represent Adam's feelings of entrapment: he being the bait used to lure his parents into their murders.

Like Adam, investors often feel alone and entrapped in investment products that are found to be confusing, complex and costly. They may feel like victims of a system that appears to be operated outside of their control. When the system fails, the trap is triggered and, as in Cormier's novel, "the cheese stands alone."

The investment and banking industry has used tools and methods that decrease risk and increase profitability. However, often times these products lure clients into complex webs of strategies that are difficult to explain and even more difficult to understand. These methods serve to lure the curious and less informed investor into unfamiliar and often dangerous markets similar to the way cheese lures a rat. Derivatives are financial instruments whose value is derived from an underlying asset (stocks, bonds, commodities, etc.). Traders can swap interest rates, take bets on whether a firm will go bankrupt, safeguard against future asset price increases, and hedge profits in uncertain times - all under the confusing umbrella term derivative. Although the concept of derivative has been around for hundreds of years, recent use in financial markets has exploded in popularity.

Derivatives are recorded in what is termed as notional value, which just equals the value of the underlying asset on which the derivative is based. So if the underlying asset equaled $10 million, the notional value would be $10 million even though large banks don't actually trade $10 million. They just trade the derivative. It becomes easier to see why the global notional value for the derivative market can reach into the hundreds of trillions, because large banks are recording the notional value not the true value of the underlying asset. This can be confusing for the investor, especially if he is unfamiliar with the concept.

It is believed by some traders that people should not worry about the notional value since it's not referencing what is actually being traded. However, if there is a failure of the underlying asset, then the derivative too will fail. We saw this in the 2007-08 financial crisis. Underlying mortgages in the housing market went bad, and then all of the derivatives contracts associated with these mortgages also failed, which worsened the crisis. So the notional value of derivatives matters, and Wall Street in 2014 is a completely different world compared to Wall Street in 2000. In other words, the dangers of the derivatives market are still very much with us.

Some derivatives, such as typical stock options, trade on exchanges. Others are simply private contracts between banks or other sophisticated investors. For this reason, it is difficult to know the total volume of derivatives now outstanding. According to the Bank for International Settlements, the notional of derivatives tripled in the five years leading up to the recession, which would make the figure approximately $600 trillion. As a matter of fact, during the post-recession few categories of derivatives have shrunk; in fact, the total value of the derivatives market has actually grown.

Derivatives allow risk related to the price of the underlying asset to be transferred from one party to another. For example, a corn farmer and a processor can sign a futures contract to exchange a specified amount of dollars for a specified amount of future corn production. Both individuals have lowered a future risk: for the corn farmer, the uncertainty of the price, and for the processor, the availability of corn. However, there is still the risk that no corn will be available because of events unknown by the contract signers, such as the weather, or that one party will not fulfil on the contract. Although a third party, called a clearing house, insures a futures contract, not all derivatives are insured against counter-party risk.

In another view of the transaction, we can see that the farmer and the processor both reduce a risk and acquire a risk when they sign the contract: the farmer reduces the risk that the price of corn will fall below the price specified in the contract, yet also acquires the risk that the price of corn will rise above the price specified in the contract. The processor, on the other hand, acquires the risk that the price of corn will fall below the price specified in the contract and reduces the risk that the price of corn will rise above the price specified in the contract. In this sense, one party is the insurer for one type of risk, and the counter-party is the insurer for another type of risk.

Derivatives trading of this kind may serve the financial interests of certain particular businesses and investors. For example, a corporation borrows a large sum of money at a specified interest rate. The interest rate on the loan resets every 6 months. The corporation is concerned that the rate of interest may be much higher in 6 months. The corporation could buy a *forward rate agreement* (FRA), which is a contract to pay a fixed rate of interest 6 months after purchases on a notional amount of money. If, after six months, the interest rate is above the contract rate, the seller will pay the difference to the corporation, or FRA buyer. If the rate is lower, the corporation will pay the difference to the seller. The purchase of the FRA serves to reduce the uncertainty concerning the rate increase and stabilize earnings.

Why are such derivatives dangerous? History teaches in the financial markets that, in the short run, the market can be very unpredictable and unstable. At this point, the participants would like to say all bets are off, but in fact the bets have been placed and cannot be changed. The leverage that once multiplied income will now be catastrophic to principal.

Banking and investment supervisors have not begun to control the buildup of leverage on the derivative. Past Federal Reserve Chairman Alan Greenspan has argued that the mathematicians are improving their formulas to make the business less risky. But the more security the math seems to give, the greater the risk on the day the highly improbable happens. Eighty years ago Frank Knight, an American economist, wrote that economists did not always make clear "the approximate character of their conclusions, as descriptions of tendency only." In theoretical mechanics, perpetual motion was possible; in real life it was not. As Knight stated, "Policies must fail, and fail disastrously, which are based on perpetual motion reasoning without the recognition that it is such."

We are working with a system that is highly speculative and easily gamed. The concept of Derivatives sacrifices the great strength of banks as financial intermediaries, the confidence of their borrowers, and the incentive to police the status of the loan. After the disturbances of 2008, a senior executive of a large Wall Street house wrote a series of rules for its executive committee to keep in mind. Among them: "When a loan is securitized, nobody has the credit watch." Researchers at the Federal Reserve Bank of New York concluded that in the presence of moral hazard—the likelihood that sloughing the bad loans into a swap will be profitable—the growth of a market for default risks could lead to bank insolvencies.[i]

Derivatives allow for dangerous practices on 5 distinct levels.

1. Derivatives allow for bad accounting – Charlie Munger once asserted, "to say that derivative accounting is a sewer is an insult to sewage." Derivatives allow firms the option to record profits today that will supposedly come tomorrow. This way a firm can speculate today and increase stock price. With this method of accounting, a seemingly

---

i. The Nation June 2008

healthy firm can suddenly implode, all due to accounting speculation—as happened with Barings Bank, Enron, and Lehman Brothers.

2. Derivatives obscure the market – Several derivative contracts can be written on a single underlying asset, a feature that adds enormous complexity to financial markets. A derivative contract on one asset might be traded in Asia and the US, while another contract on the same asset might be traded in Europe. Even more troubling, the majority of derivatives are over-the-counter, which means that they aren't standardized or traded on public exchanges. The terms of each contract can vary greatly and therefore the implications and interconnectedness of this market can be impossible for regulators and traders to see clearly. When markets melted during the 2007-08 crisis, trading halted, in part, because market players couldn't readily discern which firms were on the brink of collapse and which firms were safe. Part of the reason for this was that there were too many derivatives contracts in play on top of the crumbling mortgage market.

3. Derivatives concentrate risk not reduce – Four US banks, JPMorgan, Bank of America, Citi, and Goldman Sachs—have a notional amount of $214 trillion in derivatives exposure. That's more than 30% of the worldwide amount just in four US banks. When firms have such concentrated derivatives, exposure risk levels can increase by the sheer volume of outstanding contracts.

4. Derivatives allow financial institutions to take on more debt – Financial institutions trade risk, via derivatives contracts to another firm, while keeping the underlying asset on their books. This way they can bypass capital requirements and take on more debt. Although this allows them to make more trades, it also means that if a sudden downturn surfaces in the markets, the firm that borrowed beyond its means may quickly go bankrupt. Lehman Brothers experienced this after they borrowed 30 times more money than they had in reserve. In that case, a relatively small loss of 3% meant that Lehman no longer had any reserves, which led to their collapse.[ii]

5. Derivatives offer a false sense of security – It keeps happening. One amazing example of this is the tragedy of Long-Term Capital

---

ii. The Nation June 2008

Management. A group of highly intelligent economists and traders created a hedge fund in the late 1990s which was based on a formula which supposedly hedged risk completely. For the first few years, the fund made enormous returns and the creators of the formula even won the Nobel Prize for economics. They continued to borrow more and more money, all the while thinking they were safe in doing so, but a series of unpredictable events occurred in world markets; they lost billions of dollars and put US markets in danger. Their downfall should have been a warning sign regarding the dangers of derivatives-related risk, but several other firms suffered similar fates in the following decade. If things remain the same, we'll see the same results.

Although derivatives can have benefits in risk management, they can also lead to serious losses, if not used properly. On the dark side, financial derivatives can create unproductive activities and lower transparency. While their risk-shifting function serves the useful roles of hedging, and facilitating capital flows, the increased use of derivatives also poses dangers to the financial system and economy as a whole. The wide use of derivatives can and does lead to lower transparency between counter-parties and between regulators and market participants. They can be used unproductively for speculating, leveraging or raising risk-to-capital ratios, dodging and outflanking regulations, manipulating accounting profits and evading tax. Due to the use of derivatives, the speed and depth of the impact on the financial sector and economy in the event of a large change in the exchange rate, or other market prices, will be greater. This increases the risk of systemic failure and the vulnerability of the sector and the economy.

Derivatives can lead to transparency problems. They can distort the meaning of balance sheets as the basis for measuring the risk-return profile of firms, central banks and national accounts. When traded or booked, over-the counter derivatives lack adequate reporting requirements and surveillance. This results in distorted market information. A bank may have derivatives that bet considerably on the interest-rate levels in the financial markets and create contingent liabilities and potentially harmful losses. These derivatives then substantially alter the bank's risk exposure from that reflected in the balance sheet.[iii]

---

iii. The Nation June 2008

As Robert Cormier wrote in his classic novel, the cheese does stand alone. Serving in dual roles, the protagonist acts as both a lure for a greater action, and as a victim of abandonment. Often times we find complex financial tools performing in the same manner. They can lure both sophisticated and non-sophisticated investors into a sense of greater security, while actually increasing the potential risk of the investment. As we have seen too many times in the last several years, when there is a market failure, it tends to be catastrophic and the investor is, in fact, left standing alone with very little recourse. In the childrens' game-song, the cheese standing alone is uncomfortable, but usually the children will go on to play another game and the pain of being the "lonely cheese" is soon forgotten. In the case of the derivatives market and the potential risk to the investor, being left the lonely cheese can mean catastrophic loss. It is not easily forgotten and is definitely not a game.

About Tom

Tom A. Puentes has been in the financial services industry since 1985. His clients include family foundations, labor unions, health professionals, executives, Internet entrepreneurs, and business owners across the entire U.S.

From 1989-2000, Tom hosted a weekly financial show called "Your Money Matters," on the Business Channel, Station KWHY, Los Angeles. He was also the financial correspondent for KADY-TV in Ventura, California.

For more information about Tom A. Puentes, visit:
www.morganstanleyfa.com/tomapuentes/

About Erik

J. Erik Kimbrough was raised with the belief that giving is just as important as succeeding. In all his professional positions, he has illustrated quality and integrity because of the early philosophy instilled in him. Erik has brought this exceptional work ethic to Investment Management industry. With 11 years of branch management experience, first at UBS and now with MSSB, He approaches every assignment with intelligence and patience. In a business that is always changing, his understanding and personal approach provides his office with the comfort needed to gain the trust and confidence that is necessary to obtain growth and development. His staff is important to him and he is not satisfied until he knows they have achieved a successful outcome for all their goals.

Erik's penchant for discipline was developed in his Olympic training days on the US Tae Kwon Do training team and through his studies at Boston University, where he graduated with honors in Economics. He continued with his economic studies at the University of Madrid, his MBA at Duquesne University and now is sitting for an MS in Financial Management and Banking at Boston University.

In addition to his extensive academic and professional life, he shares his time and knowledge with the Black Achievers, the youth at the YMCA and Inroads. He received the KDKA UpLift Award for his desire to pass on his knowledge of finance to the young people of Pittsburgh, and has taught a weekly economic class at Gannon University.

Living and traveling in Europe enriched Erik's aptitude for different languages and cultures, and has allowed him to communicate easily with all types of people. Erik is a person who loves to explore different landscapes and get to know the people living there. He speaks Spanish and Italian and has exchanged ideas with people from around the world.

A native of Pittsburgh, Erik is proud of his accomplishments and is looking forward to the opportunity to continue fostering cultural understanding and an appreciation of finance with the people and staff of La Jolla, CA.